THE
ARAB
IN
ISRAELI
LITERATURE

GILA RAMRAS-RAUCH

THE
ARAB
IN
ISRAELI
LITERATURE

INDIANA UNIVERSITY PRESS
Bloomington and Indianapolis

I.B.TAURIS & CO LTD
London

Published by
Indiana University Press
10th & Morton Streets
Bloomington, Indiana 47405
and
I.B.Tauris & Co Ltd
110 Gloucester Avenue
London NW1 8JA

Manufactured in the United States of America

Library of Congress Cataloging-in-Publication Data

Ramraz-Ra'ukh, Gilah.
The Arab in Israeli literature.

(Jewish literature and culture)
Bibliography: p.
Includes index.
1. Israeli literature—History and criticism.
2. Arabs in literature.   3. Jewish-Arab relations in
literature.   I. Title.   II. Series.
PJ5030.A7R36   1989   892.4'09'35203927   88-46017
ISBN 0-253-34832-3

1 2 3 4 5   93 92 91 90 89

British Library Cataloguing in Publication Data

Ramras-Rauch, Gila
The Arab in Israeli literature
1. Jewish literature, 1900–1981—Critical studies
I. Title
809'.889'24

ISBN 1-85043-168-X

To Leo

CONTENTS

Acknowledgments

This book was written under the sponsorship of the National Endowment for the Humanities, whose generous fellowship-grant made it possible for me to take a year's leave from teaching duties. I wish to thank the NEH for their vote of confidence. I must also express my gratitude to Eli Grad and Samuel Schafler, respectively past and present presidents of Hebrew College, and to Marvin Fox of Brandeis University for granting the year's leave and for their wholehearted support of my work on this book. Through the generosity of Samuel Schafler, Hebrew College supported the cost of preparing the manuscript for publication. Marvin Fox also read some chapters of the manuscript and gave me some wise suggestions. There was help as well from Isadore Twersky of Harvard, Alvin Rosenfeld of Indiana, Nurit Govrin of Tel Aviv University, and especially Gershon Shaked of the Hebrew University. At Hebrew College, the extensive holdings of the library were placed at my disposal. I wish to thank the director of the library, Maurice Tuchman, and the library staff for their knowledgeable and unflagging help. Laura Goldberg of Hebrew College prepared the typescript and did a fine job.

My greatest debt is to my husband, Leo Rauch, who helped to bring this project to fruition. This book is dedicated to him.

Introduction

In a number of profound ways, the self-definition of the Israeli is implicitly connected to his or her ways of relating to the Arab, to the Arab's own self-definition, and thus to the ongoing Arab-Israeli conflict. For the Israeli, personal commitment to the land, to the shape and boundaries of the country, has been entangled with the Arab presence for over a century. And for a corresponding length of time the image of the Arab has made its presence felt in Hebrew/Israeli literature. The relation is clearly reciprocal.

On the most general level, the Arab can be perceived as the archetype of the stranger casting a shadow over one's existence, a presence that must be related to. (This is an interesting counterpart to the European image of the Jew as stranger.) In much of the work of Hebrew writers at the beginning of the twentieth century, there is an ever-present fear of, and fascination with, the Arab. The early archetype contains the combined sense of the Arab as "noble savage" and as constant threat. The element of fear subsides in the writing of the latter half of the present century, but the fascination lingers on in various forms. Thus the earlier allure of the Bedouin gives way to a more erotic attraction connected with the archetype of the stranger—as in Amos Oz's "Nomad and Viper" in his collection *Where the Jackals Howl* (1965) and A. B. Yehoshua's *The Lover* (1977).

It is possible to make a clear distinction between the portrayal of the Arab in pre-1948 and post-1948 literature—and still point to a shared perception. Thus in the pre-State period, and especially in the work of Moshe Smilansky (1874–1953), Yitzhak Shami (1888–1949), and Yehuda Burla (1886–1969), the writer's relation to the Arab was quite simplistic: the attraction of the Bedouin way of life stemmed from its supposed freedom from western cultural constraints, even if that freedom was paradoxically tied to a strict adherence to a tribal code. All this was connected to the theme of personal trial, a combination that proved irresistible to these authors who considered themselves "native sons." (Burla and Shami were born in Palestine; Smilansky spoke Arabic and even adopted the Arabic pen name Hawajah Mussa.) Their attempt at self-identification as "native sons" suggested a partial model for European newcomers to emulate.

In many Hebrew works of the time, the Arab was therefore presented as a stereotype: again and again, Smilansky and Shami reflect an adulation of the Arab-as-noble-savage; the stories, many in the form of folk tales and oral legends, praise the Arab ethos, its rejection of worldly goods, and its emphasis on loyalty to the tribe. Correspondingly, the negative image emerges in the form of a stereotype as well. Thus, while the image of the Bedouin excited the imagination, the image of the *effendi* (i.e., the Arab landowner) was repellent to the Socialist/Zionist sentiments of those writers who were also the sons of the Russian Revolution. This was mixed with the element of fear arising from the attacks of Arab marauders in 1921 and 1929, and from 1936 to 1939.

The claim (often encountered in commentary and criticism) that in Hebrew literature the characterization of the Arab was based on a stereotype, became a stereotype in itself—thereby overlooking the fact that early writers such as Yosef Haim Brenner (1881–1921) and L. A. Arieli-Orloff (1886–1943) portrayed the Arab in a non-stereotypical diversity of role and character. Brenner admired the Arabs' attachment to the land, and also resented what he considered the exploitation of Arabs by both Arabs and Jews. As a Socialist and humanist of high moral principles, Brenner condemned injustice in all its forms. He also perceived the complex nature of the Arab-Jewish problem in his works, from 1908 to his death in 1921. Tragically and ironically, he was murdered by Arab marauders. In the writings of Arieli, we have a gallery of Arab protagonists. In the story "The Lad Bunia," the Arab appears as a saint; in the play "Alla Karim," the Jewish heroine falls in love with a young Arab peddler of sweets; in the story "In the Days of Rain," a young Arab boy attacks two young Jewish girls and causes the death of a baby. Thus Brenner and Arieli present a more rounded treatment of the Arab as individual; and if there is any stereotyping here, it is no longer the stereotyping of the individual but rather a repetition of a familiar situation or conflict.

With the establishment of the State of Israel in 1948, and the continuation of conflict and bloodshed, the Arab once again came to occupy a central position in Israeli literature. But even if we abstract from the military/political dimension, we can point to certain basic issues the Israeli writer came to grips with, issues that did not present themselves to the Hebrew writer in the pre-State period.

There is a curious paradox at the heart of the depiction of the Arab in pre- and post-1948 literature: the greater personal proximity between Arabs and Jews in the pre-State period than in the post-1948 days. Jewish children in pre-Israel Palestine experienced much direct contact with Arabs; and although the contact was limited in scope, it was a part of the childhood landscape. Arabs are featured more centrally in the fiction of Israeli-born writers. The Arab does not feature as a protagonist in the work of some major European-born writers in the pre-State days. One could say, perhaps too facilely, that the Arab was perceived as a problem, but not as a problem of primary importance—and with this there was the tacit belief that the solution lay somewhere beyond the more pressing considerations of the present.

The 1948 War created a new sensibility in the Israeli. The state of siege restricted the areas of choice and alternative, and gave the situation something of a deterministic quality: it became apparent that there could be no easy solution (however much either side may have cherished the hope of it). On the contrary, the two nations were thrown into a tragic confrontation over the motherland. Accordingly, the realization began to dawn among some Israelis that the Arab is a legitimate contender to the land. Israeli literature reflected this attitude from the very outset—as is evident, for example, in the writings of S. Yizhar (b. 1916). Indeed, in four decades of Israeli literature since 1948, the Arab has stepped from the periphery to feature as a major character in the writings of the most prominent Israeli authors, such as Yizhar, Benjamin Tammuz (b. 1919), A. B. Yehoshua (b. 1937), and Amos Oz (b. 1939).

The Arab poses a challenge to the moral constitution of the Israeli. The self-image of the idealistic Israeli who fought in the 1948 War has been marred by the realization that blood was the price of independence. Reared on the ideals of Zionism, liberalism, and Socialism, idealistic youth of the 1940s were torn between their hard-won selfhood and the bitter truth that the victory was achieved at great cost to both sides. As a result, that generation is haunted by the now typical self-doubt, and the question of just what the portrait of the Israeli is to be.

The models bequeathed by the founding fathers did not prepare the younger Israeli generation to confront (on an emotional as well as intellectual basis) the historical fact of the Holocaust or the plight of Jews in Arabic-speaking countries—any more than the historical reality of the Arab-Israeli conflict in its protracted stages. Those early founders, refugees of the pogroms as well as of the Russian Revolutions of 1905 and 1917, came to Palestine to establish a just society, and a refuge for world Jewry, in the idealistic belief that with the establishment of a Jewish state there would be an end to the plight of Jews. The persistent conflict to which every living Israeli is born has somewhat deflated that belief and thrown it into question. The history of Israeli literature, so far, is the record of how Israeli writers have come to grips with the unrelenting self-questioning—and the image of the Arab is one of its focal centers.

The creative problems facing the Israeli writer stem from the proximity of literature to life. At times, he or she may reject the realistic approach by using allegory or pre-existing patterns and archetypes. Thus the stereotyping to be found in the realistic stories written in the pre-State period now gives way to another mode of confronting "reality": the literary reality of the modern fable, wherein both the Israeli Jew and the Arab appear as archetypes in their confrontation. An example of this is to be found in Benjamin Tammuz's novella *The Orchard* (1972). Here we have a return to the motif of the two wrestling brothers—a recapitulation of the myth of Cain and Abel, as well as of the stories of Isaac and Ishmael, and Jacob and Esau: title to the land originates in Genesis, and the image of the antagonistic brothers enables the author to allegorize the characters and the situation, to the point of adopting an inconclusive ending for the novella. Thus the appropriation of a timeless mythic pattern—creating an archetype of sorts—allows for the non-resolution of this narrative. The implication for political hopes is therefore direct and dismal.

In most post-1948 novels touching upon the Arab, the "resolution" is quite problematic. The "ending" will reflect an awareness of the irresolvable nature of the conflict itself. In the A. B. Yehoshua novella "Facing the Forests" (1963), the Israeli protagonist is entangled with his Arab counterpart in an act of destruction (i.e., burning the forest), and with the resulting exposure of the underlying Arab ruins, two opposed claims to the land are raised: the Israeli has "cleared" the land; the Arab has his village again. But it does not take much to see the inherent paradox in this situation: it is a destructive act of the Israeli that brings the Arab claim to light; the Arab has a relic of his patrimony, and the Israeli gains a memory. All in all, we can say that in post-1948 fiction—in the story, the novella, and especially the novel of the 1970s—the Arab moves beyond the earlier stereotype to become either an archetype or a character.

In treating the theme of the Arab on the land, the Israeli writer differs from his pre-1948 predecessors in the unique combination of a high moral tone and the centrality of the Arab protagonist. These combined aspects are reflected in S. Yizhar's stories "The Prisoner" (1949) and "Hirbet Hizah" (1948). In "The Prisoner," the witness-turned-protagonist projects the moral tone of the story. He perceives the Arab prisoner as a native son who belongs to the landscape, a landscape torn by political and ideological conflict. Again and again, the real protagonist will be the land, as in "Facing the Forests" and *The Orchard*. And ever again, the land seems to yearn for its original state of being—wasteland, devoid of human occupancy—for since the days of the Bible, the intervention of man has borne consequences tragic to man and to landscape.

Generally, where one has to portray an enemy or rival, and where the fictionality of the text cannot serve as a buttress against reality, there is the problem of the suspension of disbelief. Further, there is the problematic aspect of the relationship between the real author and the implied author, and between the implied reader and the actual reader. In the works of early Hebrew writers such as Smilansky, Shami, and Burla, as well as Moshe Stavi (1884–1964), the positions of the four parties were clear: the real author, the implied author, the implied reader, and the actual reader—all were in accord. All shared in one normative attitude toward the subject matter and toward its literary presentation. In the four decades since 1948, however, Israeli literature has been confronted with a new and different situation. In other historical settings, in many another such situation where the tension becomes increasingly politicized, literature tends to be pressed into the service of ideology and dogma, and therefore literary presentation lapses into two-dimensionality. But Israeli writers have found, contrary to what might have been taken as the usual historical expectations, that they cannot present Arabs as heroes or murderers (with no other possibilities available).

The Arab-Israeli conflict has deepened not only in its historical dimensions but also in its meta-historical ones. It amounts to a deepened awareness; and Israeli literature in its own ways has contributed to that deepening from within. Externally, however, the meta-historical changes have come about through a series of changes in what might be called the Jewish ontology: through the establishment of the State of Israel, the minority has become the majority; and consequently, there has arisen not only a changed political climate but also a change in the actual meaning of self-awareness. Thus, if "alienation" can no longer mean a Jew's *Entfremdung* from a culture *already* "alien" to him (e.g., Kafka in fin-de-siècle Prague), then it must necessarily mean something far more intense when his "alienation" is that of native son from native soil. It is then that the attempt to verbalize the very personal attitude creates, of itself, a new cultural climate.

Accordingly, the certainty and agreement that were so much the common property of the early writers and their readers—a network of shared meaning, feeling, intention, and tone, along with the secure inferences the reader might be expected to draw—no longer exist. What is even more remarkable is the resulting difference in narrative technique: the earlier, pre-State stories usually employed the "telling" technique (namely, they were told from a single point of view); the later, post-1948 Israeli story will employ the "showing" technique (namely, the dramatization of the situation), where the ambiguity will serve only to point up and emphasize the unclear lines in both tone and feeling. Moreover, the earlier stories had a beginning, a middle, and an end; and an all-knowing narrator presented (in first or third person) a reality that was totally comprehensible to the reader. The later Israeli story, on the other hand, is open to more than one interpretation. This is the result of several factors centered around the "showing" technique, where the author ostensibly withdraws from the text, and the ambiguity is attached to the story itself.

For example, Yizhar's "The Prisoner" ends in a very diffuse tone, and there is a question in the mind of the reader: Did the narrator release the Arab prisoner, or did he not? The story connects various approaches taken in modern Israeli fiction. First there is the unidentified "objective" narrator's voice, immersing the reader in the situation (here, the capture and interrogation of the Arab shepherd). Then there is the internal monologue, portraying the inner conflict of the speaker. And then there is the story's lack of a clear resolution; the responsibility shifts to the reader, indirectly indicating that it is up to him or her to resolve the conflict of the narrative. For the implied Israeli reader, the speaker's moral dilemma and his oscillation between what he ought to do and what he must do (release the prisoner or transfer him for further interrogation) is the essence of the tension between two normative systems—his sense of fairness that cries out for the release of the man torn from his landscape, as against his sense of duty that questions the innocence of the man and his intentions. The interpretation of the story is therefore beyond the intentionality of the author in this type of open-ended narrative. And this very indeterminate quality in the post-1948 story is consistent with the treatment of the Arab in Israeli literature as increasingly diverse and indeterminate, involving irony as well as paradox in a many-sided complexity.

One ever-present tendency has been toward a meta-realistic fiction of either a symbolic or allegorical nature. This, combined with a built-in ambiguity, opens the story to varying and various interpretations. Writing modern fables seems to be one solution allowing for a more complex and sophisticated treatment of the subject. In thematic terms, one can see a more open approach to the problem, with the acceptance of the realization, and the reality, that the land has two contenders. Thus a new and paradoxical phenomenon now appears: the Israeli writer is himself more open to the problem, and at the same time he too is now a native son. And in this light his increased sensitivity regarding the Arab claim is mixed with a strengthened awareness of his own claim qua Israeli.

Tragically, the short history of Israeli literature is closely connected to the history of Israel's wars. The year 1977, when peace seemed a real possibility, can serve as a demarcation point in the change of Israeli sensibilities in general, and in particular with regard to the realistic portrayal of the Arab in Israeli fiction. The Arab now appears as a three-dimensional character, and not necessarily involved in the immediate struggle over the land. The changed sensibility was foreshadowed by a shift in literary outlook. In 1968, A. B. Yehoshua's "Facing the Forests" showed its two protagonists, an Arab and an Israeli, guarding and destroying the very forests that represent their shared land. Thus, although the Arab-Israeli struggle had by no means disappeared from Israeli fiction, the stereotypical treatment of the Arab-as-enemy had gone, along with his function as a mere foil for the moral dilemmas of the Israeli.

This is closely connected to a wider phenomenon in the post-1977 period: the new consciousness of a "Second Israel." This period is characterized, politically and socially, by harsh voices and extreme postures. It is a period of national self-questioning and the voicing of bitter grievances against conventional Israeli society with its relentless adherence to the dictum, set down by the founding fathers, regarding the rightful hegemony by those of European stock. Against this, the voices heard in Israeli life and literature are those of the Second Israel so strongly portrayed by Amos Oz's *In the Land of Israel* (1983). This work of reportage gives a great deal of attention to those who came to Israel as refugees from Arabic-speaking countries in the early 1950s. But the rubric of "Second Israel" ought to be extended to include survivors of the European Holocaust, who came to Israel in the late 1940s. What all these people had in common was the fact that in their acculturation they were called upon to emulate the ideals of the earlier *Yishuv* (the period of settlement of the founders, from the early 1900s to 1948). The ideals of Labor Party Socialism and Zionism are now being challenged by the Second Israel. Their voices are now heard not only in the political arena but in Israeli fiction, poetry, film, and drama as well—with palpable differences in the portrayal of the Arab. What is felt is the attempt on the part of the Second Israel to find its authentic voice, which had been muffled by the process of absorption into the "melting pot." Along with this, there is the new voice of the native-born Israeli writer, questioning his ideological heritage and groping toward a new self-image uncluttered by empty symbols and dead ideals.

The emergence of the Arab in Israeli literature has taken a further step: in "Facing the Forests" (1963), the Arab protagonist is voiceless; after 1977, Israeli literature gives greater place to the Arab speaking in his own person. It is interesting that he appears in the writings of Sephardic Jews, such as Sammy Michael's *Refuge* (1977), as well as in the writings of mainstream Israelis, such as A. B. Yehoshua's *The Lover* (1977). Both pose a substantial challenge to the established stereotypes of the Arab. Michael's book gives us a look at some of the tortuous relationships between Arab and Jew, and indeed at the complexity of the interrelations among the Arabs themselves. *Refuge* points to the Communist Party as the meeting ground between Arab and Jew: here, presumably, narrow nationalism is transcended by the higher aim of world revolution. As in *The Lover* and Yitzhak Ben-Ner's *Protocol* (1982), the background is Haifa, as an Arab-Israeli city. In all three novels, the Arab sheds his stereotypical guise to become a fully rounded character.

Moreover, Sammy Michael's novel reflects a unique attempt to enter into the complex nature of divided loyalties in a spectrum of personalities: the urbanized Arab poet who is a nationalist yet has been deeply affected by contact with Israeli society; the Christian Arab, a Communist ideologue whose marriage to a Jewish woman has split his family, to the point where one son identifies himself as a Jew, while the other two identify themselves with the PLO; the Arab villager who has benefited financially from his contact with Jews, and whose national identification is shallow; the Arab woman who grew up amid the uncertainties of life in refugee camps and who now, though successful, is convinced of the uncertainties of existence itself; the Iraqi Jew who was arrested in Iraq for Communist activities when he was seventeen and spent ten years in jail, after which he was exiled to Israel.

There is an element of paradox in the development of these characters: the Arab poet, for instance, though praised in Moscow and in East Berlin, realizes that he is westernized despite himself, and that this emasculates his political self-identification as an Arab. The focal point is the October War of 1973, where the confrontation is not so much between the Jewish, Moslem, and Christian characters as between their conflicting loyalties. At the outbreak of war, the Arab poet faces arrest, and he finds refuge in the house of the Iraqi Jew, who is away fighting in the Israel Defense Force. The novel ends without a resolution, and we are left speculating as to what will happen to these characters. That uncertainty is itself the emblem of Arab-Israeli relations on a personal scale.

There are other writers to be mentioned. David Grossman, in *The Smile of the Lamb* (1983), has contributed to Israeli fiction and sensibility a moving and forceful novel wherein, through a series of monologues, the Arab and the Israeli find their distinct voices. In Grossman's book, it is words rather than deeds that are the killers of the two characters. They are captives of their words—and this captivity, combined with extremism and unyielding "certainties," sends young men to their deaths.

The frank attempt to give the Arab character a genuine voice is by now more perceptible. Yet we must not overlook the fact that some of these Arab characters are not central but rather marginal in their society: in *The Lover,* the Arab is a mere teenager; in *Refuge* and *Protocol,* the Arab protagonists are Communists, and thus are outside both the Israeli and the Arab mainstream; in *The Smile of the Lamb,* the beautifully portrayed Hilmi is a man who lives on the border between reality and dream, weaving his own fairy tales, and who is considered by his neighbors as little more than a retarded fool. It is fair to expect that future Israeli writing will overcome this marginality in its portrayal of the Arab.

In this connection, we might consider Yehoshua Sobol's play *The Palestinienne.* (In English, it was produced under the title *Shooting Magda.*) Sobol can be said to be at the cutting edge of political theatre in Israel. His aim is to find a dramatic metaphor to reflect the Israeli psyche. His plays are often rich in historical events at the same time that he indulges in an interplay of reality and fantasy, in the fashion of Pirandello. *The Palestinienne,* first produced in 1985, takes place in a television studio where a television film is being shot. Thus it is a play within a play, and we the audience are the third side of the dramatic triangle. Sobol characteristically avoids a simple, linear depiction of a love affair between an Arab and a Jew. Instead, there is one level of Arab/Jewish interrelation in the film that is being shot, another level of such interrelation in the actors and other personnel involved in the filming, and yet another level in the way the audience relates to all this. In the film, there is an affair between an Arab woman, Magda, and her Jewish lover, David. This is part of the life story of a young Arab actress, Samira, who wrote the script and is there at the shooting. In the story being filmed, Magda is a student in Jerusalem and is beaten up by a group of Jewish fanatics who mistake her for a Jewish girl dating an Arab. Later in the film, the same group will beat up the Arab Magda and her Jewish boyfriend, David.

As the story is being filmed, there is a further tangle of love affairs: Samira and the director, Benesh; Daliah, the Jewish actress who plays Magda, and Udi, the actor who plays David, and so on. Is *The Palestinienne* a metaphor for the Arab-Israeli conflict? Hardly, since other nationalities could easily be substituted for the Jews and Arabs in the play and its play within a play. More closely, it is a play about twisted contemporary existence, ruled by racism and violence; and the Arab-Israeli conflict serves here as a convenient conceit for that world of extremism and moral blindness.

Sobol had sought to be "objective" and non-committal in this play. Yet the absence of a definite point of view weakens the play, where men, Arabs and Jews, exploit women, Arab and Jewish. In the concluding scene of the play, the men in Samira/Magda's life confront her: her British lover offers uncertain promises for the future; her Arab lover, Adnan, wants her to become an orthodox Muslim woman; David wants her to convert to Judaism so that they can marry. The message of the play is the uncertainty in the choice between uncertainty, on the one hand, and the fundamentalisms, on the other. In addition, the characters quickly enter and abandon their changing social personae. David, for example, begins as a conscientious objector, then becomes a right-wing extremist fanatic, and ends up an orthodox "repentant" who adopts the rigorously orthodox Jewish way of life.

The play generated a strong reaction from the public, some seeing in it a "national disaster" in its supposed reiteration of the age-old "calumny of Israel." Despite Sobol's intention to stay away from political issues, the play is a politicization because of its reductive approach to reality, the two-dimensional representation of characters and situations.

And yet Sobol's play supports one thesis of this study: namely, that in numerous instances in Hebrew literature, the Arab is a foil for the emotional/psychological trials of the Jew. In the play, however, the problem of identity remains unresolved.

The image of the Arab in Hebrew and Israeli literature can be viewed from various perspectives. It can be seen diachronically, following the evolution of the theme over ninety years of literary activity. Or a synchronic approach can be adopted that will reveal the different mutations of the theme as these relate to certain implicit outlooks considered from a non-temporal perspective.

Hebrew and Israeli literature can be divided into two major trends, and this division can serve as an organizing principle for the wide scope of literary output. One clear trend is the realistic one, depicting the hardships and experiences of Jews first settling in the land. This trend has been prevalent from the earliest days of this century, and is still current. The other trend is qualified by its ironic, meta-realistic, and symbolic modes that try to create a literary metaphor and to moor the present in a wider framework that is cosmic, mythical, historical, or whatever. One might add that the artistic, linguistic, and perceptive achievements of the latter trend are of greater significance than those of the former—but this runs the risk implicit in all generalizati ins. The image of the Arab features in both these modes, and it is possible to say that whatever changes might occur in the modes of fiction, they will be reflected in the treatment of the image of the Arab.

T H E
ARAB
I N
ISRAELI
LITERATURE

PART ONE

EARLY WRITERS— TO 1948

CULTURAL BACKGROUND

Through two thousand years of exile, the idea of return to the Land of Israel has been integral to Jewish dreams, to Jewish hopes. The Bible, the Talmud, the prayer book, liturgy, and poetry, all were interlaced with thoughts of the Holy Land, Zion, Jerusalem, the site of the destroyed Temple. The Passover *seder* echoes with the words "Next year in Jerusalem!" And after the reading of the Scriptural passage that concludes the Sabbath portion of the Torah, a prayer is heard: "Have compassion on Zion, for it is the source of our life, and mayest Thou soon in our day save the city that is grieved in spirit. Blessed art Thou, O Lord, who makest Zion rejoice in her children." At various points in prayer, the plea is heard: "Renew our days as of old . . ."—and all of this expresses the unbroken continuation of a redemptive hope.

In modern times, this was combined with a secular hope, the hope for a redemption of the land through immigration. At the turn of the century, Palestinian Arabs undoubtedly saw the influx of Jews and the purchase of land by Jews as an unexpected, unwelcome, and even threatening phenomenon. In the four holy cities—Jerusalem, Hebron, Tiberias, and Safad—the old *Yishuv* (the old, continuous settlement) did not present a problem. What did trouble the Arabs, however, was the beginning of immigration in large numbers. In the meantime, Jews themselves began to form their various views of the Arab. Some Jews saw Jewish-Arab relations in utopian terms. At the other end of the spectrum, there were those who foresaw grave difficulties.

The emergence of the Zionist idea in Europe occurred in three stages: In the middle of the nineteenth century, Rabbi Yehuda Alkalai (1798–1878) and Rabbi Zvi Hirsch Kalischer (1795–1874) spoke of Zionism as a fulfillment of a religious promise, while Moses Hess (1812–1875) spoke of Zionism in terms of secular nationalism. The second stage was centered around Russian persecution of Jews in the 1870s and '80s. The movement called *Hibbat Zion* ("Love of Zion"), connected with figures such as Peretz Smolenskin (1842–1885), culminated with the haunting and powerful essay "Auto-Emancipation: An Appeal to His People by a Russian Jew" (1882), by Leo Pinsker (1821–1891). The third stage of this emergent period included the seminal works of Theodor Herzl (1860–1904).[1]

The Russian pogroms of 1881 were triggered by the assassination of Tsar Alexander II. Pinsker, an enlightened physician who had been cited by the previous tsar for medical service to Russian soldiers during the Crimean

War, responded to the volatile mood created by the pogroms with a call to Russian Jews to assert their Jewish nationalism. He became the leader of *Hibbat Zion*, and convened its founding conference in 1884; the aim of this movement was to encourage and support immigration to Palestine as the only remedy for the persecution of Jews.

Political Zionism began with Herzl, who convened the First Zionist Congress in Basel in 1897. With Herzl and Ahad Ha'Am (1856–1927), the topic of eventual Arab-Jewish relations became an issue. But before we consider their views on this issue, we might give our attention to the challenging essay "The Hidden Question," written in 1905 by Itzhak Epstein (1862–1943), and presented by him at the Seventh Zionist Congress in Basel.[2] There may have been those who believed Palestine was largely uninhabited, implying that an Arab-Jewish conflict could not arise. They might even have expressed the words attributed to the British writer Israel Zangwill (1864–1926): "A land without a people, for a people without a land."

Epstein reminded his listeners and readers that Palestine was not, in any sense, a land without a people, and he criticized the Zionist movement for ignoring the problem and its severity: Arabs in Palestine constitute "a full-fledged nation which took hold there hundreds of years ago." He estimates a population of a half-million Arabs, 80 percent of whom are engaged in farming, on land that belonged to their great-grandfathers. Even with the legal purchase of land by Jews, the process of displacement creates moral problems that outweigh legality.

And to those who claim that the Jew's attachment to the land outweighs that which is felt by the Arab, Epstein has this to say: "In our fervent love for the land of our forefathers, we forget that the nation whose home it is loves it as well, with heart and soul" (p. 21). He goes on to characterize the deep source of that love, in the veneration for the land in which their fathers are buried. And then he states the challenge posed by this fact: "Will the ones we have dispossessed remain silent and accept with equanimity what we are doing to them? Will they not arise to reclaim by force of arms what was plundered from them by power of gold?" (p. 23)

Nor are we to be misled, he warns, by the fact that there is no Arab nationalist movement as yet: "We should not presume to make light of Arab rights. . . . We must not be fooled by the cinders which conceal a burning ember; should one spark escape, the result would be an inextinguishable conflagration" (p. 23). And with this there is the injunction: "it is incumbent upon us to dismiss from our minds any thoughts of conquest or expropriation. Our slogan should be: Live and let live!" (p. 24)

The reaction to Epstein was immediate and far from favorable. One of the first to respond was Ze'ev Smilansky (1873–1944), a brother of the writer Moshe Smilansky and the father of Yizhar Smilansky (S. Yizhar). Ze'ev Smilansky countered in 1908 with an article titled "From Imagination to

Reality," in which he charged Epstein with being out of touch with the real world: in Russia, young Socialist Jews ignored their own interests as Jews in favor of Russian workers and peasants; now they were concerned with the interests of the Arabs, and again ignoring their own main interest, the redemption of the land.

In another article in 1908, published in the same journal in which the Epstein article had appeared, Ze'ev Smilansky continued his attack. He envisaged a period of insecurity and unrest that would eventually flare up into nationalistic confrontation. His vision was prophetic: 1908 was the year of the revolt by the Young Turks, and once the new Turkish legislation allowed for parliamentary organization on a national basis, there was an upsurge in Arab nationalism and anti-Zionist feeling, and with it a strong Arab faction in the Ottoman parliament.

In the meantime, a new image of the Jew was being formed: a worker of the land, entitled to it by virtue of his labor. The idea of acquisition by work, not by the sword, and of ownership based on tilling the soil—ideas which originated in John Locke's labor theory of property and Karl Marx's labor theory of value—now appeared in the writings of Ze'ev Smilansky and A. D. Gordon (1856–1922), the latter an ascetic Tolstoyan of the second wave of immigration to Palestine. Gordon coined the term *religion of labor* and urged the physical return to the soil, an idea he practiced throughout his life. In Gordon's view, the desolate condition of the land justified the Jewish attempt to restore it to its former state. The land has been awaiting its wandering sons, and the title to it does not expire as long as there is a Jewish people. And as the Jews may not deprive the Arabs of their rights as the current inhabitants of the land, so the Arabs must not deny the Jews the right to resettle. The greater right to the land depends on sacrifice, work, creativity. Gordon was aware of the problems inherent in land acquisition by Jews; at the same time, he felt that co-existence was possible, but only with the recognition of Arab and Jew as allies.

Ze'ev's brother Moshe Smilansky (1874–1953) rejected Epstein's altruistic and conciliatory views as a sign of capitulation. At this early stage, he saw a possibility for co-existence only on the basis of an equality in strength—even though he later was quite vocal in endorsing bi-nationality. To both brothers, Epstein's ideas were altogether too defensive, apologetic, and imbued with the defensive spirit of the Diaspora. To their way of thinking, the image of the new Jew called for a more assertive approach. (Eventually, Epstein went beyond his article, published in 1907, to advocate bina-tionality, too, although from a different perspective.)

One of the most influential intellects of the Zionist movement was Ahad Ha'Am (meaning "One of the People"), the pen name of Asher Zvi Ginsberg. Where Herzl has been justly credited with being the father of Political Zionism, Ahad Ha'Am is regarded as the father of Cultural Zionism through his activities as a theorist, reformer, and Hebraist, and his advocacy of Jewish return to the Land of Israel as a spiritual center. Thus the return to Zion must be more than physical immigration, but rather the rebirth or renaissance (he uses that very term: *Tehiyah*) of the spiritual/ cultural center of old. His contributions to that rebirth were immense—in his capacity as editor of the influential Odessa journal *HaShiloah* (which published the Epstein article and Smilansky's reply), and in his later activity in London and Palestine.

A decade-and-a-half before Epstein uttered his warnings to Jews in regard to the Arab presence in Palestine, Ahad Ha'Am was already pointing to the eventuality of Arab resistance to Jewish "encroachment" upon Arab rights. This was expressed in his 1891 essay "Truth from the Land of Israel."[3] This was Ahad Ha'Am's reaction following his first visit to Palestine, and it created shock waves not only in Europe but also among Palestine's Jewish settlers. Moshe Smilansky, who had arrived only months before, recorded the consternation produced by the widely read article. Farmers, laborers, public figures—young and old—were deeply affected by Ahad Ha'Am's forecast of trouble. Smilansky's memoirs take note of the shock felt throughout the city of Jaffa, then the center of Jewish political and civil activity. In any event, these two documents, Ahad Ha'Am's and Epstein's, register not only the beginning of political realism but also the deep sense of justice felt by Jews in regard to the Arab presence.

The "hidden question," then, was an open question to both Ahad Ha'Am and Epstein. Indeed, Epstein was the first one to draw the link between the fulfillment of the Zionist dream and Jewish conciliation with the Arabs. He combined altruism and utilitarianism with a deep sense of mission.[4] With Jewish recognition of the Arab and his rights, there would come not only the longed-for Jewish homeland but also material progress for the Arab, resulting from some sort of covenant between the two peoples.

Moshe Smilansky, who was an ardent follower of Ahad Ha'Am, and was also deeply devoted to him, even tending him at his deathbed, was moved to respond to Ahad Ha'Am's 1891 article, but then he tore his letter to shreds. With the 1907 publication of Epstein's 1905 address, despair gave way to anger. By then, Smilansky was an established spokesman for Jewish farmers and settlers: he rejected what he saw as Epstein's altruism, and he re-emphasized what he saw as the main goal of the Jewish presence in Palestine, the acquisition of land. And here we must reiterate his view that the only possibility for co-existence lay in the equality of strength (i.e., the buildup of Jewish strength to match that of the Arabs).

"Wenn Ihr wollt, ist es kein Maerchen" ("If you will, it is no fairy-tale"). In Hebrew translation, "Im tirtzu, ein zo aggadah," these words became the unofficial motto of the Zionist movement. The words are those of Theodor Herzl. In 1902 he published his utopian novel, in German, *Altneuland* (Oldnewland), in which he presents his vision of a new society wherein all human needs are satisfied, all human potentialities fulfilled, and all human weaknesses mitigated—all this to be achieved by constructing a new social order.[5] The new society would utilize science and technology in the service of social justice, thereby overcoming religious discrimination and political corruption. (The motto quoted above was the epigraph of the novel.)

The Jewish protagonist, Dr. Friedrich Loewenberg, is on the verge of disillusionment and desperation. He answers a mysterious newspaper advertisement: "Wanted, cultured and despairing young man willing to try last experiment with his life." The ad has been placed by a wealthy and eccentric Gentile, Kingscourt, who is in search of an intellectual companion for a yachting cruise to places outside civilization. They visit Palestine, and their impression is entirely negative (probably reflecting Herzl's own experience at seeing the poverty and desolation of Palestine for the first time). Twenty-one years later they return to find a new and thriving society, a Jewish state.

How does the Arab fare in the Jewish state? The Arab in the story is Reshid Bey, a Berlin-educated doctor of chemistry whose family has resided in Palestine for generations. Kingscourt asks whether Arab residents have not been ruined by Jewish immigration: "Haven't they been forced to leave the country?" Reshid responds: "On the contrary, Jewish immigration was a blessing for all of us" (p. 94). Not only has he sold some of his land to Jews, at a considerable profit, and then leased it on a long-term basis; the poorest Arab *fellahin* have benefited from the Jewish welfare institutions, schools, etc. They are better off than they were by far, and their faith and customs remain undisturbed.

As for Kingscourt's doubts about Arab-Jewish cooperation, Reshid has this to say:

> We Mohammedans have always been better friends with the Jews than you Christians. Even in those early years, when the first Jewish settlers came here, we were always good neighbours, and it often happened that in a quarrel between Arabs my people went to the nearest Jewish village and begged the Jewish mayor to arbitrate. Often enough, too, we asked for instruction or help from the Jews, which was always freely given . . . (p. 100)

The suggestion, therefore, is that the natural tendency on both sides is a peaceful one, and that any animosity that might develop would be a departure from the norm. The new society will open its ranks to whoever will cooperate in building the land.

At the very end of the book, there is a colloquy reflecting the pooling of a wide diversity of values:

Friedrich Loewenberg asks: "We see before us a new and a happier form of
human society—by what was it created?"
Old Litwak said: "Distress!"
Steineck the architect: "The united nation."
Kingscourt: "The new technology."
Dr. Marcus: "Knowledge."
Joe Levy: "Will power."
Professor Steineck: "The forces of nature."
Hopkins, the English parson: "Tolerance."
Reshid Bey: "Self assurance."
David Litwak: "Love and suffering."
But old Rabbi Shmuel rose and solemnly said, "God." (p. 217)

Herzl's utopia reflects an integrative idealism in regard to the Arab-Jewish
confrontation. Clearly, this is supported by nineteenth-century positivism,
combining a faith in the redemptive power of scientific advancement and
the myth of the perfectibility of man.

From the time of the first wave of immigration (1882–1903), the basic
tenet of Jewish settlement in Palestine was the belief that its emphasis must
be agricultural. The purpose in this was twofold: not only to create a new
model of the Jew, linked to the soil rather than to the city; but also to
provide legitimacy to his tenure of the land. This caused friction with the
Arab on both counts, not only because of Arab displacement but also
because Jews introduced new methods of cultivation.

The agrarian emphasis was by no means new. As far back as the Pro-
phets, departure from God was associated with desolation of the land, and
return to God was associated with restoration of the land to tillage:

Be thou corrected, O Jerusalem,
Lest My soul be alienated from thee,
Lest I make thee desolate,
A land not inhabited. (Jeremiah 6:8)

And Isaiah's eschatological vision declares:

I will make the wilderness a pool of water,
And dry land springs of water.
I will plant in the wilderness the cedar . . .
(Isaiah 41:18–19)

Clearly, the newcomers to Palestine wished to break away from the image
of the Jew as a non-productive member of society. This agrarian emphasis

heightened the subsequent friction with the Arab, who objected not only to Jewish immigration but also to land purchase by Jews.

From the 1880s to the 1930s, Jewish land purchase was limited to the coastal plain and the Jezreel and Jordan valleys; in the 1940s a large tract was purchased from Bedouins in the Negev. The pattern of purchases points to the desire to buy land that was sparsely populated or entirely without tenants, land that was uncultivated, swampy, and cheap.[6] However innocuous the act of purchase may have seemed, it did contribute to an open revolt by the Arab population in the period 1936–39. In the eyes of the Jewish settlers, what marked the process was the vision of turning a wasteland into a garden. The pioneering spirit was a part of the redefinition of the self, but it was also an extension of the dream of a just and egalitarian society.

In Hebrew, one does not merely come to Jerusalem, one "ascends." There is an ordinary word for immigration, but immigration to Israel (or Palestine) is always denoted by the word for "ascent" *(aliyah)*. The early days of settlement were marked by two waves of immigration (plural: *aliyoth*). The first of these ran from 1882 to 1903, the second from 1904 to 1914, and the persons involved were moved by different configurations of experience and intent. Broadly put (and with the caution such generalizations demand), we can say that the First Aliyah came to Palestine to flee persecution in Russia; the Second Aliyah came as the result of idealistic (Socialist/Zionist) commitment to rebuild the land and the failed revolution of 1905. The First Aliyah had its ideological component in a numerically small but influential group calling themselves BILU, the Hebrew acronym for "O house of Jacob, come ye, and let us go" (Isaiah 2:5). Ties between the idea of Jewish nationalism and the idea of return to the Land of Israel were in essence established by BILU, the first group to organize itself as pioneers. After two years of hardship, being unused to physical labor and earning meager wages, BILU established its first settlement (i.e., a *moshavah*) in Gedera, in 1884, while others in the movement settled in Jerusalem and Rishon LeZion. Other than BILU, the First Aliyah is remembered for establishing settlements along the coastal plain and in the Galilee.

The Hebrew literature of this period is realistic and autobiographical, documenting the everyday life and hardships of the settlers. This period was also marked by the work of Eliezer Ben-Yehudah (1858–1923), the first lexicographer of modern Hebrew, and the coiner of innumerable new words for the modern language.

This early Hebrew literature also introduced the Arab. That led to a number of possibilities in the depiction of the Arab: he could be included, as it were, in the long story of Jewish persecution; or the writer might attempt to suspend the Jewish viewpoint, and depict the Arab qua Arab; or the writer might wish to portray Arabs and Jews in non-adversarial contact, as neighbors, co-workers, lovers. In addition, as we pointed out earlier, there was the Jewish desire to become a "native son," focusing on the Arab as a model, as a way of enabling Jews to overcome the European stereotyping of Jews.

Jewish settlers of this period came to Palestine knowing very little about it beforehand. Coming from small hamlets in Russia or Rumania, they were invariably startled by their first arrival at Jaffa, a harborless port where Arabs manhandled them into shaky boats and rowed them ashore. This experience has been recounted many times. But there is also the shock of the strange climate, the sounds and smells—all realities they knew nothing about. The reaction was two-sided, and it mirrored the two-sided early reaction of Jews to Arabs: attraction and aversion, fascination and apprehension. The Arab, especially the nomadic Bedouin, was prominent in Jewish imagination as a prototype of what the biblical Jews must have been. The Bedouins, living in tents, evoked images of the biblical sons of Rechab, who were commanded: "Ye shall drink no wine . . .; neither shall ye build a house, nor sow seed, nor plant vineyard . . . but all your days ye shall dwell in tents, that ye may live many days in the land wherein ye sojourn" (Jeremiah 35:6–7).

The First Aliyah included women writers. Among them was Hemda Ben-Yehudah (1873–1951), the second wife of Eliezer Ben-Yehudah. With his encouragement and strong advocacy of the cultural equality of women, she became a writer, editor, and journalist. In her story "The Farm of the Sons of Rechab" (1903), the protagonist, Ephraim, is searching for the descendants of the land's original pre-exilic inhabitants: presumably, people whose ancestors go back to some common source of Arab and Jewish civilization. He encounters a number of Bedouin tribes, most of them hospitable, and he learns of a tribe of people near the Jordan who have kept their ancient language. The premise of the story is that the recovery of this ancient culture will liberate Jews as well as Arabs from their respective cultural constraints. A Bedouin leader (who is also Jewish) works to liberate the women of his tribe so that they can work alongside men. Arabs and Jews are seen as brothers, and all speak Hebrew.

In referring back to an early Hebraic culture, Hemda and Eliezer Ben-Yehudah can be seen as precursors of the subsequent "Cana'anite" movement, with its view that Hebrew is the rightfully dominant language of the area. Ephraim eventually locates the sons of Rechab, and miraculously they have retained Hebrew as their daily language. Nominally, they accept Jews as their brothers; yet they express disdain for them for having left the land and forgotten the language. Despite the naivete of the story, it addresses a number of vital topics of its time: the war of languages, the equality of women, the Bedouin as unspoiled "noble savage," and a linguistic/cultural solution to the problem of Arab-Jewish co-existence. Clearly the common Semitic origin and the closeness of Arabic and Hebrew enhanced the settler's desire to become a part of the East, and to speculate as to lost origins, and even to see Bedouins as lost Jews who adopted the Arab way of life.

The First Aliyah has not fared well in subsequent accounts. This is surprising, because the first wave of immigrants should by rights have been regarded as the founding fathers and mothers of Jewish settlement. Yet Hebrew literature has depicted the First Aliyah in negative terms: as pretentious, bourgeois farmers with French-speaking daughters who play piano and dream of Paris fashions. The truth is that these first settlers were of middle-class origin, who wished better things for their sons than "digging in the orchards." And if that wish led them to employ Arab labor, that too was deplored by the subsequent Socialist idealists, who believed in the dignity of labor and the equality of all mankind.

There was a more direct and concrete explanation for the poor reputation of the First Aliyah: its writers were (comparatively) crude amateurs recording their banal struggles and dreams. By comparison, the writers of the Second Aliyah (1904–1914) were far better writers (the mention of Brenner and Agnon will suffice) who were already established prior to coming to Palestine or were in some significant way connected to literary centers in the Diaspora. At their hands, the farmers of the First Aliyah came in for some disdain and even some stereotyping.

The Second Aliyah was made up of men and women who were far more committed in their idealism. Figures such as Yitzhak Ben-Zvi (1884–1963), David Ben-Gurion (1886–1973), and Berl Katzenelson (1887–1944), whose dates of aliyah were 1907, 1906, and 1909 respectively, eventually provided the core of intellectual/ideological leadership of Jewish settlement. The older farmers, for their part, had little use for these Socialist intellectuals who had trouble bearing up under the heavy labor, the heat, the typhoid— and who resented their exploitation of Arab labor. The farmers were well established, and their middle-class values were abhorrent to the young newcomers, who were dependent upon the farmers for employment. The Socialist newcomers held strongly to the principle of "Hebrew labor," i.e., that Jews, not Arabs, should work the land, and that such agricultural work would constitute the Jews' true return to the land. The farmers were much happier employing Arabs, who did not come down with recurrent bouts of malaria, were accustomed to hard physical labor, were familiar with the work and the terrain, and demanded little.

There is also the idealistic zeal of the Second Aliyah, of these former revolutionaries, with their seriousness and naivete, their persistence in refusing to compromise with the farmers. All these factors contributed to the creation of the commune, the cooperative mode of living which in turn gave birth to the *kvutzah* and the *kibbutz*. As an elaborated social system, the kibbutz is the most impressive achievement of modern Jewish settlement in Palestine. At the same time, the existing settlements required the organization of Jewish defense units in an association called "The Watchman" *(HaShomer)*. Set up in 1907 by Mania and Israel Shohat and Yitzhak Ben-Zvi, *HaShomer* set the foundation for the idea of the cooperative collective; most of its members were also members of the Socialist/Zionist *Po'alei Zion* party, advocating the right to work, and dedicated to guarding Jewish settlements and to expanding Jewish settlements in unsettled areas.

There were numerous difficulties confronting the young newcomers: the Turkish administration was corrupt, terrain and working conditions were harsh, and there was unrelenting opposition from the local Arabs. On the other hand, the image of the dedicated and self-sacrificing pioneer helped to consolidate Jewish settlement. In addition, many of the central figures involved in this early movement went on to form the political power structure that lasted into the 1970s. For these and other reasons, the Second Aliyah is justly regarded as having set the foundation for the subsequent ideology and power structure in Palestine and Israel. Moreover, the Second Aliyah can be credited with having exerted a seminal influence in shaping the Hebrew press, Hebrew literature, even the introduction and acceptance of Hebrew as the language of ordinary discourse.

1. MOSHE SMILANSKY

The work of Moshe Smilansky (1874–1953) was shaped by his many-sided activities as an agricultural pioneer in Palestine, a publicist, and a public figure. Arriving in Palestine in 1891, he was one of the founders of the *moshavah* Hadera. Eventually he settled in as a farmer/landowner in Rehovot, where he owned vineyards and groves of orange and almond trees. His literary career began with contributions to Hebrew and Yiddish periodicals in Palestine and elsewhere. Politically, he was a disciple and friend of Ahad Ha'Am; despite his admiration for Herzl's personal qualities, Smilansky opposed Herzl's plan for Jewish settlement in Uganda, and continued to follow Ahad Ha'Am's views.

Throughout his life, Smilansky was profoundly concerned with Arab-Jewish tension. On the heated question of Hebrew labor, he disagreed with the prevailing view held by the settlers of the Second Aliyah, who insisted that all work be done exclusively by Jewish workers. Smilansky, employing Arab as well as Jewish labor, believed in a mixed labor force.

Unlike other First Aliyah farmers, many of whom resented the Socialist-oriented newcomers of the Second Aliyah, Smilansky had many personal and political ties with the latter group. One of his closest friends (until a political disagreement ended the association) was Joseph Aharonovitch, the editor of *Hapo'el Hatza'ir,* the organ of the Socialist movement of that name. In the years of the First World War, many members of the Jewish population were harassed and exiled; afterwards, Smilansky was active in organizations involved in the acquisition and reclamation of land. Later he organized a farmers' federation.

Smilansky's view of the Arab-Jewish confrontation changed with the passing years. In 1908 his approach was rather hard, advocating the strengthening of the Jewish settlement and its infrastructure; with this, there was the fear that the low cultural level of Arab agrarian society might negatively affect the moral character of the Jewish population. By 1911 his approach was more moderate: as an ardent Zionist he was still a romantic believer in Jewish settlement of the land; yet the widespread insensitivity toward Arabs was a constant source of distress to him. He envisaged the integration of Jews into a greater society incorporating Jews, Arabs, and Turks—each group enjoying a national revival within the totality. By 1913 his position involved a complex of attitudes: not idealizing the Arabs although respecting their tradition and ethos; at the same time, he did not adopt the widely held attitude of dismissing Arab national identity as non-existent.

During the disturbances of 1936–39, Smilansky joined four other Zionist leaders to form a group advocating a bi-national approach in response to the ongoing hostilities. They met with Arab leaders and came to an agreement to limit Jewish immigration and land purchase over the next five to ten years. The group of five proposed a cap of 30,000 Jewish immigrants per year; Chaim Weitzman agreed to a limit of 40,000; the Jewish Agency suggested 50,000 to 60,000. Eventually, negotiations broke down.[1]

The names most often associated with the idea of bi-nationalism (i.e., the idea of two nations on one land) are Smilansky, Martin Buber, and Judah Leib Magnes. But after a number of failures to create a working relationship with Arab representatives, Smilansky's outlook grew pessimistic—and although he continued to insist on mutual accommodation as the only basis for an ongoing modus vivendi, he grew to fear that the creation of a Jewish state would present an insuperable obstacle to long-lasting co-existence.

In 1942, a group calling itself *Ihud* (Union) was formed, most of whose members had belonged to the League for Jewish-Arab Rapprochement and Co-operation. In March 1946, Smilansky, Buber, and Magnes—as representatives of *Ihud*—appeared before an Anglo-American Committee of Inquiry. This committee had been formed not only to consider the situation in Palestine, but also to look into the problem of Jewish displaced persons in Europe. The three *Ihud* representatives reiterated their basic tenet, the creation of a bi-national entity based on reciprocal independence and equality. To that end, Jewish immigration was seen as a justifiable step in an equitable agreement between Arabs and Jews, since limits to Jewish immigration would condemn the Jewish population to the status of a minority, and would make the country a wasteland.

By 1947, amid the crisis connected with the relocation of Jewish refugees and clandestine immigration to Palestine a year before the departure of British forces, Smilansky and Buber had given up on the idea of a bi-national entity as a viable proposition, and accepted the idea of a Jewish state. Smilansky was attacked in the Arab press, along with other moderates who had called for understanding and cooperation between Arabs and Jews. A leading Arabic newspaper asserted the claim that the Arabs were the legal owners of the land. Understanding and cooperation would be possible only if Jews were to give up the idea of a Jewish state and acknowledge Arab hegemony in Palestine. Further, it was urged that all Jews who entered Palestine after 1918 be regarded as foreign invaders, whose fate would be decided by the Arab state of Palestine.[2]

A year later, in 1948, war broke out.

Among Smilansky's Arab neighbors and the workers in his orchards, he was known as Hawajah Mussa ("Squire Moses"—*Mussa* being the Arabic equivalent of Moshe, and *Hawajah* the title for an eminent person or landowner). Using that appellation as his pen name, Smilansky published three volumes of stories under the composite title *Bnei Arav*.[3] This term, "Children of Arabia," is the Arabic designation for the nomadic Bedouin, regarded as the pure descendants of the original Arabs, as contrasted with the local urban population. The stories appeared individually between 1906 and 1934. Varied in subject matter, they are uncomplicated, even simplistic, close to the genre of the folk tale. Throughout, Smilansky was moved by the plight of the poor agricultural workers and the fellahin (i.e., settled Arab peasants, as opposed to the nomadic Bedouin). Their living conditions were generally deplorable, and diseases such as trachoma and bilharzia were endemic among them. Smilansky also was outraged at the exploitation of Arab workers by rich urban landowners and by the Turkish authorities prior to 1918.

As early as 1902–1903 Smilansky was writing stories with an Arab as the central figure, and this focus came to be the distinctive mark of his writing. If we look for the source of that focus in Smilansky himself, any number of possibilities present themselves: a fascination with the charm and/or squalor of the East? his admiration for the strong traditionalism of Arab society? or perhaps a desire to expose the terrible conditions of life for the Arab workers at a time when Jews in Palestine were taking their first tentative steps toward settlement and might wish to alleviate those conditions? Some commentators have viewed Smilansky's writing as escapist literature; others have seen it as presenting his own version of the "Truth from the Land of Israel." Surely the composite answer must include his Tolstoyan devotion to the soil.

One early encounter with an Arab was crucial in shaping Smilansky's complex attitude. In his memoirs,[4] published in 1928, he describes the encounter, which took place in 1891. At the time, Smilansky was a seventeen-year-old newcomer, working in a new settlement in Hadera. He took a walk to the Roman ruins at Caesaria, and he experienced a feeling of resentment toward the Romans, who destroyed the land and forced its inhabitants into exile. Amid the sand dunes, a sense of emptiness came over him, and he felt alone and forsaken. His solitude was broken by the sudden appearance of a Bedouin on horseback. As the Arab passed by, he looked at the youth with anger and contempt. He said, "Get up, Jew," and ordered him to go away. Smilansky was shocked by the tone of hatred in the Arab's voice, and he answered: "I am on my land. You go." The rider struck the young man on the head with his whip and continued on his way. For thirty-two years Smilansky did not return to Caesaria, and he kept silent about the incident. When he did return, his thoughts were taken up not with Roman cruelty but with the then-current pogroms in his native Ukraine and the Arab riots in Jerusalem. While taking a stroll with a friend who was an agronomist, they discussed ways of halting the moving sand dunes. Nothing had changed in the thirty-two years: it was the same wasteland, the same marshes and swamps—and the same Bedouin tents. "And something wells up within me: Bedouin, you have whipped me in vain. . . . Here I am again, and you, you have not done a thing, you have not changed a thing."

What had changed was no longer in Arab hands. The coastal plain—from Hadera to Zichron Ya'akov, to the mountains of Ephraim—was in Jewish hands. His "revenge" manifested itself in the draining of the swamps, the forestation of the sand dunes, the planting of crops, the building of dams. Smilansky concluded with the ironic observation that the native inhabitants who had been dwelling on the land for centuries were sterile, and it was the "foreigners" who brought life to the country. The encounter had a formative significance for Smilansky, and he used it also in his 1911 novel *Hadassah*.

Further insight into the depth of Arab animosity was provided for Smilansky by a trip to Lebanon and Syria in 1912. He had been to Europe for surgery, and his return to Palestine was like a second aliyah for him. His enthusiasm for the region led him to venture north and east. He describes the journey in the words of his autobiographical protagonist, Yehuda: In the railway carriage to Beirut he is the only Jew. He does not conceal the fact that he is a landowner, with property farther south. Hearing the hostile remarks, he muses about the source of the hostility: Is it directed at the Jew qua invader, or is it a part of a broader attitude toward all foreigners as such? Even later, when Smilansky gave up the idea of bi-nationalism, he continued to believe that the Jewish presence in Palestine was beneficial to the Arab, providing employment, education, and technological progress. Yehuda recalls one of the Zionist mottos: "We have come to the land to build and to be built through it." If Arabs and Jews both are to benefit, then it is as brothers, not as conquering invaders, that Jews return to Palestine, to redeem the land from ruin for the benefit of both peoples.

At the same time, Yehuda senses that formal Zionist thinking is oblivious to Arab feelings—and a sense of failed opportunity engulfs him. As he turns his attention to the captivating landscape, one of the travelers begins to question him, asking if he has come to spy, or to buy land and displace its tenants. He answers that he has come to enjoy the beauty of the region, but since he has already admitted that he is a landowner, the questioner asks him: "How many fellahin did you evict from the land you bought from Arabs? Clearly, you did not inherit the land from your grandfather in Moscow." (Arabs often referred to early Jewish settlers as "Moscubs," i.e., "Muscovites.")

Yehuda answers that the land he bought with his colleagues was deso-late, covered with thorns and thistles, and that the only ones evicted were the foxes. He adds that Arabs in the hundreds are at work on Jewish farms. His own Arab worker, who has been with him for twenty years, began as a poor boy and now has a house and land of his own. The Arab workers understand that Jews pay ten piasters for an eight-hour day, while the going rate in Sidon (Lebanon) is three piasters for a day that begins at dawn and ends at dusk. The Kadi in Beirut owns an orchard in Sidon and pays his workers two piasters a day.

In Beirut itself, Yehuda encounters the even stronger feelings of nationalistic college students. A Sephardic student criticizes Jews for their hostile attitude toward Arabs, ranging from condescension to the militant organization of *HaShomer* ("The Watchman"). Smilansky himself has been attacked recently, for his condescending attitude toward Arabs.[5] But such criticism can hardly be justified when Smilansky expresses just such criticism through his interlocutor. Indeed, he turned such criticism into a more fundamental skepticism regarding the Zionist standpoint as a whole. At the end of his trip, Yehuda is shattered, and asks himself: If the Zionist dream is just, why does it evoke so much hatred? Clearly, these doubts are Smilansky's own.

Smilansky's writings are conditioned by two factors: the close contact between the Jewish and Arab communities, a closeness that will vanish after 1948; and the desire of Jews to be native sons in the way that Arabs are. This serves to complicate the Jewish-Arab relation, since the Jewish desire to be native son is connected to love of the land but also to the image of the Arab as model.

In the story "Hawajah Nazar,"[6] Smilansky tells of a young man, Lazar, who was born of a Gentile mother and a Jewish father on the banks of the Volga, and comes to Palestine. He falls in love with the land. His simple affability and directness, as well as his physical prowess, endear him to the Arabs, who call him Hawajah Nazar (*Nazar* being the Arabic corruption of the name Lazar). Indeed, the Arabs give him their highest praise: "He is like one of us—a son of Arabia!" (p. 160)

In turn, he repays the compliment by studying their language, customs, manners, and modes of hospitality. In time, they would ask for his advice, and he would settle disputes between Arab villagers. As part of his acceptance into the land, he longs to replace his love for the Volga with love for the Jordan River, which he dreams of but has not seen. He is aghast when a teacher from the Galilee describes it as a narrow and shallow stream strewn with stones. Lazar entreats the narrator to join him on his trip to the Jordan, which they reach after a long ride accompanied by some dangerous confrontations with Arabs. Lazar is shocked to discover that the river is indeed shallow and lacking in the majesty he expected. On horseback they follow the river southward, and eventually the small stream becomes a broader and stronger one. In his ultimate encounter with the river, he throws himself at it, swimming and laughing as he "baptizes" himself in the gushing water. The undercurrent carries him away to his death. The narrator enters the water and is almost demented when he finds no trace of his friend. The body comes to the surface and is held by some reeds. The narrator rides to town to fetch a doctor and the Burial Society: they refuse to bury him when they discover he is uncircumcized. The narrator insists that Lazar was a better Jew than they (in his spiritual love of the land). Eventually, the river takes his body away. The narrator concludes: "You did not want to take him, so now he has been taken by the one that was most fitting—Jordan has taken him!" (p. 181)

Smilansky's "distance" from the Jewish mainstream (religious at one extreme, Socialist at the other) is paralleled by the complex ambivalence of his views of Arab values. Despite his closeness to the Arab, Smilansky's standpoint is that of a superior, criticizing values he sees as primitive. This attitude is evident in one of his earliest and simplest stories, corroborated in his memoirs as having taken place in his early years as a farmer in Rehovot. The story is "Latifa" (1906), in the *Palestine Caravan* collection.[7] It begins with a paraphrase of a Talmudic statement: "If you never saw Latifa's eyes—you don't know how beautiful eyes can be" (p. 265). Latifa is a girl of fourteen, working in the fields of the young Jewish farmer Hawajah Mussa. We may assume that the time is the mid-1890s, which would place Smilansky in his early twenties. Latifa clearly captivates the heart of the young farmer.

She declares that her father, a sheikh, will not permit her to continue working for the Jew, but will give her in marriage to the son of another sheikh, a short and ugly fellow whom she does not love. She suggests that her father would give her to Hawajah Mussa if he were to become a Moslem. At this he laughs, "Latifa, become a Jewess, and I will take you" (p. 267). We do not know how serious this is, on either side. But there is no doubt about the authenticity of Latifa's reply: "My father would slay me, and you too."

She says she would sooner die than marry the sheikh's son. She marvels at the custom of monogamy among Jews:

> "Hawajah, is it true that your folk take but one?"
> "But one, Latifa."
> "And your folk do not beat their women?"
> "Nay. How shall one beat the woman whom he loves and who loves him?"
> "Among you the maidens take those they love?"
> "Assuredly."
> "While us they sell like beasts of burden. . . ." (p. 267)

Latifa's father appears on his white horse. He strikes Latifa several times with a stick on her head and shoulders. When the narrator moves to intervene, Latifa's eyes warn him away. The sheikh storms at her: "Did I not order you to cease going to the Jew?" Turning to the laborers, he declares: "Shame upon you, Moslems, who sell your toil to the unbelievers!" When he has departed, one of the laborers says: "He is furious because he can no longer get his laborers at half the wages, and make them toil from morning to night." But it is clear that he resents Jews in general.

Latifa is married to the ugly man. Some years pass. The narrator sees two old Arab women in his yard, selling chickens. Latifa identifies herself to him. She has grown old, but her eyes still have some of their earlier luster. She asks if he has married, and asks to see his wife. She looks at the young wife for a long time. There are tears in her eyes. Latifa disappears and is not seen again.

What is emphasized here is the deterministic element which holds Moslem culture in an iron grip. Latifa is an emblem of the East—as when the narrator asks the old Latifa why she has changed so, and she responds: "All things come from Allah, Hawajah!" The suggestion is that the Arabs can no more change their age-old customs than they can dispel their hatred. And with all this, there is Smilansky's feeling of ambivalence: his admiration for the Arab, and his resentment of him.

The same ambivalence prevails in the *Children of Arabia* stories. These can be arranged in two groups: in the first, a Jewish narrator (ostensibly Smilansky himself) hears from his Arab workers—Bedouin as well as fellahin—about the hardships they have experienced in a closed society which allows no deviation from sanctified rules and customs. These are more vignettes than stories, built around a simple element that reverses the reader's expectations. The second group, more narrative and with a discernible structure, includes stylized tales about the life of Arabs. Most of these stories occur in unspecified time, and some reveal the effects of Jewish settlement on the life and fate of Arabs. In both groups, all the stories (except one) are marked by an element of determinism. The man or, more frequently, the woman is the victim of passion and circumstances. Woman and man, Bedouin and fellahin, are caught in the web of rigid social stratification and tribal codes. Any attempt to challenge these codes is severely punished, often with death. In the polarity between determinism and free choice, it is the deterministic outlook that prevails without exception. Traditional society, for its continuity, requires the suspension or submersion of personal needs and aspirations. The code of honor demands the sacrifice of all who depart from it.

The woman is clearly the main victim of this system. Often she is married off to a man she despises. More tragically, she is caught in a romantic liaison with a man, and then is condemned to death at the hands of her family. How accurate or inaccurate this picture may be is not as important for us as the fact that this is the truth as *perceived*—i.e., by Jewish writers in close contact with Arab life, wishing both to idealize and criticize that way of life. That perception could therefore serve as a basis for the feeling of cultural and social superiority on the part of those whose European background allowed for social mobility and amelioration, and who officially idealized monogamy and love between the sexes as equals.

The stories are touched by hyperbole and exaggeration. The oral tradition behind the genre allows for a balladic quality whereby dramatic events can drastically affect people's destiny. In the story "Haj Ibrahim," a generous, mild, and God-fearing Arab becomes a highway robber after his fiancée is brutally raped by a German engineer; the code forces him to kill his defiled beloved, but the injustice changes him dramatically for life. On another but related level, an object—be it a particular rifle, say, or a particular horse—takes on a metaphysical importance for some people, and they will cling to it despite all odds. This too, seen against the models of nineteenth-century naturalism and ameliorism, becomes another basis for feelings of European cultural superiority.

We are led to ask why Smilansky chose to devote his writing to stories about Arabs, rather than to realistic stories about Jewish life in Palestine. It is all too easy to attribute his choice to escapism and a fascination with the exotic East (as we suggested earlier, for speculative purposes): that fascination might presumably have been aimed at European readers who could revel in the feast of exoticism while avoiding its harsh realities. Yet if pure exoticism were his aim, he would have avoided the constant note of condemnation along with his fascination—and such avoidance is the path he did not take. Throughout his writings, moreover, Smilansky reflects the adversarial relationship between Arabs and Jews, and the effect of Jewish settlement on the Arab population as well as the cordiality in the relationship.

Smilansky did not fare well with critics in his own time; nor is he admired today for his literary qualities—he is remembered mainly in texts dealing with the history of Hebrew literature. Brenner attacked Smilansky and those who wrote "genre" fiction (corresponding to "genre" painting scenes of domestic life), that subject matter being better suited to memoirs than to fiction. The pathetic heroism, the half-baked narrative which was all too often reality with a thin patina of fictionality, entitle his writings to be called semi-documentary or semi-biographical work at the level of the familiar essay. Those who take the trouble to criticize him today find in him an element of "colonizational literature" with stereotyping of the "natives."

For us, his significance is in reflecting certain attitudes toward the Arab, attitudes held and expressed in some (though by no means all) quarters. But even beyond that purpose (and the purposes of this book), Smilansky demands interest for his unique combination of Zionist idealism and humanist sensitivity. Even in his earliest writings as a journalist and polemicist, he is sensitive to the plight of displaced fellahin, and in this he calls attention—with Epstein and Ahad Ha'Am—to a moral issue that has been a constant in the Hebrew literature concerned with the adversarial relation between Arabs and Jews. Responding to Epstein in 1908, Smilansky stresses the importance of there being a Jewish majority in Palestine. He evokes the image of the Jew who no longer wishes to be weak, and to appeal for justice and mercy from the stronger. Later, he seeks equality based on strength as the foundation of a bi-national co-existence.

Can his *Children of Arabia* stories therefore be regarded as a mere extension of his political attitudes into fiction? This is a view advanced recently.[8] It can be challenged, for the simple reason that his political stance underwent profound change (from the advocacy of bi-national co-existence to the affirmation of a Jewish state), while his fiction remained consistent from his earliest works through his entire career as a writer. This brings us to the fundamental issue of the stereotyped depiction of the Arab in Hebrew fiction.

Many commentators have seen just such stereotyping in Smilansky's fiction. His depictions of the Arab—from "noble savage" to Jew-hater; from native son to willing seller of land; from the hard-hearted effendi to the poor peasant; from the proud Bedouin to the self-effacing outcast—all are types devoid of psychological depth or individuality. The same objection can be applied, with moderation, to his autobiographical narrator, portrayed as well-meaning, dedicated, obstinate, but shallow. Smilansky wrote the fiction he could write with his limited literary powers. His work touches reality as well as the romanticization of reality, a sense of doom and an almost futile hope. In his better stories he attains a moderate degree of complexity; but in essence it is a juxtaposition of polarities of two-dimensional characters. Despite these weaknesses, his fiction is commendable for giving expression to his pantheistic love of nature, and his attempt to depict the Arab truthfully, even if the depiction falls into stereotype. The depiction of the stranger, the unknown, will always run this risk.

2. YEHUDA BURLA

If birthplace and family background are to be taken as significant in characterizing a writer, then we have here an important contrast: Smilansky, as we saw, was born outside Palestine, of Ashkenazi stock. Yehuda Burla (1886–1969) was born in Jerusalem, to a well-established Sephardic family that had emigrated from Turkey in the eighteenth century. Further contrasts appear: During World War I, Smilansky went to Egypt to enlist in the British army; Burla, remaining in Palestine, was drafted into the Turkish army. Smilansky was a farmer, Burla a teacher.

Burla also had extensive experience in civil service. In Damascus he was director of the Hebrew schools as well as of the Zionist organization. In the 1930s, in Palestine, he served as head of the Arab division of the *Histadruth* (the general labor federation), and then as envoy of the *Keren Hayesod* (Palestine Foundation Fund) in Central and South America. Later in his life he was director of information in the Minorities Office of the State of Israel. One of his last posts was that of president of the Hebrew Writers Association.

The first challenge he felt as a writer was describing the richly varied life he had known in Jerusalem, a life that mixed Eastern and Jewish elements. In an interview, he said: "If not I, who would tell the stories of Mussa and Yussuf, Bossa Reina and Bossa Rivka?"[1] He knew of no writer who wrote of Oriental Jewish life or Arab life who could serve as a literary model for him. He was, however, greatly influenced by Russian, German, and French literature, and was especially moved by the work of Gorky. For our purposes in this book, the value of Burla is in his depiction of the warmth and closeness between Arabs and Jews—in Damascus, Jerusalem, and elsewhere in pre-1948 days. Yet amid that picture of ease, there is the ubiquitous human toil and trial. Burla was drawn to writers of the realistic mode, grieved as he was by the squalor he saw everywhere around him. The best of Hebrew writers in this mode was Y. H. Brenner, and Burla sent him his first story, "Luna." Burla later admitted that if Brenner had rejected his writing, he would never again have touched pen to paper, and would even have considered suicide. Brenner encouraged him, however, and Burla's story was eventually published after the end of World War I.

Along with Smilansky and Shami, Burla expanded the horizons of Hebrew fiction: as Smilansky had opened the way for the depiction of the Arab, Burla and Shami depicted Jewish Sephardic society and Arab society in Palestine and Syria, as well as the broad milieu of the Orient, the Levant, and the Balkans. Theirs are not the introspective protagonists of European Hebrew fiction in search of their tormented inner selves; rather, their characters are externally moored in social conventions that limit the free exercise of their powers as individuals. These unsophisticated men and women are the victims of their own perception of life as much as of the reality in which they move. Burla's declared literary field was that of the Oriental person yielding to fate and superstition, renouncing all choice and free will. Many of his characters, men and women, believe in fate as an independent force even beyond the power of God.

In almost a balladic mode, the Burla character is caught in the curve of time, and is met by a catastrophe that mars him for life. In Burla's 1929 novel *In Darkness Striving*, the protagonist has his eyes put out in an act of vengeance, and his search for the reasons becomes his raison d'être. In the full tradition of the realistic novel, Burla is a writer of plot-oriented narrative: the typical story's basic presuppositions are evident in exposition, conflict, and denouement; the reader is not asked to fill in the gaps or to weave the narrative fabric out of limited material; further, the characters are fully drawn, depicted in a tone devoid of irony. Thus he does not present the self-conflicted sort of tale where the plot is one reality and the tone or point of view another. There is no mysterious subtext in addition to the tale that is told; and if there is a sense of mystery at all, it is the general one having to do with man's fate.

Burla is a traditional writer in the nineteenth-century mode, combining some characteristic aspects of European naturalism with Sephardic, Islamic, and Balkan modes: there is the familiar story within a story, and a narrator-witness listening to a narrating protagonist; but occasionally a story of his is reminiscent of the Arabic *maquama*, a verse tale featuring a rogue who relates the woes that have befallen him—and even this short narrative has a demi-epic quality in the expansion of events, time, and place. Further, there is often a sense of an oral tradition of storytelling, where the listener is almost passive in the narrative process.

The 1922 novel *Bli Kohav* ("Starless," or "Luckless"), which we will discuss more fully later, tells the story of a man whose unfortunate fate has been foretold to him. Time merely unravels the calamity in store for him. But unlike the self-assertive tragic hero of European fiction, who challenges whatever it is that has prescribed his fate, the Eastern man in Burla's tales, Jew or Arab, accepts his fate as part of the human lot. This resignation, the acceptance of a world beyond man's powers to change it, is typical of Burla's protagonists: the trials they undergo are heart-wrenching; yet his characters do not always cling tenaciously to dire reality, and some resort to suicide as the only way out.

In the novel *In Darkness Striving*[2]—the Hebrew title is "Man's Struggles"—Burla depicts Damascus at the turn of the century, where amicable relations prevail between Jews, Moslems, and Christians. The narrator is a teacher of Hebrew who is intrigued by the blind Rahamo, a Damascus-born Jew. This Rahamo is rather convivial, sitting in a coffee house, surrounded by Moslem friends, or carrying on with girls in the Jewish neighborhood. Very little is known about him, although the narrator senses that there is a story in the man. When the narrator makes inquiries, some criticize Rahamo's wayward behavior, others praise his latent goodness. His shiftless ways are attributed to his blindness.

Rahamo proves to be a raconteur. In a gathering keeping vigil over a woman who has given birth, he tells a tale in rhymed verse, the way Arab storytellers have traditionally done, "a profound allegory about 'A Prince who Became a Hermit' " (p. 12). The rhymed couplets are reminiscent of the classical Arab poets, the narrator says, "charged with wisdom and linguistic brilliance. . . ." What we should note here is something that Burla regards as so unremarkable that it requires no comment: namely, the fact that a Jew can be so integrated into Arab culture as to be able to tell a tale in a traditional Arab mode—and win respect for it. The narrator says that Rahamo recited the couplets "with astonishing ease and eloquence. . . ."

The blind bard puts off all attempts on the narrator's part to strike up a friendship. But later, in the summer, when the news of the Palestine Mandate reaches Damascus, and the Jews in the community throng to the school compound, Rahamo expresses his deep hope for Israel: Zionists are bringing about the advent of the Messiah (p. 14). It is then that Rahamo tells his own tale to the narrator. He had been a peddler, selling dresses and trinkets to Moslem women in the villages around Damascus. He met a young Moslem woman, a divorcee, and they fell in love. She was willing to convert to Judaism so that they could marry. Her family was fond of him, because he had helped them. On his way back to Damascus he was attacked by the brothers of her former husband—her deserting her former husband and taking another man was a grave insult to the honor of their family. They blinded Rahamo, and in this way the family was avenged. The love affair was over, and Rahamo was cared for by a kindly sheikh, who recited Arab tales to him, week after week. In answer to Rahamo's Job-like questioning as to why God let all this happen, the sheikh said: "Men, their lives and deeds and affairs, are far removed from God, mean nothing to him, in fact. He is the All-powerful, and we are but motes of dust, of no account to Him whatsoever. He is All, and we are nought" (p. 109). With the guidance of the sheikh, Rahamo was able to rejoin life.

As a writer, Burla has no interest in the friction between Arabs and Jews. Rather, the pictures of the easy intermingling of Jews and Arabs, and of a Jew's love of Arabic poetry and wisdom as his way of salvation combine to give us a tale devoid of hostility between the two peoples. As late as the 1960s, Burla held to this wistful childhood vision of Arab-Jewish co-existence, rather than depicting the new reality of ongoing animosity.

The earlier novel, *Bli Kohav*,[3] is set in World War I. The narrator is a Jew conscripted into the Turkish army, and serves as a translator to a German officer (as Burla did). They are on camels as part of a force traveling south toward Egypt, with the aim of attacking the British forces and capturing the Suez Canal. The Jewish narrator, David, is called by his Arabic name, Hawajah Daoud; he befriends Abed, a Bedouin scout who serves as their guide. The daylight activities of war are dissolved in the quiet desert nights when this and other stories are told. The friendliness of the two men leads to an exchange of traditional Arabic folk tales.

Over the six days and nights of the desert journey, the friendship grows, and David entreats Abed to tell his life story. The narrative and Abed's tale unfold simultaneously, and the suspense is maintained for the reader/ listener. Like a story in the tradition of the Thousand and One Nights, this tale develops slowly and is meant to be enjoyed for the telling: it stops every night, to be resumed the following night; the description of the night emphasizes the story's character as an oral tale, as Abed recreates his life to a stranger upon whom he will never set eyes again.

Both Daoud and Abed are marginal figures in the life of the military convoy. In parallel fashion, Abed is himself marginal, having been adopted by a Bedouin tribe. His desire to belong is as strong as his desire to know his true origin. The sheikh's daughter, Nahora, has fallen in love with him. Although Abed is by then a part of the tribe, he is considered to be little better than a servant. (The reason for this humiliation is not revealed until later.) The love affair of Abed and Nahora has a tragic end, and we are made to understand that Abed's fate was inscribed in his very beginning.

The mystery of Abed's origin is revealed when he meets three travelers in the desert. He learns that he is of the Kattifi tribe. Nahora's father and his men had attacked the Kattifi and had killed almost all of them. But then someone recalled a decree of the Prophet Mohammed: the Kattifi had given shelter to the prophet when he fled to Medina; when he left them he blessed them and promised that their tribe would never vanish, and that whoever killed them all would himself be killed. Nahora's father, fearing the prophet's curse, found the child Abed and saved him. But this moment of revelation is of tragic import to Abed, in almost a Sophoclean sense: in one of numerous skirmishes, when Abed was trying to impress Nahora's father, he killed a man, not knowing it was his own uncle who had come to save him.

Abed and Nahora arrange to meet in Mecca, where they marry and elope to Lebanon. After a few years of happiness they are discovered. Nahora and her children are lured by her father and brothers, to be killed cruelly; her father and his son, too, find their death in Lebanon. Daoud is moved by the tragic tale; he has further questions about Abed's presence in the desert, but he restrains himself in deference to the suffering Abed has endured.

Earlier in his life, Abed had been told by a clairvoyant that he was "without a star." Fate reigns, and any attempt to escape it must prove futile. Burla's picture of Arabs, then, is of individuals who conduct their lives in this belief—namely, that existence is the arena of fate's unfolding. Burla is saying, in effect, that despite the personal tragedy of his protagonist, there is a victory in a man's ability to tell his tale, to recount his fate in a well-wrought story. Thus, beyond the surface content of love, vengeance, bloodshed, and cruelty, these stories are about the aesthetic pleasure of telling a tale, so that the art of telling is the sub-plot, or sub-topic, and serves to override the cultural gap the stories themselves had served to emphasize, for the storytelling art touches us all.

Burla himself provides the background information for his writing of the stories, and this reveals much in regard to the rich possibilities in Arab-Jewish relations as well as the limitations that prevailed. *Bli Kohav* began to emerge when he was in the Moab, in Transjordan. He was fluent in Arabic, and grew fascinated with Bedouin lore. He remained in the area for over a year, and this stay contributed not only to *Bli Kohav* but also to four stories or sketches depicting the lives of Arabs, Jews, and Turks in the Turkish army. In these he portrays the horrors of war and the disdain for human life (the death of a mule had to be reported; the death of men met with no official notice). All this is recounted in his first publication, a documentary narrative somewhere between fiction and reportage, "Amongst the Arab Tribes" (1918).

The narrator had been exiled from Jerusalem on suspicion of harboring Zionist sympathies. When news arrived of the British entry into Jerusalem, he began to entertain the idea of desertion from the army. The terrain was harsh, dangerous, and impenetrable without a guide. Hussein, the sharif of Mecca, who later became the king of Jordan, was hostile to the Turks, and was advancing toward their position. Burla found an Arab notable, a pious Moslem, who found in the Koran a basis for friendship with Jews. He provided the appropriate disguise, and he swore three Arabs to take the narrator to his destination. The four appeared as beggars and thus avoided being robbed and killed. Arriving at the compound of the sharif, the narrator reveals his identity and is accepted.

The description of the sharif, his men, the tent, the silk kaftans evoked in the narrator the glorious period of the enlightened caliphs: "I had the sensation that I would see with my own eyes the rebirth of a new era: the beginning of the future Arab government, another chapter in the renaissance of suppressed nations. . . ."[4] The narrator's group departs. The heat and the waterless terrain close to the Dead Sea drive them up the mountains in search of water. Eventually they arrive at Hebron, where the narrator reports his tale to the city governor and then heads northward to Jerusalem. When he reaches the city he utters a prayer of thanks.

Clearly, Burla's sympathies for, and closeness to, Arab culture can be attributed to his Sephardic background. This is true as well for other

Sephardic writers, such as Burla's friend Yitzhak Shami, and more recently Sammy Michael and Shimon Balas, both Iraqi-born, who (in the 1970s and '80s) bring a fine natural quality to the portrayal of the Arab. But beside the factor of the Sephardic background, it is the actual knowledge of Arabic language and culture, of Arabic poetry, philosophy, and history, that enables them to give the Hebrew reader a look inside the Arab way of life, and to enhance the reader's knowledge of that world.

The key to Burla's narrative is his depiction of a non-adversarial relation between Arab and Jew. What interests him are nuances of human nature rather than national characteristics as such. Thus his portrait of the Arab is accompanied by deep respect for his culture and admiration for the beauty of his poetry. In effect, Burla welcomes his European Jewish brethren to the culture of the East, as well as to the subtle complexities of its traditions.

From the early days of modern Jewish settlement in Palestine, the proximity of life between Jew and Arab made it inevitable that there would be romantic connections between Jewish men and Arab women. The motif of an erotic connection across the boundaries of religion and culture is well established in Hebrew literature. In Burla the motif appears in numerous works, as in the novels *In Darkness Striving; A Man of Means;* and *The Chanteuse* (the story of a high-class Jewish courtesan whose lover is a rich Arab).

Despite the moralistic tone inherent in Burla's fiction—rather in the tradition of the nineteenth-century novel, where both the author and the implied author comment upon societal facts—the relation between Jew and non-Jew is not seen as an aberration. On the contrary, it is absorbed into the complex pattern of individual aspirations and social possibilities. This is why it is possible to say that Burla is fundamentally concerned with the human condition, as it touches men and women—and it is *that* interest that will lead him to the realistic portrayal of Sephardic Jews, Arabs, Turks, Armenians, and others.

3. YITZHAK SHAMI

We move now from writers who were prolific—Smilansky and Burla—to one who produced but seven works in all: three short stories, three novellas, and one short novel. Yet his place in our discussion is no less firm, for he occupies a unique niche: in effect, that of a Jewish writer who is so close to Arab culture that he writes what amounts to Arabic fiction—in Hebrew.

Born in Hebron, to the south of Jerusalem, Yitzhak Shami (1889–1949) received the traditional Jewish education available to Sephardic Jews. But he went on to graduate from a teachers' seminary, and he taught in Damascus, in Bulgaria, and in his native Hebron. His first story was published in 1907, and although friends such as Burla and others urged him to continue, he dismissed these suggestions, saying that it did not matter whether he died with one book under his arm or a dozen.

His entire literary oeuvre was published posthumously, in 1951, in a slim volume of 255 pages.[1] In the short introduction, the editor offers Shami's own apologia for the brevity of his output. Its six sentences contain the following: "Does everyone with creative powers have to carry on his back a heavy load of parchment in the long walk to eternity? My burden is light, and I will not stagger under it in my stride."

Like his friend Burla, Shami was thoroughly steeped in the Arabic literature of the past. In an article published in 1911, he noted the paucity of contemporary Arabic fiction, attributing it to the fact that it was a literature at the stage of transformation: unable to discard the old and unable to discover the new; a literature unable to draw the line between the sacred and the secular, or between romanticism and realism. At the same time he admits that it is a literature that cannot be judged by the criteria applicable to other literatures.

We have already noted the point (noted as well by other commentators) that Shami was a Jewish writer of Arabic fiction in Hebrew. His closeness to the Arab milieu and to Arab experience enabled him to depict these in the most authentic way. Burla's narrator remains the Jewish outsider, deeply moved by Arab culture but still looking at it from the vantage point of the non-Arab. Shami, on the other hand, could enter into the Arab experience, urban as well as nomadic, and illuminate the Arab world not only of Palestine but of Syria as well. An insightful commentator on Hebrew literature of this century has said that Shami succeeded in entering into the psyche of the Arab to a degree unparalleled to this very day.[2]

Of the seven narratives Shami penned, three focus directly on the Arab experience: "The Vengeance of the Fathers," "Jum'ah the Fool," and "Amidst the Desert Dunes." Shami depicts some of the traditional modes of behavior and the ethos of a community; yet he avoids the pitfalls of conventional modes of description, the established pictoriality and exotic coloration. Rather, the authenticity in depicting everyday ritual is gained in the density of his language and in his tight narrative.

The subject of "Jum'ah the Fool"[3] is a half-witted shepherd who is fascinated by Dervishes (a Muslim religious order noted for ecstatic trances brought on by bodily whirling). Jum'ah is given to seizures, taken as reflecting a disposition to holy possession. He is regarded as not ready for full initiation as a Dervish; but his special capacities have made him a spiritual healer. He has two wishes: to become a Dervish and to marry (i.e., to gather enough money to buy a wife). Shami does not endow Jum'ah with an inner life, nor does he beautify him; and precisely because of this restrained depiction in tightly controlled prose, Jum'ah is not a stereotype.

His "holy madness" is complex: incited by the derisive songs sung by village boys, Jum'ah's wrath is taken for the presence of the divine, his mad spells taken for God's blessing, and women who watch him are brought to ecstasy themselves. His closeness to nature, his familiarity with every subtle change around him contribute to his keen sensibility and to his ultimate gentleness. Yet in the society to which he was born he is an outsider, a man devoid of a voice or standing in his world. It is easier for the villagers to believe he has contact with demons and dark powers.

Yet it was not Shami's aim to depict social pathology but to present a unique "individual" who is out of place in society, both an idiot and one who is touched by the divine. As Shami says:

> They regarded his frenzy as supernatural in origin, a gift of the grace of Allah. They were convinced that the hidden light of the Prophet shone upon him, that the Angel Gabriel had touched him with his fiery sceptre, and inspired him with his spirit till he could contain it no longer, and must pour it forth upon the invisible spirits and devils. (p. 44)

Shami's fascination with the irrational and with ritual gives his fiction an erotic sense. Jum'ah's trances occur in the heat of summer, and their effect on women is suggestive of orgiastic rites:

> Most impressed and concerned by the scene . . . were the womenfolk. With wide staring eyes they followed the movements of the shepherd, and listened to his cries. Every groan Jum'ah gave vent to reverberated in their hearts, inspiring an exquisite anxiety and amazement at the marvelous sight. Their compassion was quickened, and often they would lacerate their flesh, tear at their hair and wallow in the dust. (pp. 44–45)

After every trance, Jum'ah experiences a sense of deprivation, and resentment against his insipid life, against the burden of fate, against those who have exploited him and robbed him of his fair wage, and against the impediments to his becoming a Dervish and marrying. In his private world of sheep and dogs he is powerful, but there alone.

The coming of the sheikh promises some acceptance, although he deplores Jum'ah's ritual performance in the village. Since Jum'ah is not an initiate his performance is blasphemous, an abomination, and he is in danger of being cast into the pit. The description of Jum'ah's preparations for curing the sheikh's mule is riveting:

> He dragged out bundles of twigs and thorns, roots of trees and ropes, then finally returned to extract from a secret cache a swollen pocket, yellow and mouldy with age and full to the brim, from the depth of which he produced an odd collection of rubbish—broken utensils, rags, glass and clay bottles with filth and mould, pieces of leather, rusty tin boxes tied with multicoloured strings. All of these he emptied carefully into his lap, and arranged them about him. Then he plunged his hand again into the bag and from its bottom drew forth his instruments—sack-needles, brad-awls, tongs and skewers. From these he selected after careful consideration what he required. . . . (p. 59)

The subsequent description of his way of lighting the fire and heating and preparing the utensils is equally captivating. Finally, he is killed by a kick from the mule he has cured.

What makes this an *Arab* tale (rather than a tale told by a sympathetic outsider) is, first, the intensely acute concatenation of objective detail; but second, it is Shami's way of entering into the ethos of the Arab village so that he not only achieves on our behalf a willing suspension of disbelief but also arrives so closely at the heart of that ethos as to make that very suspension unnecessary.

Shami's fascination with the Bedouin ethos is reflected in his story "Amidst the Desert Dunes," an action-oriented tale in the tradition of highly stylized oral narrative. There is the traditional dichotomy of good versus evil, innocence versus cunning, faithfulness versus perfidy, and personal honor versus greed. As with the stories of Burla, we can say that rationality is not a factor in the lives of Shami's protagonists—and this fact is of prime importance for our understanding of the way the Arab is depicted in this early fiction. That is, the role of reason is restricted, and it is unbridled emotions that rule. Further, Shami's characters exist in a framework of limited time and limited action. Once again we see the element of resignation to the will of Allah, a resignation that diminishes expectations and the possibility of actions that might be outside the range of character.

Shami's characters, lacking the capacity for self-reflection, are victims of fate, and a single act can shape their existence irrevocably. Shami's restrained telling voice, however, his subtly hidden point of view and his guarded style, avoid all pontification about man's fate. The internalization of the point of view and the respect for realistic detail in describing scenery and daily activities give a hard-edged quality to his fiction—but this hides a rather ironic tone in an almost unnoticeable way.

Shami's tour de force, perhaps his greatest achievement, is the short novel of 1928 "The Vengeance of the Fathers."[4] The time is the turn of the century, and the initial situation stems from the rivalry between two Arab cities: Nablus in the north and Hebron in the south. In Nablus, one Nimmer has been chosen to lead his city in the spring pilgrimage to the putative tomb of Moses according to Islamic tradition. Nimmer's counterpart in Hebron is Abu Faris, who, in a sly and cunning manner, manages to enter the tomb and is the first to place the Hebronite banner at the holy site. In a fit of rage, Nimmer kills Abu Faris and defiles the banner he was carrying. Fearing the vengeance of the Hebronites, Nimmer flees into the desert and makes his way to Egypt, where he lives as an exile. Over a long period, he succumbs to hashish and a life of debauchery, meanwhile trying to persuade his family in Nablus to appease Abu Faris's family in Hebron. Nimmer's decline, his mental and physical deterioration, is paralleled by the financial decline of his family: in addition to supporting him, they are being bilked by the Hebronites with the false promise of peace negotiations and settlement.

Nimmer is reduced to peddling soap. In his distress he seeks the help of a sheikh, who becomes his adviser and guide. According to the sheikh, Nimmer's sin is great: he killed, and he desecrated the holy place—although Allah has determined the fate of all men even before their birth. Yet Allah's mercy is infinite, and Nimmer is told that if he becomes a beggar, goes barefoot to the tomb, and asks forgiveness, he might be heard. The sheikh also orders Nimmer to go to two other holy sites: the Cave of Machpelah in Hebron and the Mosque of Omar in Jerusalem. Yet the sheikh realizes that he is sending Nimmer to his fate.

Thus the story opens and closes with pilgrimage: the first, that of a powerful man honoring tradition; the second, a pilgrimage of penitence. Nimmer arrives at Hebron, goes to the holy place, and wets the stone with his tears. Of course, he is recognized, and the men of Hebron are called out to avenge their dead leader. Yet what the crowd sees is

> a bent old man, thin, exhausted, bare of foot and head, the white hair of his head and beard descending in long unkempt braids on both sides of his face. He swayed as he walked, as if borne on the waves of a dream, slowly dragging his feet and knocking on the ground before him with his staff like

a blind man seeking his way. It was clear to everyone that he had sensed
nothing of what was going on around him. (p. 162)

He becomes aware of the crowd of men carrying their glittering swords
above them, and he collapses on the stairs, dying in front of the gathering
throng. Abu Faris's two brothers cry out, "The Vengeance of the Fathers,"
and the mob disperses in dread of the hand of Allah.

This story admits of numerous interpretations. Usually, it is appreciated
for its colorful depiction of a way of life, with its customs and ceremonies.
With this, there is also the anthropological sensitivity to Arab fatalism: the
protagonist is a captive of his temper, and his act of hubris turns his life in
the direction that has been divinely pre-ordained. The latter reading, however, suppresses the voice of any "implied author": the system of values
and the outcome of events are in conformity, giving us a tale without
elements of duality, or ambivalence in interpretation. The tragic aspect is
there throughout: the hubris and fall of the protagonist, an attempt at
catharsis, and even a moral at the end in the Vengeance of the Fathers.

At the very beginning, the narrator assumes the voice of a traditional,
God-fearing man, informing us of the details of the forthcoming pilgrimage. Eventually, this folkloric narrator becomes an epic narrator who
challenges the earlier folk wisdom. This leads to something like a rejection
of Fate as the ultimate power moving the plot and characters. With this
element of criticism, toward the end, the role of an implied author is
enhanced. Thus the story turns out to be not as simple as we had been
expecting, as the aspects of irony and criticism enter.

As we saw, Nimmer falls from his elevated station in life, and is reduced
to living as an exile. The story might well have ended there, with the
inversion from well-being to misery. But Shami opted for a further possibility: the plot-oriented narrative gives way to a character-oriented narrative—as can be seen in the way his fellow Nablusites, living in Cairo,
react to his arrival:

> The few Nablusites living in Cairo, his "brethren in misfortune," re-
> ceived him with understanding and with the joy and loyal friendship so
> characteristic of bitter and afflicted refugees when they meet on foreign
> soil. The news of his arrival and of the reason for his flight spread like
> wildfire among them. It touched and moved each of them profoundly. The
> wondrous event, already enveloped in mists of legend and bravery, capti-
> vated their imaginations. In the cruel intrigue of change from which there
> can be no escape each one of them saw his own reflection and the story of
> his own life. Before long they all found him, one by one, and came to the
> place where he was staying, to visit him and congratulate him on his
> escape. (p. 126)

There is the suggestion that he has escaped from "the cruel intrigue of chance from which there can be no escape." (The Hebrew text reads: "the evil intent of the cruel hand of chance.") There is something of an ironic tone here, carrying an admonition against self-deceit. We can therefore see the transition from the classic plot-oriented tale to the character-oriented tale—and with this we may see the author's greater awareness of the Arab as active initiator, i.e., as character.

Nimmer has a hallucinatory vision: three men in glistening robes appear, and he identifies them as the three Fathers—Abraham, Isaac, and Jacob—coming to remind him of the unavenged blood. One of them has the torn and blood-stained banner. A white bird cracks Nimmer's windowpane, and from under one of its wings it draws a dirty rag with which to cleanse a gushing wound in its chest. The bird flies at the petrified Nimmer, mesmerizing him with its glance, and terrifying him with its beak directed at his eyes.

In regard to the story's end, the folk-tale tradition sees him as dying because of the Vengeance of the Fathers. But he is evidently quite ill, and the naturalistic interpretation would see him dying of that illness. Should the story's title, then, be taken to depict the essence of the story? Or is the title an ironic reflection of the character's self-deceit? What led Nimmer back to Hebron? His gnawing guilt, confirmed in the hallucination of the three Fathers?

Prescribed ritual was to be the means of redemption. The story begins with the ritual of the festival, and with Nimmer's part in it. Presumably, his flight to Cairo was to be a flight from ritual. And ritual was his life's ending. The acceptance of that ending brings catharsis and an end to his soul's suffering. In all this—i.e., the emphasis on the psyche—the traditional narrator could have been little more than an external element, presenting the story's beginning and its end, telling of the horror felt by the Hebronites at the sight of the dead Nimmer. The tale's modern aspect is in the suggestion that personal choice can exist within the framework of a classical (i.e., predestined) form.

In the transition from a plot-oriented to a character-oriented approach, Shami endows his character with psychological depth, and with a divided self, wavering between fate and free will. This ambiguity is a further element of modernity: despite the tale's traditional form, the protagonist is in the throes of self-deception and self-destruction. None of the characters depicted by the writers of the pre-1948 generation revealed the psychological complexity portrayed by Shami in this short novel. Inverting the accepted schemata, Shami illuminated his character's complexity without "westernizing" him or giving him beliefs that would be foreign to his culture.

We have remarked on the fact that Shami's close observation of Arab lore is unparalleled in Hebrew literature. The plasticity of his language and the almost synesthetic sense of experience and immediacy give this novel a unique authenticity. But what is most significant about Shami is the ironic point made earlier: that he writes Arabic fiction, although he is a Jew and writes in Hebrew. In this light he may justly be regarded as the most prominent Palestinian writer of the pre-1948 period.[5]

4. YOSEF HAIM BRENNER

The changing depiction of the Arab follows a dual line from the simplistic to the complex portrayal, and from the placement of the Arab at the periphery of a narrative to his firm location at the center. We have begun to see something of that transition in Smilansky, Burla, and Shami. What is remarkable about the work of Yosef Haim Brenner (1881–1921) is that it displays that dual line in its entirety—so that he can even be said to have foretold much of the Arab/Jewish reality that came to prevail after his murder in 1921. In addition to his prophetic value, Brenner was what we might call a polysystem on his own account: single-handedly he trans-ferred the center of Hebrew literary activity to Palestine; as a writer, translator, editor, publisher, printer, dramatist, mentor to young writers (Agnon included), and the founder of literary organs, he secured the continuation of Hebrew literature among a small population in Palestine in the first two decades of this century.

This dual line is exhibited in Brenner's fiction and essays as he portrays the Arab in the naive mode, the realistic-humanistic mode, and the psycho-logical mode. Thus we can see the historical evolution of that transition, but we can also see it synchronically and synoptically in Brenner, who pene-trated to the very heart of the Arab-Jewish problem as he expressed his deepest fears and guilt, while he envisaged a new human being in a new country.

Brenner was born in a small town in the Jewish Pale of Settlement, in Russia. The traditional religious education, a loss of religious faith, and the search for some other source of meaning haunted his life. The seventeen-year-old needed a substitute for the God that had failed. He joined the Jewish Workers' Bund, but was disillusioned by the Communism of its members and their reaction to the pogroms, and to the Jewish problem in general. Eventually he came to Zionism and became an active proponent of settlement in Palestine, although he also became the severest critic of that policy.

Drafted into the Russian army, he served for a year, then deserted and went to Germany. Prior to coming to Palestine in 1909, he resided in London, where he founded, edited, and published the Hebrew periodical *HaMe'orer* (The Awakener). Arriving in Jaffa, he soon failed as an agri-cultural laborer, as did many another Socialist-Zionist leader. Instead, he resumed work as a writer and editor—but also became a teacher, a roving

35

lecturer, and the foremost literary voice of the era. In May 1921, he was murdered by Arab marauders.

Brenner's influence has survived—in writers such as Yizhar, A. B. Yehoshua, and Amos Oz. His passion for truth left no place for complacency or comfort. This passion also informed his view of the growing problem of Arab-Jewish relations. His most characteristic qualities are his Dostoevskian self-laceration and self-doubt, which he combined with his Jewish soul-searching to produce the most intense attack on Judaism and the Jewish way of life.

His short stories, novels, drama, essays, and letters, and his day-to-day reactions to the events of the time give us a unique picture of the twelve years he lived in Palestine. His fiction has often been compared to that of Dostoevsky. (His Hebrew translation of *Crime and Punishment* is still regarded as a classic.) A dark despair marks his protagonists, along with a tireless quest for truth and values in a world that offers no metapersonal basis for them. Life does not offer them a clear set of alternate possibilities, although his protagonists continue to seek new beginnings amid their despair. His loveless characters are sunk in hardship, disillusionment, and alienation—all abhorring compromise.

In the story "Nerves,"[1] written a year after Brenner's arrival in Palestine, the protagonist, in conversation with the narrator, looks at trees planted twenty-five years before. The young trees stand for the young new country in its self-imposed poverty—as against the established culture of Europe. The question is what the treetops "see":

> Let's say they can forget the great cities [of Europe and America]. Let's say they can't even see them and needn't compare them with our pitiful Jewish village. They still can't help noticing their surroundings. And I tell you, my heart goes out to them . . . my heart goes out to anything that is forced to put forth branches before it has time to strike root. . . . (pp. 32–33)

If the comparison to Europe is suspended, how do these new Jewish settlements compare with the indigenous Arab villages?

> Those that belong, that have their own sun to shine and their own rain to fall on them, that aren't a quarter-of-a-century old . . . well, they may be filthy beggars themselves . . . but at least they're not the outcasts of the earth. When I think that those treetops are doomed . . . and always, always, the same wretched Jews on the run. . . . (p. 33)

In a highly compressed manner, this passage contains references—direct and indirect—to most of the problems that will plague the newcomers: the instability and impermanence of the new settlements; the inevitable shadow and memory of life in Europe, with the implicit comparison to the disadvantage of the present; the "roots" that are not genuine but are rooted in the mentality of the Diaspora; the desire to be "at home," a native son, with the inescapable sense of estrangement from the land. (The Arabs, despite their primitive way of life, are native sons, and the sense of a Diaspora does not exist for them, nor do they bear a burden of exile at this time.)

Despite the optimism that might be suggested by the new trees, and by the dunes that have been transformed into lush orchards, there is a sense of doom over it all, and of a rootless existence. But the vision is not finished. It needs some personal reversal, very much in the tone of the soliloquy of Dostoevsky's Underground Man:

> And do you know what else I wanted to say? . . . Here more than anywhere . . . here of all places, where our ruin, the ruin of our people, is most obvious . . . here I've had some of the best days of my life . . . which . . . which at times I've actually thought was taking on direction, some meaning. . . . To this day—it's been a year and a half now—I can't get those first moments out of my mind: so this is what our promised land is like! . . . (p. 33)

Brenner clearly expresses his view of the Arab in "Pages from a Literary Notebook."[2] This work was written in response to views expressed by his friend Rabbi Benjamin, the literary name of Yehoshua Radler-Feldman (1880–1957), a polemicist and a founder of the conciliatory movement that came to be known as Brit Shalom (Covenant of Peace). Radler's ideas were attacked by Brenner. In 1907, Radler had written a piece urging his compatriots to love the Arab and help him. He rebukes those who want to deprive the Arab of his land: the proper role of the Jew is to revive the land, not to deprive its inhabitants of it. The shared Semitic heritage means that there is no substantial difference between Jew and Arab, and the Jew therefore has the obligation to help the Arab with medical services and new methods of agriculture. Radler believed that the intensive cultivation of the soil would enable the two nations to co-exist peacefully. In 1913, he proposed building a "Temple of Peace" where the three major faiths might worship together.

Brenner attacked these views for setting forth an ideal that could not be realized. The idea of joint tillage of the soil as a way of bringing the two nations together was not feasible because the greater part of the Jewish nation was not in Palestine at the time; the land could not absorb the European Jewish population; nor could that population equal the Arab birthrate.

Where Radler had opposed the Socialist/Zionist ideal of Jewish labor, hoping by that opposition to get Jews to hire Arabs and thus foster cooperation, Brenner argued that the only way for the Jew to overcome the mentality acquired in the Diaspora was to return to the land, to manual work and productivity. At stake was nothing less than the Jewish future and the Jew's future character. There are, he says, a half-million Arabs willing to work for very little—hardly the recipe for a dignified co-existence of mutual respect.

Brenner mocks Radler's notion that Jews ought to build clean sections of their cities for Arabs. Moreover, he argues that the idea of a Temple of Peace, together with the other utopian notions, is idle, blind to the deepest human instincts and to the bitter reality: Arabs and Jews, he says, are "soul-enemies." Idealism is therefore baseless and irresponsible. The Arabs in Palestine are the actual masters of the land, despite their poor condition and lack of culture, Brenner says. And here we Jews come to live among them, forced by necessity. There is a hatred between us, which will continue into the future. Since they are the strong, and we the weak—and we accustomed to live as the weak among the strong—we shall have to be prepared for the outcome of this hatred.

But above all, Brenner urges a clear understanding of the situation, without sentimentality or idealism (pp. 321–23). It is a delusion to relate to the Arabs as though it is *they* who are 10 percent of the population, not the Jews. It is the Arabs who give the tone to the country. And as for the future, Brenner foreshadows what has by now become a truism of Arab-Jewish interrelatedness: namely, the realization that the Arab has learned his nationalism—doctrine as well as language—from the Jew. And thus Brenner gives a prescient forecast with the remark that "the Arab cultural and political renaissance is not a fairy-tale either" (alluding to Herzl's motto: "If you will, it is no fairy-tale"). Brenner does not offer a solution. He clearly rejects the utopian answer, yet he emphasizes the historical necessity of the Jew's coming to Palestine.

The image of the Arab as indigenous to the surrounding landscape—an image so powerfully expressed in the writings of Yizhar, Shamir, Shaham, and others—was already established in Brenner's fiction. In the 1910 story "Bein Mayim LeMayim" (Between Water and Water),[3] a young Jewish woman raises her eyes from the literary periodical she is reading and sees three camels in a convoy, one rider swaying on the camel's hump; the sound of their bells, and their repose are an emblem of something unknown. Here, and in the pre-State literature in general, the Arab is perceived as maintaining the wholeness of the land by symbolizing rootedness and continuity.

In this story Brenner supplies a number of vignettes: a proud-looking Arab woman carries a heavy load on her head with grace and pride. Young Arab boys run alongside their donkeys which are carrying stones from a quarry. After them, a pale Jewish yeshiva student slouches toward the ritual bathhouse to prepare himself for the Sabbath. The mere juxtaposition of these images reflects Brenner's attitude regarding the need for major change. There is also a concern with more immediate problems: the Jewish farmer knows that many laborers will leave the land. A Jewish watchman is killed by Arabs when he tries to prevent them from uprooting new plantings. In the memorial service, lofty words are said. There is another image: poor fellaḥin, barefoot and wrapped in their robes, walking "on their soil," weary, and sunk in their unknowable ruminations. They are dirty, their sores are infected, their eyes have a certain cunning—and so they pass along the streets of Jerusalem as their forefathers have done for centuries, humming a fragmentary song. Their lives are mired in poverty and backwardness, yet theirs is an enviable inner peace.

Ghettoized Jerusalem is the continuation of the Jewish malady. Pitted against the Jewish ghetto-dweller is the young farmer in a new settlement, saying that the meaning of Palestine is the new beginning, the beginning of Jewish agricultural labor, Jewish industry, education, spoken Hebrew (instead of its use for liturgical purposes alone), the beginning of Hebrew theatre—all of this is presented against the background of the quiet Arab, who is constantly there although only intermittently displayed. Despite the limited space devoted to the portrayal of the Arab in Brenner's fiction and essays, his work is remarkable for its honesty, and its refusal to ignore what threatens to become a situation of confrontation and conflict.

MiKan U'MiKan (From Here and There),[4] a 1911 novel by Brenner, and S. Y. Agnon's *Tmol Shilshom* (Yesteryear) are the two major novels concerned with the Second Aliyah. In Brenner's Introduction/Apologia, a narrator tells us of notebooks found in the knapsack of an anonymous young and seemingly uprooted Jewish man (Brenner loved this narrative device). The notebooks seem to be a formless record of incidents, characters, random observations, dreams, letters, and other modes of expression. Yet in actuality they constitute a complex and well-crafted novel as well as Brenner's aesthetic credo. This work combines the variegated traditions of the confessional novel, the social novel, the *Künstlerroman*, as well as elements of stream-of-consciousness technique, where the minutiae of everyday experience evoke existential themes of despair and suicide.

The main protagonist has the symbolic name Oved Etzot (the phrase for "void of counsel"—as in "for they are a nation void of counsel," in Deuteronomy 32:28). In his perplexity and confusion, he is the prototypical character to be found in almost all of Brenner's works—and the autobiographical source is quite clear. The novel's other focus is Aryeh Lapidot, fashioned after the Tolstoyan philosopher/pioneer A. D. Gordon (1856–1922), who sought salvation in return to the soil. Brenner's paradoxical convictions appear here: advocating a return to the soil, Brenner is negative in regard to his religious heritage; yet he sees in Jewish self-identification the bridge to future redemption.

The Arab presence is to be found in this novel as well: Lapidot's older son is attacked by an Arab and dies of his wounds. When the two brothers are accosted by the Arab, the younger pulls out his automatic but forgets to release the safety catch. The bitter story suggests that the Jew can nowhere escape vulnerability, and that Jewish blood will forever remain unavenged.

Brenner's ambivalence enters: Oved Etzot tries to tell himself that this is his homeland; yet he is repelled by the sight of the Arabs, their poverty, their primitive behavior—including some evidence of homosexuality and bestiality. All this adds to the general nausea he feels at the current state of affairs. There is the gnawing thought that the biblical prophecy of destruction is being materialized: the killer of Lapidot's son was a native of the land, whereas the Jews are strangers. The theme of the Jew as native son runs through this novel as well as Brenner's last major work, *Breakdown and Bereavement*. In both books, the dominant view is that the Jew *can* become a native son, i.e., someone belonging to the land, but only if he sheds his Diaspora mentality so that he can relate to himself, his present and future, directly and without that impediment. As an existential ailment, the Diaspora has become an inborn element in the Jewish psyche, so that nothing is left but the ability to form questions without hope of answers.

Until the time of his son's death, Lapidot had been known as an "Arab-lover." He held that Jews, as Europeans, must not pass judgment upon Arabs; that Arab culture is ancient and noble; and that it is incumbent upon the Jew to revivify the Arab. And if it were not for the fact that the Jew needs to work the soil with his own hands, as the way to his own revitalization, Lapidot had felt, there would be nothing wrong with employing Arab labor and providing for Arab livelihood.

From Here and There can be read in either of two contrary ways: as one of the most pessimistic literary documents, or as a statement offering some form of redemptive hope. One never knows how to separate Brenner's mockery from what he unambiguously intends—and it is a tribute to his skill as a writer that, in the context of his fiction, either approach is fully plausible. Toward the end of *From Here and There,* Oved Etzot has left a document that amounts to his last will and testament:

> Life is bad, but always mysterious . . . death is bad.
> The world is torn, but also versatile, and sometimes beautiful.
> Man is miserable, but occasionally he is also marvelous.
> The Jewish nation, according to the laws of logic, has no future.
> Nevertheless, one should work.
> As long as you are alive, there are elevated deeds and there are exalted moments.
> Long live Hebrew labor! (p. 369, translation mine)

The paradoxicality of Brenner's ideas is reflected in his complex relation to the Arab. He sees the Arab as an enviable model of what the Jew lacks—i.e., belonging, continuity, and rootedness in the land. And at the same time he sees him as the target of fear and abhorrence. This duality pervades his writing, so that the Arab is the object of both attraction and aversion for him, fascination and revulsion.

In all this, and through his highly fictional devices, Brenner introduces the ineluctable issues reverberating within Zionism in the second decade of this century, and ever since. The aesthetic distance he achieves between himself and his text, and the irony such distance allows him combine to indicate the complexity of his thinking. Compared to the single-surfaced narratives of Smilansky and Burla, the dense and paradoxical unraveling of the human psyche in Brenner's work is unmatched in Hebrew letters—with the possible exception of his close friend Uri Nissan Gnessin (1879–1913). Brenner's is no simple realism, but rather a complex realism that touches on naturalism at one pole and existentialism at the other, enabling him to exhibit an array of attitudes and feelings toward one subject. Thus the Arab is the Gentile whose presence bodes trouble (evoking memories of the Jew's suffering at the hands of European Gentiles, in pogroms, etc.). On the other hand, the Arab is the native son the Jew would wish himself to be, without any self-doubt.

Brenner's last major novel, published in 1920, was *Breakdown and Bereavement*.[5] It is the story of Yehezkel Hefetz, an agricultural laborer who suffers a physical and mental breakdown. The novel relates his experiences in Palestine, to which he has returned after a stay abroad. The introduction by a narrator tells of notebooks found in a knapsack (again). The knapsack was abandoned by a thirty-three-year-old man who had fallen mentally ill; the notebooks have a "memoiristic flavor" to the narrator, who decides to expand them into a work of fiction, but offers here the notebooks themselves, uncorrected.

The presence of the Arab in this novel, although marginal, is important for its impact on the mind of the central character. This marks an evolution in a sense: in "Between Water and Water," the Arabs are figures in a landscape, to emerge only when they kill the Jewish watchman; in *From Here and There*, the Arab is there as the killer of Lapidot's son, but he is also presented in an additional dimension, as native son. In *Breakdown and Bereavement*, the Arab enters the psyche of the Jew—and with this step, Brenner opens a new level of fictional possibilities. Forty and fifty years later, A. B. Yehoshua and Amos Oz would go further along the same road, portraying the Arab as a part of the Israeli psyche in a psychological siege whereby the enemy has invaded the character's dreams and hallucinations, as in Oz's *My Michael*.

Hefetz's madness incorporates the "Arab problem," therefore, by virtue of the fact that the Arab has taken up permanent occupancy of Hefetz's innermost consciousness. Hefetz seeks to exorcise the occupant by talking:

> The more remote a problem was, the less he or anyone else could do anything about it, the greater his concern. He talked a great deal, for

example, about the Arabs; he spoke of their national awakening and of
their hatred for the Jew; he was obsessed . . . by the possibility of a
pogrom, over which he wracked his brain, soliciting advice and making
endless plans for rescue and relief. Once an Arab woman from one of the
families in the village had stopped by the inn, which was near her house,
to inquire of those seated on the bench outside whether they had seen her
little brother, who had gone off somewhere unannounced. He, Hefetz,
who had been sitting in the doorway, turned as white as a shroud. He
didn't attack her or lay hands on her—it hadn't yet come to that—but
when he heard the word *zrir*, meaning child, he jumped to his feet like a
shot and leaped backward over the threshold as though looking for a place
to hide, from where he began to stamp his feet and to shout: "*Zrir, zrir*, I
know what she's after! We're not cannibals here! We don't drink human
blood! But just try to convince her that we don't have her brother when the
Arabs are awaking and the germs of hatred have infected them too. . . .
See where it gets you!" (p. 14)

Jewish history haunts him; his reality returns as nightmare, evoking memories of blood libels and pogroms. Personal experiences have merged with
collective Jewish memory, so that the Jew is the eternally haunted individual. Hefetz's compulsive speech precedes his admittance into an asylum in
Jerusalem. There too the image of the young Arab woman looking for her
brother re-emerges:

Just a few days before he had paced wildly about in the garret above
him, and softly groaned "rocks, rocks, rocks" without knowing why . . .
knowing only when he did know that he would not be killed by the mob
. . . it was enough that he had been imprisoned on a false charge . . . a
charge brought against him by the Arab woman in the colony . . . before
the Passover . . . the woman who had lost her child . . .—And he knew
then too, knew he would prove that his blood wasn't Jewish at all . . .
Gentile blood flowed through his veins . . . he had been born exactly nine
months after the first pogroms . . . he wasn't a Jew at all, but a *goy*, eighty
per cent Slav . . . how could the woman not understand that he didn't
have her *zrir*? (pp. 113–14)

There are elements of self-negation, even self-hate, in this delusive raving.
It is of no small significance that Brenner was born in 1881, the year the
pogroms began; and the subsequent reports of rape, pillage, and massacre
undoubtedly contributed to the later episodes of self-negation in him (not
merely in his fictive character).

Brenner's open-ended novels typically remain unresolved. His protagonist moves in a circle, of which we see only selected "stations." Thus an
"ending" is not all characteristic of his writing. Most often, the "ending" is
little more than a change of tone or mood, if that. Here in *Breakdown and
Bereavement*, the closing paragraphs have Hefetz's uncle watching some

Arabs swimming in Lake Tiberias. He admires their skill as swimmers. But then the uncle muses, gloating, that it is the swimmers who drown, while he and his nephew, who were no swimmers and never waded far from shore, always stayed alive.

Perhaps the best-known work of Brenner is a short piece he composed toward the end of April 1921, a few days before his murder on May 2. It is regarded as amounting to a last will and testament, perhaps his spiritual bequest. The piece was widely circulated and deeply pondered. To writers such as Yizhar and his generation, it amounted to nothing less than a direct personal message; and in that light it influenced their perception of their moral responsibility toward the Arab. Because of its prophetic significance, and the increasing significance it has acquired with the years, I have decided to quote the piece in its entirety. (In a private conversation, Yizhar suggested that I use the piece as a motto for this book.)

Towards evening I had been straying along the paths of the Arab groves just below the city of Jaffa. I happened to pass an effendi's house. On the doorstep there sat an effendi in the company of two elderly neighbors and a young fellow of about twenty in a cap. I greeted them; they did not answer. So I went on. As I happened to glance back I noticed by their looks that their silence was a purposeful and mean one. The young fellow had already stretched himself upon the ground and cast about a triumphant expression, as if to say: We didn't answer that *Yahud*.

I went on. Suddenly, from one of the groves an Arab jumped out, dressed in a short tattered topcoat, with a spade slung across his shoulder.

"Hawaja!" he exclaimed upon overtaking me.

I noticed that he was not as old as he seemed at first, but only a lad of 13 years. He asked me something in a small, shrill voice, emphasizing each and every word. Unfortunately, since I didn't know any Arabic, I couldn't answer him. I replied with only one word:

"From Selima?" (i.e., From the nearby town Selima?)

He replied: "No, I come from this neighborhood, from the grove."

Then he went on with his story. I asked him, pointing my finger:

"Effendi?" (i.e., Does the grove where you're coming from and where you seemingly work belong to that effendi sitting there on the doorstep?)

He nodded with his head, "yes" and then continued to tell me his story in the same manner. From a few of his words and more from his movements and gesticulations I gathered that his parents had died during the war and that he was an orphan. He also understood my next question:

"Khadesh?" (i.e., How much do you earn a day?)

He answered in a dignified manner: "Eight grush."

"That's not so good," I told him. For a moment he was puzzled and did not know what I had meant by "no good." Was it too much or too little? Then he went on to tell me that there were workers in the grove who received fifteen grush a day, and some even got twenty a day. But these

were the big workers . . . and he had a younger sister . . . they had to eat
and live . . . and he only made eight grush. Allah deemed it so.

Just then I reproached myself, rather severely, for not having learned to
speak Arabic. Oh, if I could only have conversed with you better—my
orphan worker! My young comrade, whether it is true or not what the
scholars say about your being my blood relation, I feel responsible for you.
I should have opened your eyes and let you enjoy some human kindness.
No! Not only revolutionary machinations in the Near East, not on one foot,
not at the command of some committee or agents of some socialist politics.
No, not any politics! Maybe this isn't even any of our business. We'd
probably have to do this by force, out of despair or the lack of an alternative! No, we don't want this! We want only a soulful relationship . . .
today . . . for centuries to come . . . for many, many days . . . with the
meaning to be brothers, comrades.

"Farewell, *Hawaja!*" the young Arab bid me, as we took leave of each
other, noticing how absorbed I was over our conversation. His farewell
greeting imparted a feeling of satisfaction over his having had a chance to
speak to a grown-up expertly and manlike.

"Shalom, my brother!" I whispered through my lips, my heart beating
for both myself and him.[6]

Brenner was intensely aware of the gravity of the "Arab problem." He firmly
believed that the Jewish settlers would be facing an organized national
power, and he was equally convinced that an upsurge of Arab nationalism
was imminent. Yet unlike his friend Radler, he did not endorse pacifism.
The 1920 Jerusalem riots enraged him, as did the attack on Tel Hai, the
small settlement in the Galilee where Trumpeldor was killed.

The lasting significance of Brenner's work, in addition to its intrinsic
value as literature, is that it depicts for the first time the entrance of the
Arab into the Jewish psyche. Other writers of his time may be evaluated for
their "distance" from, or proximity to, the Arab and his culture—as a mark
of the writer's willingness to understand the Arab and to enter *his* soul.
What Brenner examines is the other side of that relation: the internalization
of the image of the Arab into the consciousness of the Jew, with his
inchoate fear of losing his spiritual integrity as a result of the confrontation.
The effect on the Jew, and in turn on the Israeli, is a point of major
importance, since, as we pointed out earlier, the self-definition of the Jew
as Israeli must include the relation to the Arab, as well as to the very Arab-
Jewish conflict itself.

5. YITZHAK SHENHAR

Each wave of immigration to Palestine had its unique socio-economic mixture; but it was marked even more by certain characteristic reasons for making the arduous journey. Thus each aliyah was more typically composed of people from, say, poorer or middle-class origins; and motives for their coming range from various shadings of ideological idealism to the immediate need to escape danger. The Third Aliyah began at the end of World War I, and some of the reasons for it can be discerned in the works of its writers, who sought to give literary expression to the Jew who seeks his national/Hebraic rehabilitation in his ancient homeland. This wave of about 35,000 (including my parents) brought with it a renewed emphasis on pioneering (*halutziut*) in an agricultural setting. This was very much in contrast to the Fourth Aliyah of 67,000, arriving between 1924 and 1928, mostly from urban middle-class Polish backgrounds, and preferring to continue life in an urban environment.

This extravagantly complex mixture of cultural sources and motives will also color relations to the Arab. Each aliyah may be said to have its characteristic slant in this regard, and in giving emphasis to it we risk cultural stereotyping. Yet each aliyah had its own way of responding to two encounters: the encounter with the unfamiliar landscape, and the encounter with the Arab. And in the literature of the pre-State era, those two encounters may be said to constitute some of its most prevalent thematic material. The Palestinian landscape—its intense Mediterranean light and heat, its star-filled skies—contrasted, for all these writers, with the northern landscape familiar from their youth. The novelty of the exotic is soon submerged under the unchanging summer skies, the harsh, dry, and yellow land, lacking in water and forestation.

There is also a broad variety of responses to the Zionist ideal. Hebrew writers in Palestine in the first half of this century were not Jews who happened to live in Jaffa, or Tel Aviv, or Jerusalem, or Petah-Tiqva (as someone might "happen" to live in Warsaw, Odessa, or wherever). Rather, their presence in Palestine attested to their commitment to the Zionist ideal—and it is safe to say (as the critic Dan Miron has said) that even into the 1980s Hebrew literature continues to be imbued with the modes of expression associated with the Zionist dream. But this does not lessen the fact that they are at the same time wrestling with the ideal. Thus Brenner, and in turn writers as diverse as Yizhar, A. B. Yehoshua, Amos Oz, Shaham, Shamir, and Megged, are still coming to terms with Zionism's implications. And lest we be tempted to think of any of these writers speaking of Zionism as untroubled self-fulfillment, we need only read Brenner—or Agnon or Shenhar—to realize the complexity of their dialogue with Zionism. One writer, Haim Hazaz, goes so far as to have one of his characters exclaim that Zionism and Judaism are not the same, that they may even contradict each other, and that "Zionism starts from the place of the destruction of Judaism."[1]

The intense self-examination of these writers, especially in regard to the matter of justifying the Jewish presence in Palestine, led to a myriad of questions, all centering around the "return" to Palestine: What is the nature of that return? Is it primarily a secular action, devoid of a historical/religious basis? Or is it a revivification of past ideals? Is it a part of a cycle repeated throughout Jewish history? Or is it something altogether new and without precedent? Each of these views will have its advantages, but will also pose certain limitations. Thus the Socialist dimension may have its attractions in raising the ideal of a new birth of a rational society; but then the locus of that new birth need not necessarily be centered in Palestine. And to the extent that we give emphasis to the Judaic base of the return, Zionism's departure from Judaism (as noted by the Hazaz character) would seem to negate its justification. Is Zionism an old "text" revived, or is it a new text? Is the Jew to be the guardian of *time* (i.e., the religious, spiritual, historical dimension), or the guardian of *space* (i.e., the land, here and now)? Both Brenner and Agnon look for an equation that will combine both these aspects—even if, in Agnon's text, the Jew is a guardian of time, and of the old text, in a modern absurd reality.

One of the outstanding writers of the Third Aliyah was Yitzhak Shenhar (1902–1957), who was born near the border between Galicia and the Ukraine. His commitment to the literature of the past is seen in the fact that he was one of the outstanding translators of his era, translating works from Russian, German, French, and English literature into Hebrew. His own fiction was written in Palestine in the 1930s and '40s. His earlier stories depicted the pogroms in the Ukraine during the Revolution and after; later, he wrote of the life of Jewish settlers, and then of the Holocaust. His style is of his own making, stemming from his characters' sense of individual uncertainty and self-questioning. Like Brenner and Agnon, he admires the individual who is totally committed to tilling the soil and who is also devoid of Jewish guilt and the Diaspora mentality—beyond the obvious pains of adjustment his characters must go through in the new land. Very much conscious of the Arab presence, Shenhar poses existential questions as to the nature of the nation that is being shaped and reshaped by the diverse waves of immigration. There are two main centers of concern in his fiction: the shift in mentality from the Diaspora to Palestine; and the co-existence of Arab and Jew.

In his stories dealing with the Palestine reality and experience, Shenhar often introduces biblical topics and motifs. His language, laden with biblical allusions beyond the actual story line, evokes another reality. Land and landscape become the meeting place of past and present:

> The level expanse had been desolate for ages. The desolation was chequered with thorns and briars, and a narrow trail passing through the midst of them. The course taken by the country's early days unrolled here like a threadbare shabby carpet, all the way to the horizon. There the hills touched the lower reaches of the sky, while night scattered its stars far and wide across them, as of old. In bygone days that carpet had been trodden by the feet of the long-legged, hook-nosed Amorite, whose ravaging smile had hovered on his shaven upper lip and run down into his wedge-shaped beard. Here the Danite bands, masters of stratagem and seekers of combat, had flowed to make a heritage of their new homeland. Here Crusader knights had ridden, their armor jingling like muted bells, their arm-pieces and leg-pieces fashioned of beaten copper which glowed in the hot sunshine. Thereafter came the desolation; and it blotted out the traces of tribes and peoples, of graves and tombs and mighty deeds.
>
> In the spring little flocks spread out across the flats, moving to and fro like shadows. In autumn days a wind comes from the west and beats against the thorns. Sometimes a camel caravan slowly plods its way from the north to the south.[2]

The story's title, "The Tamarisk," evokes any number of biblical echoes, many having to do with one's strangeness in the land, counterbalanced by faith. For example, in Genesis 21:33, 34, we read: "And Abraham planted a tamarisk-tree in Beer-sheba, and called there on the name of the Lord, the Everlasting God. And Abraham sojourned in the land of the Philistines many days." In Shenhar's story, the young tamarisk, beginning to grow in the middle of the plain, corresponds to the first Judaic acceptance of God—and to the tragic end of the first chosen king of Israel, Saul, whose bones were buried "under the tamarisk-tree in Jabesh" (I Samuel 31:13). For Shenhar, the tree simply grows (no man planted it) as a solitary object in the heart of the plain.

The story's opening (quoted above) provides the basis for all that follows. Moreover, there are words uttered here which will reverberate throughout Shenhar's oeuvre—words such as *desolation, thorns and briars, night* (i.e., the historical night), *shadows, stars.* The word *stars* evokes the promise made to Abraham: "Look now toward heaven, and count the stars, if thou be able to count them; . . . So shall thy seed be" (Genesis 15:5). The tamarisk, then, becomes for Shenhar the totem not only of Abraham's tenure of the land, but of the modern-day Jew's presence in it. Land touches sky by means of the tamarisk; man creates a place amid primordial desolation—and the land has returned to desolation in the cycle of time. There is the suggestion that that desolation is the land's natural condition, and that history itself will be effaced by time, leaving only a wasteland under the sky.

That motif, of the wasteland as natural state, has found its way into a number of works since Shenhar's. For example, there are A. B. Yehoshua's "Facing the Forests" and Benjamin Tammuz's *The Orchard* (both of which will be discussed later). The motif is given an interesting reversal in Shulamit Hareven's *The City of Many Days*.[3] Here a young Arab resents his father's selling land to Jews, and he therefore longs for the silence of the wasteland, lands which would belong to no one but God. Cities, too, would be no more. . . . Cities have been the ruin of Arabs, he feels, making Arabs into Jews and Europeans. Instead, he imagines himself saying to his friends, "Brothers, does the Arab still know how to keep the desert alive in his heart?" (p. 113)

In Shenhar's story a rich Arab owns the desolate plain with the tamarisk. He has never gone out to inspect his land. Instead, he spends his time dreaming at home, or sitting in a cafe and sucking at his *nargileh*, as the wind from the west puts fantasies into his mind. His tenant farmer is a poor and starving peasant who has left his village to live on the plain; he must give the rich Arab two-fifths of all he produces. He and his wife have a child each year, but the child never lives. After each death, the peasant beats his wife; she sits in the shadow of the tamarisk, wailing, and only the jackals respond.

Two representatives of the "Geula" ("Redemption") Company come to buy the land. The peasant is discharged of his debts and is given money; he leaves the plain, and desolation spreads out again, sending forth thorns and briars. A man is sent out by the company to guard the land. The man is a figure of mystery, so that his actions take on something of a legendary significance. His name, Yemini, is an allusion to the tribe of Benjamin. An old member of a neighboring kvutzah (collective settlement), he feels reborn with his new task as guardian:

> Yemini felt his youth restored, as of old. Once again he found himself in the familiar listening moonlit nights, when there was not as much as a single shadow in which to hide. The secrets of the countryside imbued him with their dread, which he had so long known. During the long dark nights the desert admitted him to its secret marvels, so that his loneliness seemed to him like life's loftiest peak. Sometimes he was afflicted with boundless, helpless, hapless sorrow, and then at heart he wished to join in the distant chorus of the howling jackals. At such times he would feel grateful to his all-too-familiar mare for her living warmth, and to the tamarisk which rustled for him in so familiar and neighborly a fashion. From time to time he would act as host in the shadow of the tree to the Arab villagers from the hills, and would establish relations with those of their inhabitants who were most liable to keep busy in the nights and in the dark. But on the Sabbath he would return to his *kvutzah*, take a shower and spend his time like an honored guest who had ample deeds behind him and brought with him the scent of distant parts. (p. 21)

Meanwhile, the rich Arab landowner talks the peasant into giving him half the money he received, in exchange for which he will receive a parcel of the rich man's land in perpetuity. The landowner fails to keep his part of the bargain, and a lawyer consumes the other half of the peasant's money. In his anger, the peasant gathers some men around him, and they embark on a life of banditry. In a foray, Yemini is killed by the peasant and his men: some bullets hit the tree, but one hits Yemini in the chest. "He fell on his face and his blood coursed out over the root of the tamarisk" (p. 22). The notables in Jerusalem decide that he is to be given a hero's burial, under the tamarisk (and the symbolic link to King Saul, also a Benjaminite and buried under a tamarisk, is implied). When his body is placed on the ground, the tamarisk rustles its branches over him, and he seems to undergo a metamorphosis, to become one substance with the roots of the tree.

The tamarisk rustles twice in the story, once to the desolation of the land (in something like a dialogue with it), and once to the dead Yemini (who, in his death, becomes a part of the myth of the place). With the phrase "as of old" there is the repeated suggestion that whatever happens is an eternal return to something of biblical significance. "Yemini felt his youth restored, as of old." And the story ends with the haunting words: "And once more there was nothing to be seen, save a nameless tamarisk as lonely as of old, rustling its branches over the desolate plain" (p. 24).

Yemini's life and death suggest a historical cycle: a metamorphosis of days of old suffuses his life; and his death evokes the mystic connection between *dam* (blood), *adam* (man), and *adama* (earth). And then there was the historical night that shone over the solitary guardian of the desolate expanse. Night is the realm of eternal myth, day that of the transitory and unreal. For Shenhar, then, death is the bond between man and earth, in their mythic continuity. Biblical reality and current reality link myth and history in a dialectical relation of both opposition and resolution. In the landscape, the ultimate "presence" is desolation: absence. The tree—a presence in myth as well as in brute reality—rustles over Yemini, but not over the Arab peasant whose lot was equally tragic. Yet the two are the guardians of the same landscape.

Shenhar does not merely tell a simple tale, to be taken as allegory and structured on its contrasts. There is also the element of irony, especially in connection with Yemini's funeral and the utterances of the mourners. One of them cries repeatedly, in agitation, "Watchman, what of the night? Watchman, what of the night?" (Isaiah 21:11) For anyone familiar with chapter and verse, there are the haunting (but here unspoken) phrases "The burden of Arabia" (21:13) and "all the glory of Kedar shall fail" (21:16). Shenhar uses this device of unspoken allusion once again, when the speaker, moved by the sight of the body under the tamarisk, cries: "Surely the Lord is in this place; and I knew it not" (Genesis 28:16). These words of Jacob follow immediately upon his vision of the ladder, where the Lord says: "The land whereon thou liest, to thee will I give it, and to thy seed. . . . And, behold, I am with thee . . . and will bring thee back into this land" (28:13–15). To those who know this passage, the mourner's words are enough to evoke the rest—and to do so more powerfully and subliminally than if the additional words were actually spoken aloud. Jacob's vision parallels that of Abraham in Beer-sheba when he calls on the name of the Lord and plants the tamarisk tree. Jacob gives the name Beth-el ("House of God") to the place where he had his vision, and it is the approximate place of Shenhar's story.

Ultimately, the mere title "The Tamarisk" carries all these allusions, and more, to those with a first-hand acquaintance with the Hebrew Bible—thus evoking all these "arguments" far more effectively than any discursive argument would do. But in addition to these allusions "back" to biblical passages, there also are allusions "forward" to more recent Hebrew literature. I have already mentioned the link between Shenhar's story and A. B. Yehoshua's novella "Facing the Forests." In the way that Shenhar endows his tree with an importance beyond the here and now, Yehoshua's forest is given a symbolic significance as well. Yet unlike Shenhar's Yemini, who, by guarding the land and by his death, becomes a part of the land and literally a son of the soil, Yehoshua's protagonist is, at the outset of the novella, a tourist in his own land, a guest for a night. Only toward the end of the novella, when he walks the land with the Arab, when he realizes that destruction and desolation are part of the unwritten "script" for the land, does he acquire a memory and thus become a native son in that sense, when the ruins of the Arab village alert him to the past and present.

Further, the burning of the forest in Yehoshua's novella is linked to the theme of desolation in Shenhar: the burning releases the land from its historical shackles and returns it to the condition of wasteland; in Shenhar, the land becomes wasteland by being abandoned. But in either case, the regression to wasteland wipes out all historical claims; time is thus the true ruler of the land, offering the possibility of a new (yet mythic) return to the land.

Shenhar's fabula is intertwined with unspoken allusions that are very much there and very much a part of the *intended* story. All this adds to the irony, even sarcasm, directed at those mourners who are mere "tourists" in the land. (Shenhar did not set out to create three-dimensional characters having psychological insights.) The allusionary technique marks Shenhar as a transitional writer, linking the fiction of the interwar period to that of the 1948 period. His stories devoted to the presentation of the image of the Arab, in both friendly and an adversarial relation to the Jew, provide another such link, adumbrating the moral dilemma that came to prevail.

PART TWO

WRITERS
OF THE 1948
GENERATION

CULTURAL BACKGROUND

The State of Israel was established in 1948. That was the official starting point of the process of becoming Israel—a process that began more than a half-century earlier and is still continuing. But the process itself, which can be regarded in physical, political, and demographic terms, is also marked by its spiritual/literary dimension: from 1948 on, writers have called themselves Israeli writers, creating an Israeli literature (rather than a Hebrew literature per se).

It is no exaggeration to say that the writers of that generation were marked by the declaring of statehood as the central fact of their existence. The concomitant fact, for them, was the War of Independence. The first generation of Israeli writers, the generation that matured during the war period, is referred to as the "Palmach Generation" (the word *Palmach* referring to underground military units operating against the British authorities during the time of the British Mandate). In addition to their deep bonds to the land and the language, a factor in their growing up was the youth movement, which provided the ideological framework for their eventual world outlook. Despite differences in their political standpoints, most shared the same Zionist and Socialist values, which they were expected to express by joining a kibbutz, a collective agricultural settlement.

In 1948, when the establishment of the state was met by war, the young generation was called upon to translate national aspirations into reality. Yet the earlier values often were not in accord with the reality of the war: the shared experience of the "we," with its mentality of collective belonging cultivated in the youth movement, was now challenged by the experience of the "I" who is the fighting individual. Thus the war threw the individual back onto his personal responsibility, as his sense of collective belonging was confronted by bloodshed and horror. All this entered the literature of the era.

One writer who gave voice to the dissonance between self and reality is S. Yizhar. His typical protagonist is a captive of his own sensitivity and sensibility. He is passive—because activity involves choice and commitment that are equally irrevocable. Decisiveness and certainty are attitudes that are entirely foreign to him. Thus the time of bliss for the Yizhar protagonist is the period of childhood, prior to initiation into adulthood and war; child and landscape are then in harmony, in a world without boundaries. Reality therefore entails a call to reassess the ways in which we belong to the land, and the land to us.

The war also raised issues of personal morality for the protagonist in Israeli literature: What is to be one's relation to the enemy? to the prisoner? What is an act of good faith, and what is *mauvaise foi?* Where are we to look for the basis of justice—in our personal convictions or in the collective national need? Yizhar's protagonist does not pass judgment, nor does he undergo an essential change of outlook; the situation is but a stage for his unceasing interior monologue, a monologue filled with self-mockery. He tries to escape time and self-consciousness. He sees the ambiguity and irony in the world of "reality," and he is unceasingly aware of being an outsider in the stand-off between his self-searching sensitivity and the actions of others.

Of course, this standpoint is by no means that of all the Israeli writers of this generation. Moshe Shamir, for example, rejects the separation of the "I" from the "we." Recognizing the tension between the collective emphasis and the individual as a recurring theme in Israeli literature, he stresses the shared experience as a key motif. And therefore the Shamir protagonist of the war period is characterized by self-assertion rather than self-doubt, action rather than contemplation, and he is at one with the demands of his time.

Not only did the 1948 War of Independence provide most Israeli writers with the initiation into reality; it also produced in them a more complex relation to the land. It meant the personal participation in making history— with certain ramifications that were problematic for some, but not for others. For most Israeli writers it meant a heightened self-awareness as an individual—although not all writers were led to a sense of isolation as a result. All in all, we can say with some certainty that the declaration of statehood and the war that began immediately thereafter, two types of events not necessarily connected with any particular literary effect in other literatures, served as the formative crucible for the first generation of Israeli writers.

6. S. YIZHAR

S. Yizhar was born Yizhar Smilansky in Rehovot in 1916. He is thus one of the oldest native-born Israeli writers now living (and is even "pre-Israel," his first story having appeared in 1938). His was a family of farmers who were also writers, and the family was associated with the first wave of immigration, of 1882 to 1903. Two of Yizhar's uncles also were writers—one of them the Moshe Smilansky we discussed earlier, whose stories were among the first in modern Hebrew literature to portray Arabs.

Yizhar's is a complex personal heritage, combining the First Aliyah mentality of that early Rehovot with the enhanced social consciousness of the Second. His father, Ze'ev Smilansky, was a modest man who worked his own farm and contributed articles to the Socialist/Zionist organ *Hapoel Hatzair*. And although he employed Arab workers in his orchard, he believed in the concept of "Hebrew labor" as an essential element in the Jew's return to the soil. To this day, Yizhar continues to live in the house his father inhabited.

His deep connection to the land—and to the people of the land, rather than to the Jewish Diaspora—has led Yizhar to use the Bible as a major source for the imagery in his works. These biblical topoi, together with biblical allusions, evoke the early Hebrews as an essential element in his fiction. His love for the land also evokes his nostalgic affection for the Arabs of his childhood, although in Yizhar's stories the image of the Arab is many-sided, as nomad or villager, as friend or foe. But whatever the character may be, the Arab is always a native son tied to the soil—thereby calling into question the Jewish birthright to the land.

Yizhar's contribution to Hebrew and Israeli literature is tremendous. His unique language places him among the masters of Hebrew style, along with figures such as Uri Nissan Gnessin (1879–1913), whose work influenced him greatly. With Yizhar's first novella, in 1938, he emerged as a writer of a deep sensitivity that has not been surpassed. He is a master of the stream-of-consciousness technique, as he places his protagonist in the very midst of his tale. The stories are usually simple, consisting of a few episodes; the fabula is quite basic and uncomplicated. The stream-of-consciousness technique, which he has used from the outset, minimizes external time and place, enhancing the protagonist's reactions to the unexpected situations into which the author throws him. Yizhar's landscape is entirely personal, experiential, *a*historical. It is the landscape of a child's discovery of the boundless, the desert wherein a man is turned back upon himself, as a solipsistic character untouched by society or outer conflict. Here the protagonist can see the Arab as a son of the soil, grazing his sheep as his forefathers did.

Individualism and solipsism typify most of Yizhar's protagonists, thus creating what may be called an "epic of one voice." His characteristic protagonist is a child or young man caught in an unforeseen situation. Where there is a historical framework, the protagonist gets his perspective from time and events. Yet apart from this, the vision proceeds from the protagonist outward, as the land itself is shaped through his eyes.

Already in Yizhar's early novellas and stories the builders of the land confront the Arab presence—the few facing the many. The siege mentality becomes a dire reality when new kibbutzim are attacked by surrounding Arab villagers. Yet Yizhar's first story, "Ephraim Returns to the Alfalfa" (1938), does not touch upon an Arab-Jewish encounter, but takes place in a kibbutz. The matter seems trivial: one of the members, Ephraim, asks to be given a different task, and the kibbutz committee refuses. The Arab-Jewish conflict is not addressed in this story; yet the story is significant for projecting a Jewish archetype that will figure in Yizhar's further writing on the conflict.

Ephraim belongs to the Third Aliyah of the early 1920s. His sensitivity and self-doubt make him a Yizhar prototype: he is derided by one of the other characters as a "bleeding heart" (*yefe nefesh*; literally, "beautiful soul"), an unfocused romantic forever in search of open spaces and personal freedom. In a reverie about the wide, wide fields, Ephraim dots the landscape with a passing Arab:

> Here is loneliness. Here is silence. What is there to meditate upon, . . . to distract the soul, to give her any substance of hope at all? . . . A camel stalks down the path; alongside, an Arab rides on his donkey at a leisurely pace.[1]

The Arab is conceived as a part of the environment; the Arab and the land seem in accord. An ironic implication is embedded here: If the Arab is part of the "place," and the new Israeli has found his own connection to that place, then his connection to the Arab would seem similarly intrinsic and unproblematic, at least in his own eyes.

Yizhar's perception of landscape is synoptic; his fiction is pictorial, with the pictoriality changing as the text unfolds. Yet what this means is that the depicted world is pitted against human consciousness. Yizhar is not concerned to present a complete portrait of an individual—say, with a family and a past. Rather, the character's presence in the narrative line is itself spatial, as Yizhar moves from one character to another, one consciousness to another. Frequently, the inner time of the character is loosely connected to the "objective" time that unites the story. Yizhar's stories are often rich in movement but poor in events. And just as often, a story is poor in dialogue, and the omniscient/omnipresent authorial voice is not dominant. Yet although his tales may be contextually sparse, they create an epic totality. (All these features will, of course, have an immediate bearing on the portrayal of the central character, and thus on the portrayal of the Arab.)

Between 1938 and 1941, Yizhar published four novellas. Three of these were subsequently republished in one volume. "Paths in the Fields," however, was not reissued and is therefore confined to the pages of the now extinct organ *Gilionoth*.[2] "Paths in the Fields" (1938) marks the first appearance of an Arab in Yizhar's writing, although he does not appear qua Arab, and is not referred to directly. The Arab gradually encroaches on the territory of the Jewish settler. From the innocuous picture-postcard image of the eternal Arab on his donkey, the Arab grows into an ominous presence.

The novella *On the Edges of the Negev,* which first appeared in 1945, is the story of a group of Jewish settlers—two dozen young men and women—drilling for water in a temporary encampment in the Negev, Israel's southern desert.[3] It is a story of human effort rewarded, of young love, and of the life-affirming spirit of the settlers who make the desert bloom. Yizhar's involvement with the Negev will lead to a dichotomy that remains unresolved in him: on one hand there is his fascination with the unspoiled emptiness, and his deep desire to preserve the landscape with all its biblical echoes; on the other hand there is the Zionist dream of settling the wasteland. That dichotomy will rise to a tragic level in "The Prisoner" and "Hirbet Hizah."

In *On the Edges of the Negev,* Arabs not only become centrally present, they are given names and identities: Abu Sayid and his shepherd son guard the drill site. The older man is described in his sagelike slowness, his inner power and knowing hands. Yizhar evokes a contrast between the Arab, who is entirely "at home" in his world, and the Jewish settlement with its barbed wire evincing newness and fear; between the distant sounds of a camel's bell and the voice of its Arab owner, and the sounds of the Jewish settlement in its furtive defensiveness. Abu Sayid's slowness is a part of the ritual manner with which he approaches everything: his way of dissecting a watermelon, in the heart of the wasteland, has an almost ceremonial quality. He offers to serve as a guide in the search for further drilling sites.

When the truck loses its way in the wilderness, neither Abu Sayid's experience nor the settlers' map can find the route. A lone Bedouin appears—white shirt, dark cloak, white kaffiye, red boots, white horse with red tassels—a handsome man with parched skin and squinting eyes. Dismounting and tethering his horse to a bush, he places his sword on the ground; he walks up to the truck to show them the way back. He will not lose his way in the open desert, and the narrator continues, "and he is certain that no one will touch his possessions, a man in the midst of what is 'his,' a man at home" (p. 129).

The story ends on an upbeat note: water will change the face of the arid desert, and the young people will create a home of their own. And despite the ceremonial element, the presence of the Bedouins is described in a non-stereotypical way in this story. Although they are ubiquitous, it seems that they will remain unaffected by the new culture.

Kibbutz Hulda, in the Judean foothills, came under attack from Arab rioters in 1929. Its twenty-four defenders held out heroically, though their commander was killed. Although Yizhar does not usually borrow his plots from actual events, "The Grove on the Hill"[4] is based on what happened in Kibbutz Hulda: a young settlement is attacked; the defenders are few; their leader is killed; eventually the British come and compel the settlers to abandon the place, hardly allowing them time to bury their dead.

One difficulty in interpreting Yizhar's fiction stems from the elusive nature of the authorial voice. Thus he will employ the "telling" technique in handling nature and landscape; yet the "telling" technique is not a neutral presentation of mere background, but rather an indirect expression of the author's values as he puts a distance between himself and the events. That distance is what enables him to enhance the stream-of-consciousness technique and the inner voice, so that external events become a springboard for the inner ones. And this will apply increasingly to all his protagonists, regardless of the intensity of their external situation. In this way his narrative acquires its epic dimension and deliberate pace.

The protagonist, too, withdraws into an internal landscape, so that the two systems, inner and outer, can be seen as running in tandem, with or without a causal connection. As a result, continuity and plausibility are no longer essential requirements of his narrative. The narrator's withdrawal into the inner landscape is by no means a withdrawal into fantasy; rather, it is a withdrawal into a divided self, an inner theater where personal and societal values are in conflict. As we might well expect, this will lead to ethical dilemmas for Yizhar's protagonists—and these dilemmas will reach their climax in the treatment of the Arab.

We find the typical Yizhar protagonist existentially "thrown" into a situation for which there is no precedent to provide guidance. The result is self-doubt—introspection which leads to action that is ambiguous and opaque, rather than clear-cut and decisive. Does his protagonist embrace group values as a refuge from the angst of his solipsistic self? Can we simply go along with Yonatan Ratosh, the "Cana'anite," when he says that Yizhar's aim is to exhibit the self-tormented European Jew for whom the conflicting values remain unresolved (in contrast to the self-assured native Israeli)? To dichotomize in this way is to create a normative vacuum, whereas the Israeli reality has been, and continues to be, the *troubled* co-existence of the two worlds: the individualistic and the collective, the inner and the outer. Time does not bring hope of change or resolution to Yizhar's protagonist, who, in essence, has not changed in more than three decades. Change necessarily occurs in time; yet time itself is often suspended for the Yizhar protagonist, as his consciousness becomes non-sequential. The narrating voice will sometimes employ a roving camera-eye technique as a way of detaching itself from what is seen—even to the extent of being devoid of a point of view.

Where does the Arab feature in Yizhar's approach to the individuated protagonist? And how does the Arab's presence figure in the Israeli protagonist's perception of the world? Increasingly we shall be seeing that the only complete portrait to appear consistently throughout Yizhar's work is that of the Arab. Clearly, the individual will shun the false values and "bad faith" of the group more and more as he sees the group fail—in understanding, compassion, humanity. And this will be true, moreover, regardless of whether the group is Jewish or Arab.

We shall also see that Yizhar's Israeli protagonist has a deep covenant, as it were, with the Arab. Meeting on the same ground, each is forced by circumstances to fight his "brother in confrontation." As the Arab comes to the foreground, he will feature as friend and as enemy, as the narrative plucks him from the village and places him in the midst of war and suffering.

We shall now go on to discuss four war narratives of Yizhar: "Before Zero Hour," "Midnight Convoy," "The Prisoner," and "Hirbet Hizah." All relate to the 1948 War of Independence, and all appeared soon after.[5]

"Before Zero Hour" is not a story in the conventional sense of a series of episodes shaped by change. Rather, it is the depiction of the moods of some men prior to setting out on a military action. The men are apparently members of the Palmach (one of the unofficial military forces prior to the establishment of the State of Israel), and they are to leave from a kibbutz. The unidentified narrator gives voice to his feelings and doubts: "Nervous, no, not that much. Sad, maybe that's the word" (p. 10). The atmosphere gradually intensifies into a sense of urgency and imminent death. Another voice is heard, life-asserting, foreseeing a short action and quick return. Yet another voice expresses hesitation, confusion:

> If you could perhaps call on someone, like father and mother back then, when you could call them in from the other room. Suddenly strange skies surround you, unknown earth protrudes . . . a strange fog. And hurrying and shooting . . . and people appear . . . shoot them, shoot them. . . . And suddenly you're shot dead and that's it. Namely, ha ha. Nonsense. . . . Between us . . . what nonsense war is. . . . Shots are heard then a funeral . . . and it's finished . . . and someone might be moved to

quote a nice verse, instead of yelling, before death: "You asses! You're being cheated. Don't go. What fatherland? You'll be killed!" (p. 31)

The voice goes on to yearn for the simple life—as against the voice of duty. Weapons and equipment are distributed. The story ends with the departure of the unit. One of the men whispers, "What a beautiful night, isn't it?" And the speaker answers, "A night full of magic."

The Arab presence looms heavily in the speaker's consciousness, as it leaps from the time prior to departure to the possibilities of death or safe return. Thus once again we see the Arab as a major element in shaping Israeli consciousness, even when not directly present to that consciousness.

Like so many of Yizhar's narratives, "Midnight Convoy" is set against the background of actual events, here again the 1948 War.[6] Six soldiers are assigned to mark the way for a convoy that will bring food and arms to a Jewish settlement beyond enemy lines, in the Negev. The soldiers, working through sand and marshes, are trying to find a road, but it has already been obliterated. The length of road to be marked is three kilometers, with the enemy beyond the road and hill. Yizhar does not tell us whether the convoy eventually manages to pass through the danger zone and reach the besieged settlers.

Once again, the central character is a sensitive young man, lanky and diffident, who admires his commander and secretly yearns for the girl who operates the communication unit. And again we are given the contrast between the individual in his inwardness and the "group" outside. Where "Before Zero Hour" presents nothing more than the inner voice of the unidentified protagonist, "Midnight Convoy" is more of a war novella, and includes external action. Yet the inner voice is not abandoned; on the contrary, the novella is made all the more complex by giving us two such voices and two points of view. The authorial voice (one of the two main voices) gives us the framework for the tale, while the five men and one woman enrich the fabric of the story by providing action and background. The other main voice is that of the sensitive young man Zvialeh, who will withdraw into his inner world.

The action going on in the surrounding war gives the novella its depth. Yet Yizhar avoids giving us an account of actual combat. Moreover, he avoids the conventional story structure of a beginning, middle, and end. The tale as such could come to an end at any number of points. At the same time, "Midnight Convoy" comes closer to the experience of war than most of his tales. "Fear sweeps lightly . . . there's an enemy here somewhere" (p. 116). The repeated use of the word *enemy* suggests the inevitability of confrontation in the dark. There is the suggestion that the enemy are Egyptians; but that is not as significant as the point that the soldiers in this unit feel themselves surrounded as the defenders of the settlement. The commander echoes this apprehension: "One lousy shepherd could spoil everything. There may be mines where we crossed the road—we're not sure" (p. 117). Shepherds serve almost as icons in Yizhar's fiction. They are an integral part of the landscape, suggesting a connection to ancient times and ancient tenancy of the land.

Yizhar's landscape is, in essence, personal, ahistorical, yet mythic—stemming from its presence in the childhood experience of limitless vistas. As Yizhar's protagonist grows up (typically) and wanders beyond the familiar, he is attracted all the more to the desolated land and its monotony. It is only in the heart of the wasteland, undisturbed by progress or boundaries, that he can experience what it is to be a native son. The war will deprive the Yizhar protagonist of this spatial experience. He is thrown into a world of imposed commitments which cannot be readily questioned. The war has broken the intimate connection to the landscape, just as it has questioned ownership of the land. Yizhar's way of questioning that ownership is through a protagonist's estrangement from the land. Thus, instead of confronting the historical issues, Yizhar approaches the problem via the individual's personal perception.

There is another element of complexity: On one hand, Yizhar hears the land ring out with its biblical past, the past which established Abraham's title, and thus the title possessed by Abraham's seed. Indeed, the epiphany undergone by Zvialeh has overtones of the reaffirmation of the covenant of Genesis 15. Yet the difference between a biblical claim and that of Yizhar's protagonist is that the biblical has a temporal basis, while Yizhar's is spatial. For his protagonist, it is the soil itself, not history, that is the basis for tenure of the land. On the other hand, that same spatial emphasis includes the Arab as an intrinsic part of the landscape. Without that temporal link, however, the result can only be estrangement:

> For some reason, that oppressive feeling came back again. It was your uneasy conscience, though this perhaps was no more than your consciousness of being a stranger here, far from anything that was yours and not close to anything belonging to this place. (p. 149)

Despite that very estrangement (and perhaps even because of it), Zvialeh studies the terrain closely, and it is this that gives him a sense of belonging. Symbolically, his growing familiarity with the terrain only raises the fear that he will step on a mine—i.e., the land itself is dangerous, and growing closer to it only increases the danger. With this, there is the realization that there is no escape from the state of war.

Yizhar's "The Prisoner"[7] and "Hirbet Hizah" are two of the most controversial literary works to emerge from the 1948 War. "The Prisoner" recounts the Israeli maltreatment of an Arab shepherd in that war, while "Hirbet Hizah" tells of the Israeli pillaging of an Arab village and the abuse of its inhabitants. Understandably, the publication of these stories (in November 1948 and May 1949 respectively), during and toward the end of the victorious war on which the very life of Israel depended, created a political uproar in the newly established state, and evoked a wide variety of reactions. At one extreme, there was praise for the moral courage of an Israeli writer who was not hesitant to portray a serious lapse in Israel's own conduct of the war. At the other extreme, there was indignation at the "bleeding hearts" who were casting doubt upon the moral uprightness of an entire generation of young men, thrown into a war they did not start and from which they emerged with glory.

Obviously, then, these two stories have had a powerful impact. Yet to regard them as nothing more than political statements is to misread them as works of literature. They were not intended as political tracts in fictional guise, but rather as stories having a universal scope, displaying some of the dehumanizing effects of war. Further, they say something about the corrupting effect of power—made all the more poignant by the sudden reversal in the role of the Jew, from the eternally hunted to the hunter. Yet the political inferences are inevitable, since the stories take place in an identifiable locale and time. But these are not stories of the "good" versus the "bad," or about a morally neutral narrator pitted against the heartless "others." Rather, the narrator/protagonist, in his moral sensitivity, indirectly accuses himself, and thus challenges the reader.

By this time, Yizhar had given up the collective standpoint of "The Grove on the Hill," and had gone back to the earlier mode, that of the individualistic protagonist who sets the tone and point of view. In "Before Zero Hour" and "Midnight Convoy," the individual is still in accord with the values of the group, and although the main protagonist is revolted by war, he does not hesitate to join with others in military action. Zvialeh, in "Midnight Convoy," may wish for "a different kind of war," a war which is in essence constructive; yet the preparations for the ensuing battle cement his sense of belonging to the group. As we shall see, this standpoint will change in "The Prisoner" and "Hirbet Hizah," where the main protagonists question the need for what takes place, as well as the morality of the group.

In "The Prisoner" the platoon, consisting of the narrator's comrades, is depicted by the use of metonymy. No character is fully drawn. We see gestures, parts of the body, but neither names nor portraits are given. The Arab shepherd, on the other hand, is roundly drawn, given a name and a totality of appearance.

At the outset of the story, the narrator is a mere observer of the capture and interrogation of the Arab. Toward the end, the narrator has become a protagonist, with a vital moral decision to make. It would be simplistic to see the story as a depiction of a righteous individual pitted against the group. Rather, it points to the complexity of the conflict between moral and prudential values. It presents the plight of a modern protagonist who knows the limitations of his knowledge and the indeterminacy of his own state of being; who shares the values held by his group yet is the critical voice of their conscience. At the same time that critical voice is silent; it is left to the stream of consciousness, to which only the reader is allowed access.

The fabula of the story is not complicated: an Arab shepherd, a Bedouin, is captured by an Israeli patrol, and is brought to their base for interrogation. He is ill treated (his requests for a cigarette are ignored). Eventually he is transferred to headquarters for further questioning. The narrator is assigned to transfer the prisoner.

Each one, the narrator and the prisoner, is torn from a well-knit fabric of existence. The narrator comes to realize the evils of power (including his own). The capture of a single shepherd in an unimportant military action unravels what had been a complete world for each. And both participate in a drama they don't belong to. Or do they? Is the Arab potentially "the enemy" simply because he is Arab? And should he be treated as such? (How does one treat "the enemy"?) Is the Israeli committed to certain actions merely by virtue of his being a member of a military unit? Yizhar challenges the assertions that would be positive answers to these questions. As for the Arab, the war has not only violated his pastoral landscape, it has uprooted him from it in a tragic way.

Moreover, Yizhar's way of limiting the story to the viewpoint of the observer undercuts the author's own position as all-knowing. It is an opaque technique that must leave some doubt as to the reliability of the narrator. Thus the shepherd could be either innocent or cunning, a victim or a participant. And the narrative technique Yizhar has chosen serves the purposes of that ambiguity—not only within the framework of the story but also in the wider framework of Arab attitudes toward the Israeli and Israeli attitudes toward the Arab.

For writers of a later generation (e.g., A. B. Yehoshua, Amos Oz), the value of fiction is in presenting the tragic clash of right versus right in all its complexity. In Yizhar the conflict goes even deeper, where loyalty to the land (with its biblical associations of which the shepherd is a part) conflicts with loyalty to the group and its aim. Thus there is the idyllic reverberation in the second paragraph: "In the distance quiet flocks were grazing, flocks from the days of Abraham, Isaac, and Jacob" (p. 294). Yet the aims of Zionism, independence and peace—contrary though these may be to the shepherd's tranquil existence—cannot be rejected. The conflict is mirrored in the inner ruminations of the narrator; and so it is an additional dimension of complexity to have transformed the passively observant narrator into the real protagonist. When the narrator is ordered to transport the prisoner to headquarters, there arises the moral dilemma of whether to free the prisoner. This is not an abstract moral problem for the narrator, but the culmination of the clash between two loyalties: loyalty to the land as against loyalty to an ideal. Any sensitive reading of the story must not only feel that conflict, but must also see it exemplified in Jewish/Israeli life as such.

In effect, Yizhar has the narrator ask us what *we* would have done in his place. We might want to evade answering, by asking what did in fact happen. Did the narrator release the prisoner? It remains an unanswered question. The story must remain as indeterminate on this score as the tragic situation itself remains to this day.

The conflict between "we" and "I"—that is, between collective values and individual conscience—is central to Yizhar, and it is there in his work from the beginning, in 1938. In the four war stories, we see him placing greater emphasis on the individual voice than on the collective. Thus we can see the typical transition from "we" to "I"—but the transition is never conclusive. And it is a testimony to his power as a writer not only that he can leave the conflict unresolved, but that its irresolution is entirely plausible. It is plausible because Yizhar, in the scope of a short story, has masterfully shown us a man who on one hand identifies himself fully with the Zionist dream, and on the other hand is appalled by the cruelties of war.

The cruelty of war is obvious. Yet despite the protagonist's clear separateness from the group, he shares its system of values. He is simultaneously one of them *and* their conscience, albeit (as I pointed out) their *silent* conscience. What is of lasting significance is that for the protagonist/narrator, the victorious War of Independence is at the same time the undoing of previous certainties. One of these certainties was his deep love for the land—expressed so sonorously in the opening of the story—a love which (as we saw) becomes a part of the problem:

> Shepherds and their flocks were scattered on the rocky hillsides, among the woods of low terebinth and the stretches of wild rose, and even along the swirling contours of valleys foaming with light, with those golden-green sparks of rustling summer grain under which the clodded earth, smelling of ancient soil, ripe and good, crumples to gray flour at a foot's touch; on the plains and in the valleys flocks of sheep were wandering; on the hilltops, dim, human forms, one here and one there, sheltered in the shade of olive trees: it was clear that we could not advance without arousing excitement and destroying the purpose of our patrol.
>
> We sat down on the rocks to rest a bit and to cool our dripping sweat in the sunlight. Everything hummed of summer, like a golden beehive. A whirlpool of gleaming mountain fields, olive hills, and a sky ablaze with an intense silence blinded us for moments and so beguiled our hearts that one longed for a word of redeeming joy. And yet in the midst of the distant fields shepherds were calmly leading their flocks with the tranquil grace of fields and mountains and a kind of easy unconcern—the unconcern of good days when there was yet no evil in the world to forewarn of other evil

things to come. In the distance quiet flocks were grazing, flocks from the days of Abraham, Isaac, and Jacob. A far-off village, wreathed with olive trees of dull copper, was slumbering in the curves of hills gathered like sheep against the mountains. But designs of a different sort cast their diagonal shadows across the pastoral scene. (pp. 294–95)

This is the language Yizhar reserves for the pristine landscape (although we should take note of the ominous reverberation at the end of each paragraph). He has quite another language for the narrator having to do with military events. The glee of the soldiers over their meager capture is described through their own voices. Yizhar rarely involves his main protagonist in dialogue, but leaves him to his interior monologue and stream of consciousness. All this serves the purposes of "we" and "I"—to sharpen or blur the distinction, as needed. The description of the prisoner's "palpable misery" as he is led away blindfolded is interspersed with the description of the sun and landscape, like a fugue, interchanging ground bass and theme.

Although the questioning is conducted by a group of officers, and the setting is rather formal, the entire tale is characterized by the upset of balances—some tragic, others grotesque. The Arab is not believed, which adds to the general ambiguity throughout. (The narrator, again, is not all-knowing.) The following paragraph in *erlebte Rede*, reflects that ambiguity:

It was clear he would lie at this point. He had to lie. It was his duty to lie, and we would catch him by his tongue, the dirty dog, and we would show him. And just as we understood that with these tactics he would reveal nothing, so we knew that this time he wouldn't fool us. Not us. It's his turn to talk! (p. 301)

The Arab is questioned as to the number of Egyptian soldiers in his village. The investigators expect him to deny the presence of the Egyptians, but (to the dismay of the officers) he confirms their presence. This takes the investigators by surprise, and the reaction is, "That's a lie."

The barrage of questions continued without a break. The kicks landed like lightning, more naturally and freely, cool, deliberate, increasingly skillful. If at times they seemed unavailing, they nonetheless continued.

Because if you want the truth, beat him! If he lies, beat him! If he tells the truth (don't you believe it!) beat him so he won't lie later on! Beat him in case there is more to come. Beat him because you've got him at your feet! Just as a tree when shaken lets fall its ripest fruit, so a prisoner if you strike him yields his choicest truths. That's clear. And if someone doesn't agree, let him not argue. He's a defeatist, and you can't make wars with that kind. Have no mercy. Beat him! They have no mercy on you. Besides, a goy is used to blows. (pp. 303–304)

That last sentence created shock waves in the readers of the *Molad* quarterly, where the story first appeared: an inverted world, where the Jew is now the persecutor who beats the defenseless.

Nowhere does Yizhar assert the prisoner's guilt or innocence (even if these considerations were at all relevant). The uncertainty becomes indecision about further action:

> Well, what now: to the village quarry or perhaps a little more torture to open his mouth? Was there any other way to get rid of him? Or . . . perhaps one could give him a cigarette and send him home. Get out and let's not see you again! (p. 305)

Once the narrator is ordered to take the prisoner to main headquarters, Yizhar inserts the question, "Who could foresee how it would end?"—and it is not clear whether he is referring to the fate of the prisoner, the action of the sentry/narrator, the subsequent military action, or even the narrative itself.

Yizhar heightens the indeterminacy by creating an interior dialogue in the conscience of the sentry/narrator. He is his own tribunal and defense. The urge to free the prisoner is countermanded by the plea that "I am only a messenger." Yet he realizes that he cannot evade making a choice, and he cannot escape into "I'm a soldier . . . It's an order." Now, he realizes, he is naked and facing the force of moral duty (p. 307). Let the shepherd go back to his wife and home—and to hell with the slogans. *They* made this outrage possible in the first place. Yet am I responsible for what others have done to him? Again, this is seen as an evasion: "That's the way every son-of-a-bitch escapes from a fateful decision and hides himself behind 'I have no choice' " (p. 308). Yet: "I'm nothing but a messenger. What's more, there's a war, and this man is from the other side. . . . What would happen if we all started to set prisoners free?"

The irony, as he himself points out, is that someone with less moral sensitivity would already have freed the man and forgotten the whole thing. "But you, with all your knowledge, arguments, proofs, and dreams, it's clear that you won't do it." And then, it's the mess he'll get into that gives him further doubts. Yet he feels that someone must stand up against "this habitual swinishness" that is cruelty made the norm, the cruelty to which he has been the passive accomplice. This is his chance to stand up and be a man! (p. 310) Yet behind the misty evening there is the "Who knows?" felt by the wife of the prisoner—but also the "Who knows?" belonging to us all "which will remain here among us, unanswered, long after the sun has set" (p. 310).

How shall we come to terms with this ending? A number of possible indeterminate "explanations" present themselves: One might say that the story shows us man "thrown" into an existential predicament which would make any pat resolution unbelievable. One might even say that the theme of indeterminacy is the very point of the story, so that no resolution is to be sought by the reader. The indeterminacy could be merely a device of the author's to challenge the reader to examine his/her own values, to ask, "What would you have done?" Or one might see in the story a portrait of a tragic hero challenging his own beliefs by juxtaposing them to other values. Obviously, the values he criticizes throughout are the very ones he holds. Yet when these values clash with the demands of humanness, the protagonist's only way out is the disturbing skepticism of the repeated phrase, "Who knows?"

These are the thematic/literary interpretations, attempting to view the story from "within" its own narrative boundaries, as it were. There is also the possibility of looking at the story from "outside"—as a sociopolitical document reflecting actual Israeli attitudes toward Arabs. Thus the indeterminacy of the story's ending could be seen to indicate the Israeli bafflement in regard to the Arab.

If we look at Yizhar's Jewish protagonist not as an existential hero but rather sociopolitically, as someone who cannot act—someone who cannot free the prisoner, yet cannot continue to keep him in custody because the "justification" (either way) is clearly not there. The prudential justification is there, but what he seeks is the *moral* one, a justification that would resolve all doubts. In the English translation, the story ends with the words, "and still another 'who-knows?' belonging to us all, which will remain here among us, unanswered, long after the sun has set." In the Hebrew original, the term is not "unanswered" but "uncompleted" *(lo gamur)*—and it comes at the very end, to "complete" the story.

Although one can say that "Hirbet Hizah" is one of the most controversial works of modern Hebrew literature—together with "The Prisoner"—the controversy concerns ideology rather than aesthetics. The two stories belong together, as we noted, because their common theme is the maltreatment of Arabs vis-à-vis Israeli conscience.

"Hirbet Hizah" is the story of an Israeli platoon that rounds up the inhabitants of an Arab village. After a display of cruelty, the platoon goes on to expel the inhabitants and to demolish a part of the village. (The able-bodied young men of the village have fled to join the Arab forces; the remaining inhabitants are women, children, and the elderly.) The name of the village, Hirbet Hizah, is fictitious. Yet the presence of a first-person narrator lends the story the effect of first-hand reportage. Moreover, Yizhar has said that he himself witnessed what went on—so that the story is not a "fiction" to be dismissed out of hand.

Its publication in May 1949 (in a small volume that included a reprint of "The Prisoner") created a furor in public circles: Yizhar was branded a "pacifist" and a "defeatist," someone who was serving the aims of Arab propaganda. In 1978, the controversy erupted anew when the drama department of state-owned Israeli television prepared to offer "Hirbet Hizah" as a docudrama. On the eve of its airing, the presentation was canceled by the Ministry of Education and Culture.[8] In a radio interview, Yizhar stated: "People must ask themselves questions such as: What are the limits of war? . . . My sense of justice could not let me stay quiet." Twenty-five writers protested the ministry's ruling.

This was not a transitory issue. It touched not only on the issue of freedom of expression but also on the question of whether Israeli public life could find the moral courage for genuine self-assessment. Although the controversy quickly became ideologized, few of the participants could acknowledge this. One astute journalist, Mark Segal, observed that perhaps the aim of the filmmakers "was not to achieve an artistic reflection on the end of innocence which war always is for young men, but to convey a political message—the Jew as invader, the Arab as martyr."[9] With this, Segal recognized the film's anti-Zionist implications, which focused on the Arab as mythical Noble Savage evicted from his pastoral paradise by the Wicked Jew. Ultimately, a petition against the cancellation reached the High Court of Justice, and the issue was raised as well in the Israeli parliament: Had the government the right to censor what would be aired or screened?

The ideological reverberations were deep and many-sided. In the glowing aftermath of the victorious Six-Day War of June 1967, a number of volumes of conversations with soldiers were published.[10] In those discussions, mostly with young kibbutz members who had been in the midst of the fighting, and who were as strongly committed to Zionism as anyone, there was nevertheless some concern as to the moral justification for some of the action taken in the (then) twenty-year struggle. For this reason, some even questioned the validity of the Zionist enterprise and its very right to the land.

Had Yizhar's stories exerted some influence on these young people, directly or indirectly? Was *all* moral sensitivity untenable—as "pacifist," "defeatist"? Could cruelty be made acceptable, in response to the all-too-numerous massacres perpetrated by Arabs? A Knesset member, Geula Cohen, argued that "Hirbet Hizah" should be aired—but along with some docudramas of Arab massacres where Arabs killed and mutilated Israelis. Eventually, the ministry did rescind its cancellation; Israel Television aired "Hirbet Hizah," and Jordan TV made a copy and showed excerpts of it—which caused a further uproar in Israel. Since then, the film has not been shown on Israel TV. (In a conversation I had with Yizhar in February 1987, he told me that after the controversy connected to the television presentation, he was approached by an Arab journalist who said, "I congratulate you for giving expression to Arab pain." Yizhar responded by asking, "Is there an Arab writer who has given expression to Jewish pain?" The Arab, who was holding Yizhar's hand, took offense, dropped his hand, and left without another word.)

Yizhar has always been reluctant to discuss—or defend—his work. But amid the 1978 clamor, he did grant an extended interview to Rochelle Furstenberg, in which he declared:

> I was not crying out against the War of Independence. . . . There were many admirable things in that war, and our finest hour, the declaration of the State, came out of it. . . . [But] one or two events concerning injustice to the Arabs, which I witnessed at the end of the war, events which were peripheral, the exceptions and not necessarily the rule, demanded that I write. . . . They created an explosion in my life, which made me a writer. On the day I witnessed these injustices certain axioms of my life crumbled. . . . I was brought up—in Rehovot—with the belief that there are certain things that Jews just don't do. They don't inflict injustice. . . . [I was also brought up to believe that] there was no basic conflict between Arab and Jew. Both can live together on the land. It was the trauma of that personal fall from innocence that led me to write my stories.[11]

In an interview given to Chaim Nagid, however, Yizhar stated that although "Hirbet Hizah" related to actual events he had witnessed during the 1948 War, his was "a fictional treatment of this certain event, not reportage."[12] He went on to say that he did not write it "as a Jew versus an Arab," but "as a person who has been hurt. . . . something took place there that my whole consciousness refused to accept. . . . that contradicted my entire world-view." When Nagid asked whether the story could be construed as challenging the Jewish right to the land of Israel, Yizhar replied that such an interpretation deserves pity or psychiatric treatment. Could the story be construed, then, as representing the path of Zionism from the beginnings of Jewish settlement? To this, Yizhar replied, "God forbid!" The story describes a *deviant* event in classical Zionism. What he was concerned to describe, he said, was the gulf between the necessity of certain actions and the realization of what their outcome would mean—the gulf between that necessity and one's pre-existing values. Classical Zionism never spoke of banishing Arabs, but rather of co-existing with them. Everywhere we see the gulf between that ideal and the reality.

The poet Chaim Gouri, in a mock-serious write-up, attempted to delineate some of the polarized attitudes relating to the film:[13]

a) The action in "Hirbet Hizah" is an exception, and we must protest vigorously against it;

b) It is a mere joke, compared to what the Arabs have done to us;

c) It creates a falsehood, a new myth of crucifixion;

d) The whole country is Hirbet Hizah—and whoever denies it is a hypocrite and should leave;

e) The whole country is Hirbet Hizah—and it is time to grant justice to the Palestinians;

f) Whoever says "the whole country is Hirbet Hizah" defiles Zionism;

g) "Hirbet Hizah" is merely a story about people faced with the anguish of moral choice;

h) "Hirbet Hizah" is a story cut off from the context of time and place, and it lacks a serious protagonist who can argue with the author;

i) "Hirbet Hizah" is part of reality and will remain so, a lamentation over the loss of innocence.

Some of these points are quasi-political, others quasi-literary. The most searching literary criticism of Yizhar's "war literature" appeared in a 1950 article by the right-wing critic Mordechai Shalev. In his view, Yizhar's main weakness is the presentation of his main protagonist. What is supposed to give depth to the story is the emotional struggle in the narrator, who is carried along by the sadistic behavior of his comrades who torment the Arab villagers, while he is burdened by a sense of guilt. The depiction of this struggle, Shalev says, is rather schematic, using the narrator's two voices in a facile way: one good, the other bad. Thus Yizhar fails to give complexity to the dualism of good versus evil; and his inability to give shape to a complex literary character is a reflection of his failure to create a bridge between his earlier characters (the men of Socialism and morals) and what are now the "young Jewish murderers." Shalev asks: What happened to the ideals of "The Grove on the Hill" and its dedicated defenders? What is the point of transition from these men to the sadists of "Hirbet Hizah"?

The phrase "bleeding hearts" (*yefe nefesh*) came up repeatedly in discussions of Yizhar's typical protagonist—and the narrator in "Hirbet Hizah" even applies the term to himself, sarcastically. When Chaim Nagid, in his 1978 interview, asked Yizhar about this (i.e., could it be an overly rarefied conscience that gives the narrator his trouble, and not really any genuine problem about putative "injustice" to Arabs?), Yizhar responded by saying that the phrase "bleeding hearts" is a mediocre term used by those who want a license for crudeness, and who want to sweep such crudeness under the carpet—while it is for the good of us all, and for our maturity, to bring the unpleasantness into the open.

This point is relevant to Shalev's criticism regarding the absence of a bridge between the earlier protagonists and the later ones: "How did the 'bleeding hearts' who had tried to hide their sensitivities turn into the 'sadists worse than Nazis'?" According to Shalev, history outran Yizhar, who failed to foresee the coming reality, and then it surprised him. (Of course, these criticisms increase in significance if they are seen to be applicable not to Yizhar's fictional characters alone, but to the Israeli as such—however much that extension must be acknowledged to be questionable on methodological grounds.)

Moreover, Shalev argues that Yizhar personally shares in the vacuity of his characters, which stems from the "we have no choice" ethos of his old models. At the center of this malaise is the claim that the war was necessary because Israel was attacked—and once the attack is over, there is no further cause for war, presumably. The resulting frustration breeds the sadism we see portrayed in Yizhar's men, the frustration of men fighting for no discernible aim other than survival.

Against this, Shalev's vision of Israel is the Greater Israel of the Bible. He deplores the "defeatism" that undermines solid and morally founded claims to the land. For Shalev there *are* positive reasons for hatred, but when Yizhar's protagonists kill Arabs it is not because of hatred for what the Arabs did, or for revenge. Thus Yizhar fails to acknowledge the ultimate and absolute right of Jews to be masters in their own land. This failure in his characters is what leads to their sadism (and presumably to actual sadism directed at actual Arabs). It is the result of animosity reflected back inward on the part of the "second generation" Israelis who lack the mental stamina of the founders, and who are depicted (in Yizhar) as spineless men with "humanistic" qualms.

The point that is ignored, of course, is that Jews, through centuries of uprootedness and persecution, have become humanized to the point of actually feeling the pain of those people they have now displaced. Such awareness and empathy can be the beginning of a solution to The Problem. Whether such "humanistic" attributes are a sign of weakness or of strength, however, is a question for one's moral sensitivity to answer—but it is this triumph of humanness, in all its vulnerability, that Yizhar has undertaken to explore in his main characters.

The opening paragraph of "Hirbet Hizah"[14] carries the implicit suggestion that the narrator *must* tell his story, that it is his only way out from under his burden of guilt—his haunting memories of inhumanity and of his own powerlessness to change anything. Thus the story itself is a failed attempt to change what did happen. The theme of silence versus outcry indeed unites the story, just as it unites the narrator with the Arab villagers—although his moral anguish is not to be compared to their physical suffering. The story opens and closes with the significance of silence and outcry:

> Then we saw a woman walking among a group of three or four others. She held by the hand a child about seven years old. There was something special about her. She looked strong, self-controlled, taut in her grief. Tears, as if they did not belong to her, rolled down her cheeks, and even the child was whimpering, tight-lipped, as if to say, "What have you done to us?" Suddenly we saw that this was the only woman who knew exactly what was happening to her, so that I felt ashamed in front of her and lowered my eyes. It was as if a cry escaped from their gait, cursing their enemies. We saw also how she was too proud to pay us even a morsel of attention. We understood that she was strong-headed, and saw that the

furrows of restraint and the will to suffer heroically had hardened the lines
of her face, and how, when her world had perished—she did not want to
break before our eyes; and exalted in their pain and suffering above our
existence—our wicked existence—they passed on, and we also saw how
something was happening within the child so that when he would grow
up he could not be other than a poisonous serpent, this being who was
now nothing but a whimpering, frail child. (pp. 329–30)

I have touched on the familiar theme of the Jewish humanization that
resulted from centuries of uprootedness and persecution, and I pointed to
this experience as the basis for the Jew's identification with all those who
suffer. This identification is not an abstract *Mitgefühl* based on philosophic
principles but a vital element in the Jewish psyche drawn from Jewish
experience in history. Thus, to ignore it—intentionally or otherwise—is to
ignore a significant part of the Jewish past. Yizhar's hero sees that historical
link, derived from Jewish exile (*Galut*) and the Diaspora (*Golah*). But he goes
one step farther—a step in the direction of tragic identification with anyone
displaced—and he sees the Arab woman as being in a Galut of her own:

> Something suddenly became clear to me in a flash. At once I saw
> everything in a new, a clearer light—Galut. This is Galut. Galut is like this.
> This is what Galut looks like. (p. 330)

As a result, the collective experience and the personal experience coalesce:

> I had never been in the Golah—I said to myself—I had never under-
> stood what it was . . . but they had spoken to me about it, told me stories
> about it, taught me and kept on dinning into my ears, wherever I turned,
> in books and newspapers, everywhere: Galut. They had played on every
> fiber of my being. It had come to me, so it seemed, with my mother's milk.
> What really had we done here today? (p. 330)

Yet that same historical perspective could make us see everything in a
relativistic light, an attitude of lessened concern for the immediate pain of
those now suffering. The narrator turns to one of the men, Moyshe:

> "Well," said Moyshe, "what do you want?"
> I did want something. I had something to say. Only I did not know how
> to say something sensible and practical and not just to say how I felt.
> Somehow I had to shock him. At once, and in a very few words, I had to
> make him understand how serious things were.
> Instead, Moyshe spoke to me,. . .
> "You listen to what I'll tell you," said Moyshe, and his eyes sought out
> mine.
> "To Hirbet, what's-its-name, immigrants will be coming. Are you listen-

ing? And they'll take this land and they'll till it and everything here will be fine." (p. 331)

Is that to be the consolation? Jewish settlements built upon Arab ruins? The narrator's reaction is sardonic.

> Of course, what then? Why not? Why did I not think of that at first? Our Hirbet Hizah. There will be problems of housing and absorption. Hurrah, we shall build houses and absorb immigrants, and then we shall build a grocer's shop, we shall put up a school, perhaps also a synagogue. There will be political parties here. They will debate about a lot of things. They will plough fields and sow and reap and work wonders. Long live Jewish Hizah! Who will dream that once there was a place called Hirbet Hizah which we removed and to which we then moved in? We came, we shelled, we burned, we blew up, we pushed and we shoved and we sent into exile.
> What, in the devil's name, are we doing in this place? (pp. 331–32)

> I felt I was on the edge of a slippery slope. I managed to control myself. Everything within me cried out. Colonizers, it cried. Lies, it cried. Hirbet Hizah is not ours. . . . Oh! oh! the voice cried within me. What did they not tell us about refugees? Everything, everything for refugees, for their welfare and their rescue . . . of course, for our refugees. These people that we are driving out—that is another matter altogether. Wait; two thousand years of Galut. What did not happen? Jews were killed. Europe. Now we are the masters. (p. 332)

Can one, then, still the outcry?

> But these people who come to live in this village—will not the walls cry out in their ears? Will not those sights, those cries which were uttered and those which were not uttered; the alarmed innocence of a startled flock of sheep; the submissiveness of the weak and their strength—the one strength of the weak—that they do not know what to do and are unable to do anything, these mute weaklings—will they not make the air alive with shadows, voices and hidden looks? (pp. 332–33)

The narrator's impotence to change anything accompanies his moral indignation:

> I wanted to do something. I knew I would not cry out. Why, in the devil's name, was I the only one here to get excited? What sort of useless stuff was I made of? Now I had tied myself into knots. There was something rebellious in me, ready to blow up everything, to deny everything, to curse everything. To whom could I speak and be listened to? They would only laugh at me. I had gone entirely to pieces. I knew one thing and that fixedly, that it was impossible for me to come to terms with anything, so long as tears were springing from the eyes of a sobbing child, walking by the side of a mother tense with the fury of silent tears, and

> going out into exile carrying with him such an anguished cry of complaint
> against evil that there could not fail to be found in the world someone to
> hear it in due season. . . . (p. 333)

At the end, the story rises to a crescendo of biblical wrath and calm. But
here the "outcry" theme takes on the added dimension of accusation.
Yizhar closes the text with the word *haketza'akata*, taken from Genesis
18:20–21 (the phrase in underlined here):

> And the Lord said: "Verily, the cry of Sodom and Gomorrah is great, and,
> verily their sin is exceeding grievous. I will go down now, and see whether
> they have done altogether *according to the cry of it*, which is come unto Me;
> and if not, I will know."

This, then, is Yizhar's closing paragraph, with *haketza'akata* as the final
word. But this time the word leaves us with the question of whether the
deed that was done has justified the cries of those who suffered:

> The valley was growing quiet. Someone already was talking about sup-
> per. Far along the dusty road, swallowed up by what looked like a sand-
> storm, the distant lorry was disappearing, becoming darker, swaying, as
> heavy lorries do when laden with fruit or grain or the like. Even the pain of
> disgrace and the anger of being unable to do anything were giving way to a
> kind of indefinite pin-pricking. Everything became suddenly so open, so
> large, so very large. We all became small and unimportant. Soon that hour
> would come to the world when it is pleasant to come home from work, to
> return tired, to meet people, or walk about alone, walk about silently. All
> around silence descended, and soon it would descend upon the final
> scene, and when silence would blanket everything and no man would
> disturb the tranquillity, and there would be a quiet murmuring beyond the
> silence—then God would come down to the valley to see if the deeds that
> were done matched the cries.

Innumerable questions are raised here, as we saw, and these questions are
"internal" as well as "external" to the story: Is Jewish "self-hate" a factor in
the narrator's sense of guilt? Is the story primarily confessional, or is it a
"J'accuse"? Is its main focus the theme of moral anguish, or is its intent to
make a political statement? How reliable is the story as an "eyewitness"
account, as Yizhar claims, if he also says that it is fiction? The questions will
return in his major novel.

Days of Ziklag is a monumental two-volume work of 1,143 pages, the most
extensive novel about the 1948 War.[15] Yet its epic size does not give us an
epic novel in the tradition of *War and Peace*, where the lives of individual

characters are set against the background of vast historical events. Yizhar does not try to encompass the totality of one individual's existence, let alone that of an entire era. And although he here devotes somewhat more space to the depiction of his characters than he had done in previous works, the characters are by no means placed in the midst of the war (as the epic tradition would demand).

The plot is rather simple and spare. It is the story of three attempts to capture a hill of some strategic importance, situated on the main road leading into the Negev. The first two attempts fail, but the third succeeds. (In view of the limited scope of the story, a novella would have been a more suitable form for this material. Indeed, some critics have suggested that *Ziklag* is in essence a chain of novellas strung together to amount to the size of a novel.) An important change from Yizhar's previous writing is the fact that he has now given up the omniscient narrator as the unifying element. *Ziklag* is carried by the voices of a number of young men, whose interior monologues provide the raw material of the novel.

Once again we find the element of incongruity in Yizhar's fiction. Man, time, and action are repeatedly at odds. Yizhar also allows for greater irony and a lighter tone in the initial depiction of his characters. Although they are better crafted than their predecessors, they are still the typical Yizhar protagonists in transition. These are young men out of their milieu, temporarily located in the Negev, in a desert situation that is foreign to their usual mode of existence (about which Yizhar tells us still very little). Indeed, the truncated picture of existence is a permanent feature of Yizhar's war fiction, perhaps because war itself is conceived by him as a mutilating experience.

The name Ziklag evokes biblical allusions: "Then Achish [King of Gath] gave him [David] Ziklag that day; wherefore Ziklag belongeth unto the kings of Judah únto this day" (I Samuel, 27:6). Yet the hill of the novel is mistakenly identified at the very outset. One of the young men, a scholarly type, is Barzilai, named after the loyal friend of King David, who supported him when he fled from his rebellious son Absalom (II Samuel, 17:27; 19:32–40). The bookish Barzilai incorrectly identifies elevation point 244 on the map as the biblical Ziklag. He is soon made aware of his error, but the name sticks.

Are we to take this error as in some way emblematic of Zionism's biblical claim? To understand this assertion we must bear in mind the central place given to study of the Bible in Israel, even in secular education, from second grade through the twelfth, and from the earliest days of Jewish settlement in Palestine up to the present day. The Bible is therefore a fundamental part of the cultural substance of the Israeli, and many are no doubt weary of it by the time of young adulthood. It is therefore in a tone of irony (on Yizhar's part) that the persistent Barzilai further wearies his comrades by reading from the first chapter of II Samuel. ("And it came to pass after the death of Saul, when David was returned from the slaughter of the Amalekites, and David had abode two days in Ziklag. . . .") As Alter puts it, "He is trying to give depth and significance to the experience of the present moment by identifying it with a parallel moment in the heroic past of the Jewish people" (p. 216). Yet stories about the glorious past are not welcomed by Barzilai's comrades.

There is comic/grotesque incongruity between the young fighters, all under twenty-one, and the lofty elegy of David at the death of Saul. Yet this very tension—between present and past, between the anxiety-ridden boys and the majestic tale of a king who turned a curse into a blessing—is also to be seen as a facet in the personality of the young Israeli. The encounter with the Bible may be negative, but there is a certain weight to the mere juxtaposition of the novel's present and the biblical past. Barzilai's enthusiasm may be ill-timed and out of place, but its presence in the novel allows the reader either to moderate or to accentuate the connection. It is as though Barzilai is using the Bible to settle any doubts on the part of his comrades, doubts to the effect of "What are we doing here?" David, too, experienced doubt, anxiety, fear, loss; and he too was thrown into situations he could not have foreseen. But while the emotional identification is admissible, a nationalistic identification is something entirely different.

Thus in reading the final chapters of I Samuel, one might come to realize that Ziklag was connected with the nadir of David's life, farthest away from his people and from his mission. As a gift to David, Ziklag was linked to his brutal slaughter of the Amalekites (under the guise of an attack upon the Israelites). Thus Ziklag hardly denotes historical grandeur or heroic idealism. David, in fear for his life from the elderly and failing Saul, embraced his enemy, the Philistines; and Ziklag, far from being won in battle by David, was rather the gift of a master to his servant. And far from the place itself being evocative of glory, Ziklag was the place where the Amalekites took their revenge on David, his family and belongings. To any of the 1948 fighters who remembered their school Bible, the choice of Ziklag as a place with which to identify could hardly have been inspirational—a further irony of Yizhar's.

Another biblical theme that is frequently evoked is the Binding of Isaac. Just as God commanded Abraham to sacrifice Isaac as a test of his (Abraham's) faith, so the sacrifice of Israel's young men in her frequent wars can be seen as a sacrifice of the young upon the altar of the ideals of foregoing generations. Robert Alter is correct in pointing to the theme of Isaac's sacrifice (*Akeda*) as being of central importance in *Ziklag*—as is evidenced by the identification of the young fighters with that idea, and their resentment at being made to live and die for a system of ideals they did not themselves construct.

Here is Alter's translation of the relevant passage:

> There's no way around the *Akeda*. You only imagine that you can leave
> everything and run. You can't. You're denied the possibility of run-
> ning. . . . I hate our father Abraham going to sacrifice Isaac. What right
> does he have over Isaac. Let him sacrifice himself. I hate the God that sent
> him to sacrifice and closed all other paths for him—only the way to the
> *Akeda* He left open. I hate the fact that Isaac is nothing but material for an
> experiment between Abraham and his God. To slaughter sons as a proof of
> love! To use force and interfere and take lives in order to win a quarrel.
> And that the world remained silent and didn't get up and scream: Scoun-
> drels, for what do the sons have to die? Hate all necessity to get something
> at the price of causing ruin. Or destruction. Or torture. Or compulsion.[16]

Here, Yizhar challenges the hard, heroic trial-branded forefathers whose
personal ideals (and not necessarily divine grace) supposedly endow their
achievement with promise. In the ancient world, war presents the occasion
for the exercise of virtue and valor. In the modern world, war spells horror,
uprootedness, and futility. The young Israeli, idealistic and unsophisticated, and confined to a "radius of twenty kilometers," is thrown into a war
which was no part of the idealistic context of the founding fathers in the
Second and Third Aliyoth.

Yizhar's pacifism is a stance based on intellectual conviction: the reality
of the war damned the young, whether they fought or did not. The tragic
absence of choices or alternatives, intensified by the danger to survival,
brought them to a state of self-questioning doubt. Yizhar's protagonists in
Ziklag are not "sofa-heroes"—nihilists and pessimists in a safe and restricted world. Rather, they create a dialogue with the enemy, talking war,
blood, and mutilation—and simultaneously questioning the goal. *Akeda*
without faith is murder. Their fathers' ideals are not sufficient justification
for the new sacrifice.

Ironically, it is the technique of interior monologue that enables the
Israeli to address his external enemy—and to display through his consciousness the complex variations of his reactions and feelings. For example, the sense that the land belongs to "us" alternates with the sense that it
belongs to "them." A sense of defeat, even total desperation, alternates
with the sense of camaraderie after the grueling seven days of fighting.
Ziklag is the only narrative of Yizhar's describing actual battle—but again
this is conveyed through the inner consciousness of the fighter, so that the
objective reality is filtered through subjective time. One of the fighters,
Gidi, is alone in a dugout under mortar attack. The description of the
attack, as perceived by Gidi, is suffused with wry humor oscillating between two extremes: "Watch out there you, Yousuf, or whoever you are
behind the shed," and "How is it to be dead? How is it not to be?", and
"God damn it . . . I hate you, hate, hate."

Oscillation and polarization are typical throughout the entire monologue: a cry to God the master of the universe gives way to a sense of

disgust with language itself. Wisdom, folly, and the silences between them, all are to no avail. A similar oscillation overtakes the Israeli soldier who is thrown into the intimacy of life in the Arab village—and he faces the Arabs, now as co-inhabitants of the land, now as the enemy. At the end of the novel, the Israeli knows that in this round of fighting, on this particular hill, he is the victor, and he extends his feeling to the entire land his eyes see. Yet although the battle is over, the haunting question remains: But is the war over? Yizhar has his protagonist ask it in 1948; Yizhar himself asks it in 1958; it is a question that persists into the present, as we know all too well.

Throughout Yizhar's work, war mars the reality which he depicts through the romantic innocence of his characters. His young protagonists come to early maturity through war. The stream of consciousness is no longer caught up in the solipsistic self. The sight of burned bodies, the awareness of fate's mutability, the experience of pain and the inflicting of pain, hate and compassion, alienation and belonging—all combine in an interiority that experiences the extremes of the human situation.

In its classic form, the epic novel has a cumulative effect, as the reader is made more and more familiar with characters, events, and their details. Background and foreground are brought together, as the main characters are at center stage. Yet Yizhar does not perceive the battle over this one hill as representing the entire war of 1948—and, indeed, the incompleteness of his account (when compared to the classic epic novel) is a mirror for the radical incompleteness of all human acts, purposes, and achievements. It is as though the self-imposed limits of his narrative technique are deliberately chosen to reflect the limits of all that we do.

Yizhar's technique creates an immediacy which is not typical of the war novel, where the omniscient narrator engulfs the totality. *Ziklag*'s concluding interior monologue presents a voice that is itself divided by inconsistencies and contradictions, and this makes perfect sense since it is the stream of consciousness of someone immersed in actual combat:

> It's sickening to kill you! Why did you come here! Why are you stuck here, making killing you the only way to get rid of you, God damn you. . . . What a despicable road one has to go in order to win. It's terrible to be this way. Shut up, it's not terrible. . . . (p. 1139)

And the short sentences before the concluding paragraph:

> The hill is ours, the fields, the open spaces, the land. Have we finished? (p. 1143)

As we saw, the question is raised not only because the conflict cannot be conclusively resolved, but also because the individual soldier cannot know the course of the entire war. In the classic epic, one does know; but not here, because there is no link between foreground and background. And as a result, the limited perspective of the individual fighter lacks the overall sense of justification that is needed.

Yizhar's men, therefore, are products not only of existential uncertainty; they are as much the products of his narrative technique. They are enmeshed not only in the futility of action per se, but also in the stream of consciousness from which they emerge only fitfully. Yizhar's paradox (as we noted) is in his unique creation of the solipsistic protagonist who yearns for the open spaces, a protagonist whose objective uncertainty is the projection of his extreme inwardness.

Yizhar's latest work of fiction is his 1963 collection of four novellas, *Stories of the Plain*.[17] Two of these novellas, "The Heap of Dung" and "A Story That Did Not Begin," touch upon the subject of the Arab and Yizhar's younger days. "The Heap of Dung" is a first-person narrative of an event experienced in childhood, the selling of dung by Bedouin Arabs of the Negev to Jewish farmers. The dung is brought in on camels, and the weighing and bargaining are done in a ritualistic manner. The child/narrator is shocked by the deceit involved. When his older brother tells him that that is the way of the world, the young narrator says that it does not have to be this way. The brother replies that he doesn't know if it has to be this way or not, but this is how things are.

Although most commentators tend to see the moral emphasis here as characteristic of Yizhar, primarily in regard to the relations between Jews and Arabs, and although the Arab is interwoven into both settings, Yizhar associates him with the old world of his own childhood—a world that came to its end for him with his brother's death in a railroad accident in 1942, and the establishing of the State in 1948. For Yizhar, the Arab is associated with innocence—and moral indignation arises only in the reality of war.

"A Story That Did Not Begin" is Yizhar's epitaph for that early world, pointing ironically to silence and to the limitations of language vis-à-vis human experience. The first-person narrator addresses someone who is walking with him to a site familiar to the narrator from his childhood days. The account touches on the death of Yizhar's brother, as he and an Arab associate were riding a motorcycle over a railroad crossing, were struck by a passing train, and were killed instantly.

In one section entitled "The Silence of the Villages" (pp. 145–64), the narrator and his companion arrive at a hill with new carob trees. The hill is all that remains of what was once an Arab village, a village the narrator knew. Referring to the Arab rioting of the 1930s, he notes that the village was known as a "wasps' nest," a "ravens' nest," even an "eagle's nest":

A "murderers' village" it was called in the newspapers in those days, without anyone trying too hard to know what it looked like or where it was, exactly. But it's always good when people have a place they can visualize, as a cave of violent men and a pit of vipers. It's hard to live in a world that has no such horrible places. And maybe it was even the place of the terrible Abu Jilda, once so well known for his deeds but now forgotten. Here he slept, or at least he passed by to instill fear, here he had a sip of coffee, murdered a bit, mounted his horse and disappeared. However that may be, this is what the place is today. (p. 147)

Does the narrator really question the reputation of the village as a haven of marauders? The same question was raised in connection with Hirbet Hizah.

Abu Jilda was well known in the 1930s as the head of one of the gangs that brought terror to the local Jewish population. There was a Hebrew jingle about him sung by children. Arab attacks on the Jewish population were heaviest in 1921. In 1929 there was the Hebron massacre, and the attacks began again in 1936, lasting to 1939. Although the narrator clearly states that a Jew could not go near the village in those days, he now adopts a rather light and condescending tone about the dangers of the village and Abu Jilda. The narrator admits that vicious crimes were committed against innocent people. "But are we the judges of the world, to judge of good and evil . . . ?" He says that he is "only a man who sees, a man in pain from seeing." And all that is left is a place that left its place, a story in past tense. He has not come to eulogize or to condemn, he says. Where in the world did it not happen? (pp. 149–50)

The narrator's first encounter with the village occurs when he is in a military unit that has taken the hill and is conducting a house-to-house search. There are corpses and there are people fleeing; a barn is set on fire; then the land is silent, back to its original state. To him it seems, however, that the earth in its depth does not forget—only men do.

The author has only sarcasm for any attempt to eradicate the past by giving new names to such places. The new names are more "cultured," and some are from the Bible. Modern agriculture yields richer crops, more "cultured" crops. Yet in his view a certain basic balance has been destroyed. He misses the innocence of those who lived then and were devoid of all self-consciousness. The senseless death of his brother and his Arab partner, the hill, the forgotten village—its cries and its silence mark their eulogy. Although the villages that were there are no longer, and new ones have sprung up in their place, the hill and the land are still there, even the deserted railroad tracks. The narrator says, "I drag with me the tale of my sermons, wherever I go" (p. 193).

Stories of the Plain is a parting collection, a farewell to the land that has changed, and to those in it who have changed even more, a farewell to the old pre-State Land of Israel under Ottoman and then British rule, a farewell to the Arab village and to the Bedouins the author knew as a child. It is an ode to a way of life of which the Arab was an integral part. "A Story That Did Not Begin" is a summation of all the themes in Yizhar's work.

Yizhar as Political Essayist. Yizhar Smilansky has always been vocal in the Israeli political arena—not only during his six terms in the Knesset, but even now as a professor of Hebrew literature at Tel Aviv University. And his writing, political articles as well as fiction, has always created controversy. In addition to the storm of discussion in connection with the film *Hirbet Hizah,* there was also a massive outcry against his being awarded a number of literary prizes in the 1950s. He continues to voice his decisive political views in the press.

In his contribution to a 1985 symposium at Tel Aviv University on "The Israeli Situation and Hebrew Fiction of the Last Decade," Yizhar took an unpopular stand.[18] He challenged the notion of a definitive connection between literature and political reality. First, he challenged the sociocultural/historical emphasis in literary criticism. Then he went on to challenge the mimetic approach which sees literature as a reflection of political reality and as the expression of its era. Finally, he challenged the assumption underlying the symposium topic by arguing that the "Israeli Situation" in the last decade can be of no interest to literature. In his view, it is not the function of literature to represent reality—and he stated this as a principle governing literature of the past, present, or future. Since questions posed in historiography differ from those posed in literature (or in the study of it), there can be no necessary connection between them.

Moreover, the events that occurred in Israel during its few decades did not "make" literature. Rather, literature "used" these events—just as it will always find its "matter," and press it to its own needs. Even in "war literature," he argued, we do not have a reflection of the "war event"— which is why the historian cannot admonish the writer of fiction for not "placing the cannons in the right position," just as the political scientist has no right to say that the central figures in a work of fiction are not represented "as they were."

Since the historical events are but the raw materials of fiction, the writer is responsible only to the fictional world of his creation, Yizhar said. This is because literature goes beyond the present time, and so the writer's main concern must be the creative act. To interpret literature as a sociopolitical document is to drag it into the mire of journalism. Thus literature begins when it severs its dependence on reality, and even departs from it.

It is not at all ironic that Yizhar, the writer of fiction who has been most heavily attacked on political grounds, should renounce the connection between literature and politics. Clearly, Israeli literary critics in the 1980s have retained the tendency to evaluate works of literature for their political *effect.* The contention is that the abnormal situation in which Israelis have lived in the last four decades must affect writing and writers. The assumption is that any literature written in a continuous state of siege—and especially a literature dealing with encounters with the Arab (whether as friend or foe)—*must* reflect that anxiety as its milieu. As we have seen, Yizhar's fiction is itself an expression of a generation caught in existential dilemmas. Yet Yizhar wants literature to transcend the daily raw material out of which it is wrought, and to be read and regarded in that purer light. Can the reader be expected to do this? Identifiable realities in history and in the countryside compel the Israeli reader to fill in the gaps in the story with what he or she knows, and thus makes the reader an active partner in the creative act. But can the Israeli reader read about Hirbet Hizah in a framework of *fiction* if Yizhar himself has said he was present at the events described? Can Yizhar reflect on moral issues that are raised by actual events, and then claim that he uses war as mere "raw material" for the literary process? In response to the man who says he was there at Hirbet Hizah, we might well ask, Is literature really a departure from reality?

What is more, Yizhar, in order to safeguard the "purity" of literature, overlooks its normative function. A literature beyond moral judgments, beyond good and evil, threatens us with a world devoid of a moral code. Yet Yizhar's fiction emphatically does not present such a world (despite the appearance of moral skepticism in the "Silence of the Villages" section of "A Story That Did Not Begin"). In the footsteps of James, Yizhar seeks to protect his House of Fiction, and that is understandable. Yet in the light of the fiction he has produced, we may well challenge him when he denies making moral judgments and denies having a point of view. Is not his typical protagonist torn by having to take a moral point of view? And could Yizhar himself be above having a point of view, when we know that his outlook (and his relation to the Arab) was shaped by the pre-State experience? Yizhar's readiness to take a moral stand was evident after the 1967 war in a newspaper article in which he asks: "Does one acquire land by conquest, by force?" And: "What [rights] does a military victory bestow?"[19]

After all this, can Yizhar still claim that literature and politics must be separate entities? In a 1986 article, he again endorsed their separation.[20] In an interview following the appearance of the article, he stated: "Those who turn poetry into politics diminish poetry. They use poetry as a tool, an applied means, like a newspaper or a placard. The poem by its very nature has the quality of being beyond politics. A work of art is not merely a reaction to something."[21]

Yizhar creates a unique narrative bearing his own unmistakable stamp. He has always been fascinated by the perennial clash between individual free will and the force of the societal code. His protagonist exhibits the typical awkwardness which comes from trying to live according to both.

Yizhar pushes his protagonist to the verge of conflict: that is, he confronts basic realities that touch upon the continued existence of society, yet his moral code denies him the power to accept those realities.

Moreover, the Yizhar protagonist is a man of words, not of deeds: existentially, any action on his part would not change things. At the same time, the war is paradoxically *his* war, just as it is the litmus test for the Israeli conscience. For these reasons, the Yizhar protagonist is in a situation from which there is no way out. It would seem that all this gives us the paradigmatic tragic dilemma of a man facing two incompatible but equally valid sets of claims. In classic drama, the two systems are represented by two characters; in modern literature, the conflict is internalized, and the protagonist himself represents the two. Classically, moreover, the tragic dilemma is heightened by irreversible action, while Yizhar's protagonist remains in the domain of speculation, rather than taking action.

The war typically overturned the prevailing relations between Jew and Arab: the Jew came from a multifaceted cultural milieu, the Arab from a uniform culture; the uprooted Jew tried desperately to sink roots in the land, while the rooted Arab was uprooted. This perennial situation is aggravated by the fact that Yizhar's protagonist is a man of conscience and moral sensitivity. Shall we therefore read "The Prisoner" and "Hirbet Hizah" as Jewish guilt and Jewish self-doubt in a new guise?

There is no doubt that Yizhar's protagonist, whoever he is, was traumatically affected by the 1948 War. Although this can be seen as a transition from innocence to experience, it is a transition that is never fully realized; the protagonist never achieves mature self-acceptance but is forever in the throes of self-questioning.

If it were not too naive to think in this way, one might expect that some of his doubts—at least those regarding his relation to the Arab—might have been settled for him by the establishment of the State of Israel. Yet Yizhar never gets as far as writing about the post-1948 reality, perhaps because that pluralistic reality must clash with the simpler mentality of the pre-1948 world. A native son belonging to the land and to the landscape—that identification of his is overturned by the war, and it calls for a re-assessment of the protagonists' relation to themselves, to the land, and to the Arab. On the other hand, one can see the Yizhar protagonist as a continuation of the existentially torn and indecisive character to be found in Hebrew literature for the last hundred years—and then Yizhar can be seen as a part of the tradition of Yosef Haim Brenner and Uri Nissan Gnessin, whose fiction affected Yizhar's style and language profoundly. Is Yizhar's protagonist, then, the last phase in a secularizing process wherein individuals take on the load of Jewish conscience, angst, and inaction?

How does one become owner of the land? This question will appear and reappear in the narrative literature related to the Arab-Israeli conflict. In

Genesis 13:17, the Lord commands Abram: "Arise, walk through the land in the length of it and in the breadth of it; for unto thee will I give it." One imagines that walk as Abram's act of "taking title," establishing ownership. In our own time, the ownership will be based rather on the blood that has been shed. However that may be, the land remains for Yizhar the meeting place of Arab and Jew—whether it is a "meeting" of co-existence or hostility.

7. MOSHE SHAMIR

Moshe Shamir belongs to the generation of writers whose coming of age is linked to the 1948 War. It is the generation of Yizhar and those others who fought in the Palmach—and we have had ample evidence of the extent to which the war experience shaped Yizhar's subsequent writing as well as his view of the Arab. But there was more that shaped this generation, and separated it from the writers of the post-1948 period (such as Amos Oz and A. B. Yehoshua). In a 1973 interview,[1] Shamir acknowledged some of these distinguishing influences on himself and others of his generation: he spoke of childhood hardships, the Tel Aviv sands, the struggle against the British, and the sense of growing Jewish strength; there was also the active participation in the Socialist/Zionist youth movements; and the ominous influence of World War II and Rommel's advancing army.

Another differentiating mark of the 1948 generation is that its writers were not academicians (as Oz and Yehoshua came to be); on the other hand, this generation showed a strong leaning toward political activity: just as Yizhar served in the Knesset, Shamir, too, became a member of the Israeli parliament (in 1977). Shamir sees his generation as more deeply involved in national issues of security and defense, as reflected in the flood of articles by Aharon Megged, Chaim Gouri, Hanoch Bartov, Benjamin Galai, and Shamir himself, and he attributes that active political interest to their having grown up in kibbutzim and the Palmach. All went through military courses together, and those courses spawned not only this generation of writers but also the eventual upper echelons of Israel's army. "We were friends who grew up together," Shamir says, "and when my generation went into the Jewish Brigade [in the British Army in World War II] it had a meaning." These, then, are hardened veterans.

Shamir was born in Safad in the Upper Galilee in 1921. The family moved to Tel Aviv when he was one year old. Two more sons were born, and one of them, Elik, was killed in the 1948 War. Moshe was a kibbutz member from 1941 to 1947, when he moved to Tel Aviv with his young wife. He was very influential from the start in the literary life of the country, by establishing and editing numerous literary and political journals (*Yalkut HaReyim, Daf Hadash, BaMahaneh, Masa,* and others) in addition to his work as a political essayist and dramatist. At that time, he had been associated with the left-wing Mapam Party, and had been powerfully influenced by Marxist doctrine.

One of his central themes was the relation of literature to life. His views on this topic had been shaped by the writings of Plekhanov and Lukacs.[2] In an early manifesto, "With My Contemporaries," he urged a naturalistic approach, whereby everything in human life is to serve as raw material for literary treatment. Israeli literature was to avoid the separation of literature from life; it could do this by clinging to the ideals of Socialism/Zionism. The arguments used are reminiscent of the Socialist Realism of A. A. Zhdanov (1896–1948), a member of the Soviet Politburo whose task it was to root out "cosmopolitan" Western influences from Russian cultural and scientific life. Marxist ideology reached Shamir and his generation in a diluted version, mainly because these young Israelis were for the most part monolinguists, and could read neither Russian nor German; it was for the Socialist/Zionist youth movement to transmit these ideas and make them the idealistic tokens of total dedication to the cause.

Modern Hebrew literature was, from the outset, closely linked to the ideals and ideas of Zionism, especially in the interwar period of 1920 to 1940. Shamir's manifesto is filled with youthful enthusiasm and naivete, and this was the idealistic *Zeitgeist* whose totems were struggle, progress, and equality.

Shamir was to undergo a turnabout in his political and literary outlook: speaking in a public forum in the 1950s, he stressed the sui generis nature of literature as being outside the life it depicts; literature, in its opposition to the State, is faithful to the ideal form the State should take. The Shamir once so closely tied to Mapam, the party on the far left of the political spectrum, was to be found in the right-wing Likud Party in the 1970s, and he was a major force in establishing the Tehiyah (Renaissance) movement, a right-wing party with a strong nationalistic and irredentist orientation. His changeover began in the 1950s, with the revelations of the Stalin excesses. In a moving article, "Broken Tablets," which appeared in 1956, Shamir attacks the so-called Dictatorship of the Proletariat, and tries to identify evil per se, quite independently of party lines. The response was fierce: he was accused of apostasy, of being unfaithful to Marxism. In a rebuttal article titled "No Way Right," Shamir conceded that without Marxism, one would be lost in a chaotic world without direction. Yet he pointed to the clash between the Zionist element in the ideology of Mapam and its Marxist base; and he saw that clash as irreconcilable. He was, however, emphatic on the point that there was for him no way to espouse the ideology of the right within the framework of Mapam, and that therefore a new self-appraisal was required of the Mapam-oriented person. In a confessional tone, Shamir admitted that his knowledge of Marxism is fragmentary, that it was for him more a matter of feeling and supposition than well-informed doctrine; yet it was embedded in his mind, he said, and for the rest of his days he would be affected by Marxism as a way of thinking.

The topic of the Arab was a part of Shamir's ideological stance in 1957. He felt that the left-wing Mapam has a special pioneering role in weaving the fabric of understanding between Arabs and Jews, and establishing peace between Israel and its Arab neighbors. He saw this as quintessential to the future of the Jewish people as a nation—and thus the revival of the Jewish people is to be inextricably tied to the revival of other peoples: Israel's other political parties were still clinging to ways of thought involving quasi-fascist, chauvinistic, and religious-metaphysical notions, of which they ought to purge themselves, he claimed.

His early attitude toward Arabs can be found in a Hebrew article with the Arabic title "Alsalam wa'almasawe fi Al'Hukuk" (Peace and Equal Rights); his giving it an Arabic title reveals much about his feelings on the subject. The article was published in October 1956, on the eve of an Arabic-Jewish conference in Haifa. In it Shamir declares that the time is ripe to extend complete equality to the Arab citizen in Israel, just as the time is ripe for an Arab participant in the conference to call for the opening of negotiations between Israel and the Arab countries, without prior conditions; he ends the article with a call for universal peace and brotherhood.

In the three decades that followed, Shamir's political orientation saw remarkable change. In an interview of June 1987, on the occasion of the twentieth anniversary of the Six-Day War, Shamir recalled an incident that initiated his transformation.[3] On May 1, 1967, he was given leave from his duties in the army reserves. Approaching his house in a suburb of Tel Aviv, he saw his wife and three children digging a deep trench, apparently in preparation for street combat.

> This gave me the blow of my life. Except for the death of my brother Elik in the War of Independence, I can't recall the day I was so shocked. Nineteen years after the establishment of the State, and all that has happened since, and all my books and plays—and suddenly we are in the Warsaw Ghetto and the Nazi legions are surrounding us. The sense was that everything had turned overnight, and we are in a state of siege.

He goes on to say that as a man seeking ways to peace, and attending public meetings against military rule, he felt that his world had crumbled under him, and that his ideology had collapsed. Up to that point he believed that peace would come if Israel desired it: we give a bit, they give a bit—compromise for compromise. This, he said, showed itself to be an illusion.

Shamir's turn to the right was politically costly to him. He and Yitzhak Rabin had played football together as children, and he certainly could have held a top post in the hierarchy of the Labor Party coalition; but the turn to the right, which he had deemed impossible for himself, became in his view the only option available to him. In a conversation I had with Shamir in September 1986, he told me, "There is no Arab problem. There is a Jewish problem." As he explained, it is not the Arabs who will destroy the State of Israel. The Jews will destroy it—those who won't come and those who leave. Allowing for the rhetorical flourish in his words, it is clear that Shamir does not actually believe that the Arabs pose *no* danger. But in any case he has given up the conciliatory stance—compromise for compromise—which he took when he was a member of Mapam.

In 1977 Shamir became a member of the Knesset for the Likud Party ("the four black years of my life"). In 1980 he established the Tehiyah movement in conjunction with Geula Cohen, who (prior to 1948) had been a member of the militantly nationalistic Stern Group. In recent years, he has given up all political activity to devote his time to writing. As for his views on other writers, Shamir told me he felt it was time for Israelis to overcome the inferiority complex permeating the national climate, as expressed in works such as Amos Oz's *My Michael* and Yizhar's "Hirbet Hizah" and "The Prisoner."

In his early days, Shamir was the active spirit behind the newly emerging literature produced by the young writers who reached maturity around the time the State of Israel came into existence. A prolific writer, he was one of the prominent voices addressing the compelling issues of the time. By 1945, when he was twenty-four, he had already published twenty stories. In the next few years he won the three most prestigious literary awards that Israel can bestow: the Ussishkin Prize for *He Walked through the Fields* (1947), the Brenner Prize for *With His Own Hands: Stories of Elik* (1951), and the Bialik Prize for *King of Flesh and Blood* (1954) and *The War of the Sons of Light* (1955). Later (in 1987) he received, with Chaim Gouri, the Israel Prize for Literature.

Shamir's work includes novels, stories, memoirs, plays, essays, and articles—and the Arab presence figures in much of it. Further, that presence concerned Shamir as a Socialist, as a committed Zionist, as a native son, and as the cofounder of the Greater Land of Israel Movement. The latter was established after the Six-Day War and called for the integration of the vast territory of the once Greater Israel of Biblical times.

His first major novel, *He Walked through the Fields*, was received with tremendous acclaim. Undoubtedly this was due in part to the picture of its main protagonist, a youthful Uri Kahana, kibbutz-born and devoid of Jewish *Weltschmerz* and self-doubt, at a time when Israel itself was going through its birth pangs and political turmoil. Just as the Yizhar protagonist takes on a life of its own, so does the Shamir protagonist, though he is an entirely different individual. In *He Walked through the Fields*, in the novel *Under the Sun* (1950), and in the literary tribute to his fallen brother Elik, *With His Own Hands* (1951), the main personage is part of a kibbutz or a moshavah (an agricultural settlement); he has attended an agricultural high school, and is involved in military activity. And unlike the Yizhar protagonist, Shamir's man is not intellectual, is even anti-intellectual. *With His Own Hands* begins with the sentence "Elik was born of the sea."[4] Gershon Shaked adopted a part of that phrase as the title for his article on the modern Israeli hero.[5] Surely a great part of the success of that new image is traceable to the fact that this is the way Israelis like to think of themselves. As Shaked puts it:

> In their conduct and language these heroes are closer to the Bedouin than to Diaspora Jews. Not only do they speak Arabic more fluently than Yiddish, but their simple dress is a metonymy both for their closeness to the Arab way of life (the *shabariye, keffiye* and *finjan*—the dagger, the headdress, the Bedouin coffee pot, all symbolizing liberty and manliness) and to the Labor Zionist movement, whose values permeated their social existence. These traits, language and closeness to the soil, indicate that the figures are more bound up with space than with time or Jewish history. The authors following the Yizhar lead, tend to describe figures as part of the landscape. Synecdoches of the landscape, standing for the land of Israel, permit the authors to make their characters into part of the land, and the land into part of their characters.

The sentence "Elik was born of the sea" underlines the emergence of the young independent man—carefree, mature and immature at the same time. Thus *With His Own Hands* gives us a new version of the *Bildungsroman,* where the initiation into manhood culminates in the death of the young man in the war (the fate shared also by Uri Kahana). The group, the immediate social unit, provided the support system that discouraged individualism. In school, then through activities in the youth movement, the kibbutz, the Palmach, and Haganah—in all of these areas, the young Israeli protagonist (in the fiction associated with the Socialist/Zionist milieu) was part of his immediate group. And by a social osmosis he absorbed its values and goals.

The political reality of the 1940s, World War II, activities connected with aiding illegal immigration under the regime of the British Mandate, friction and skirmishes with the Arabs, all contributed to the psychological infrastructure of the Shamir hero. Observing these young men as they discover their manhood, girls, camaraderie, and self-imposed dedication—and finally meet their death—the reader is left with a tragic sense of loss. The non-contemplative nature of Shamir's hero, the way he avoids individual sensitivity or closeness, makes his death all the more enigmatic. Elik was escorting a convoy to beleaguered Jerusalem. The seven young men were in an open truck because the British prohibited the use of armored vehicles. The truck hit a mine, and all seven were killed.

Once, as Elik was watching a family of fishermen, he became mesmerized by the simple way they broiled their fish: "That is life, deep down at the core of things, right next to the fundamentals—the sea, the fish, the sand, and the wind" (p. 11). This simple and uncomplicated attitude toward the surrounding world typifies Elik and Uri. Theirs is the basic experience of the native son who can do things with his own hands as he gives shape to his existence. Unlike Yizhar, Shamir does not dwell on the inner life of his protagonist. Rather, his gaze is always turned toward the wider framework and the current cultural mood.

As he is the chronicler of his autobiography, he is also the chronicler of his generation, concerned as he is with the interaction between the individual and the collective, the "I" and the "we." In any case, Elik and Uri do not reiterate their parents' experience, but carve a world of their own, so that they become emblems of their own era. Their parents are of the Third Aliyah, which came to Palestine for ideological reasons, by and large. Yet it was a generation still connected in many ways to the Diaspora, and it was only the generation of 1948 that succeeded in translating the ideology of the Second and Third Aliyah into action. The Shamir protagonist is that man of action, a fighter and leader.

The success of his novel *He Walked through the Fields* prompted Shamir to produce it as a play.[6] Its first performance, during the 1948 War, became a public event, and it set the tone for the depiction of the sabra hero. Some of the atmosphere of the time is described by Mendel Kohansky:

> The premiere was the first in independent Israel, a fact much stressed by the newspapers which in those heady days were much prone to point out "firsts." On the day of the opening, newspaper headlines read: "Tulkarem, Jenin Bombed," "France Will Take Strong Measures Against Arabs for Damaging French Property in Jerusalem," "Victims of Gas Attacks in Jerusalem Hospitals," and there were columns of announcements of deaths. The subject, plus the timing, made the play a symbol of the War of Independence, a morale builder for the troops who jokingly called it a "secret weapon." Performances were held in army camps, in places where the mortar fire and explosions occasionally drowned out the voices of the actors. The trucks bearing the cast and set rode into Jerusalem in the wake of the troops who had liberated the city after a long siege, and a performance was given the same evening.[7]

The 1950 novel *Under the Sun* (considered by some to be Shamir's best) achieves a unity of background, characters, and action to create the reality of life in an agricultural settlement in the 1930s. The title, evoking Ecclesiastes, sets the novel's tragic tone, steeped as it is in sun, sand, and blood. The story of a family in a moshavah—its relations with the neighboring Arabs; the older Jewish population with the characteristic Diaspora mentality; the efforts of the younger people to defend the place—all these elements are typical of the fiction of the 1930s and '40s. The novel employs an interesting narrative technique: each chapter is given over to the inner voice of one character, but there is the implied voice of the storyteller who unifies time, place, and events. The narrator provides the landscape, while the characters provide their individual perspectives, linked by their streams of consciousness.

Like Yizhar's "The Grove on the Hill," Shamir's *Under the Sun* concerns the Arab riots in connection with Kibbutz Hulda in 1929. Much of the autobiographical source can be pieced out from Shamir's *My Life with Ishmael* (1968), and all the events cited there had found their way into *Under the Sun*. For example, in *My Life with Ishmael* there are two very revealing passages:

> I went to the village where Grandma and the uncles lived. Be'er Ya'acov—a quiet little place surrounded by Arab villages without even a road between, no electricity and no telephone. Just a secluded happy home, quite innocent. An Arab shepherd by the name of Shak'r, who is like one of the family, takes the farmers' cows out in the morning and brings them back in the evening. A friend to everyone, including little me, who steals out every now and then to spend a whole day with him and the cows.
>
> Then suddenly someone is standing by my bed, and it is dark all around, and he quietens me with a kind hand: "Night. Get up. It's all right." By the light of the paraffin lamp in the other room I find my clothes and see my uncle groping in the chest under the bed and taking something out and thrusting it into his belt. Apparently I am still sitting on the bed, goggling in astonishment. Grandma comes in. They dress me. There is no time for sandals, and they push them into my hands. Tumult in the house, they hustle the women and children outside. Other figures are hurrying about in the cold dark of the village street. They rush to the one and only stone building, on the hill across the street—the schoolhouse. Words are flung in hushed tones. To the south-east, beyond the cypresses in the yard—like a premature sunrise—a pale rosy stain on the fringe of the sky. "Hulda is burning."[8]

The autobiographical incidents related in the 1968 memoir *My Life with Ishmael* had served as the basis for the 1950 *Under the Sun*. In the novel, the younger generation is pitted against the older, whose members are individualistic and unyielding (except for the father of the Kramer family, at the center of events). Friction with the nearby Arab population prompts the kibbutz members to approach the elders of the moshavah to suggest setting up a combined defense. The elders are depicted as Diaspora Jews who resent the kibbutz. The kibbutz members, for their part, rebuke the moshavah farmers for employing Arabs and exploiting them. We ought to bear in mind that the issue of "Hebrew Labor" was central in the confrontation between the idealistic young kibbutz pioneers and the farming gentry of the older moshavah. The novel stems from Shamir's Socialist period, and so the 1930s moshavah is represented negatively, as reflecting something like a colonialist mentality.

The attempt to set up a unified defense fails. On their way back to the kibbutz at night, two kibbutzniks in a cart are set upon by Arabs, and one of them is killed. That death, combined with the self-deception of the old farmers, who believe they can prevail with little or no manpower, stirs up the Kramers' son, Aharon, who organizes the defense, beginning with an attack on the Arab village.

The old farmers are depicted almost as Dickensian characters: Gedalia is a handicapped and lecherous old man who is the direct cause of the suicide of one of his three successive wives. There is Solomon, the chairman of the moshavah committee, who narrow-mindedly prefers his Arabs and trusts them more than he does the kibbutzniks. (Nevertheless, the Arab shepherd, Shak'r, is dismissed.) Solomon's only son is a spineless character who leaves the moshavah, lives off his aging parents, and joins a right-wing terrorist group. (One of his successful missions is throwing a hand grenade into the house of a sleeping Arab family.) Another despicable character is Shapira, a farmer who lives closest to the Arab settlement. In his own yard he houses an Arab family that looks after his estate. He sires a daughter with one of the Arab women, but as tension builds he evicts the family. In addition to exploiting his Arab tenants, Shapira has no hesitation about expelling them with little or no compensation. At night the Arab tenant farmer returns with two men and kills Shapira. Aharon Kramer eventually defends the moshavah with the help of the kibbutz members.

Arabs were closely associated with Jewish moshavoth from the 1880s. Shak'r works for all the Jewish farmers, and it is significant that the same persona, Shak'r, appears in the novel (Under the Sun) and in the autobiographic/historical essay (My Life with Ishmael). The opening and closing chapters of the novel feature the grandson, the young Moyshale who is the author's namesake and the implied protagonist, visiting his grandmother. For him the moshavah is the place for awakening and epiphanic experiences. But the novel's concluding sentence encapsulates the novel as a whole, and points to the future: "and he did not know that blood and sand and sun will accompany him all his life, to the very moment when his quick blood is absorbed into soft sand under a hard sun" (p. 397). The moshavah organizes itself, as men, women, and children enter a new reality.

Aharon is the prototype of the Israeli whose roots are in the land. He desires the nineteen-year-old Balfouria, Gedalia's daughter. (She was probably named for Lord Balfour of the 1917 Balfour Declaration—children were often named for momentous and immediate events during the Yishuv era—and that would date the novel as taking place in 1936, although the Hulda burning dates from 1929.) What he says to her at one point says much about him and his feeling for the land:

I don't know you yet, Balfouria. I want to know you as well as I know so many things. I know this region of mine, I know it better than any unwashed Arab who was born here, along with his ancestors for centuries, because I was born here, together with my ancestors three millennia ago.

Men like me don't pose many questions. The world belongs to men like me in an absolute way. They take it, and that's that.

Take this piece of earth and place it on your hand. I'll close my eyes. With the touch of my fingers, I'll show you every little point, every fold of land, every ravine and every hut. . . . There is nobody who loves this land the way I do as I trace my footsteps in it. (p. 96)

Aharon "measures" the land with his feet—and one thinks again of the Lord's command to Abram: "Arise, walk through the land in the length of it and in the breadth of it; for unto thee will I give it" (Genesis 13:17). That, too, is Aharon's way of making contact with the land.

The moshavah Be'er Yoseph in the novel is based on the Be'er Ya'akov, where Shamir's grandmother settled with her family in 1923. Shamir's *Not Far from the Tree* is a family history going back one hundred years.[10] Here he describes the relations between the Jewish settlers and their Arab neighbors. The years of the riots had been tense and strife-ridden, but personal relations with Arab neighbors were easy and cordial. He argues that it was the bravery of the people of the small moshavah that averted many a confrontation.

The Arabs in *Under the Sun* are not represented in a stereotypical way. The novel depicts the paternalistic attitude taken by the first moshavah residents toward "their" Arabs. This elitism served only to widen the gap, and to reinforce the stereotype of the Arab peasant as an inferior being. It also allowed Socialist parties to ignore their own ideals regarding the equality of all the world's workers, and to give first priority to Jewish labor: the Arab had the right to work, but Jewish needs superseded Arab rights.[11] The Zionist view regarding the need to settle the land and to create a Jewish state was shared by almost all political parties.

In the 1950s, Shamir's protagonist is a self-reliant Israeli, "walking through the fields" but with a metaphoric bullet in his heart. A decade-and-a-half later, in *The Border,* a novel written between 1959 and 1965, his protagonist is no longer Israeli-born. He is European by birth and mentality; he does not walk through the fields, but to the no-man's-land between east and west Jerusalem. Instead of the open vistas so characteristic of Yizhar's and Shamir's early fiction, there is now the reality of a border, of separation and siege.[12]

The protagonist, Rafi Orlan, is a millionaire and a high official in the Israeli government. He cancels his trip abroad and tries to cross the border. The act is a quest for something, but it is also an escape from Israeli affluence and insensitivity. It is an escape as well from the responsibilities of position, power, and family. This is a common theme in the fiction of the Palmach generation, especially for Aharon Megged. Some of the Palmach-generation writers expressed deep disillusionment with the non-idealistic, so-called pragmatist aspects in the Israeli power structure and society. The fiction of the Palmach generation, while realistic in tone, nevertheless sets

certain ideals by which to judge a "realistic" society. Shamir and his contemporaries have stayed with the realistic novel, where the values of the
implied author give the tone and point of view to the narrative (in contrast
to the early work of Amos Oz and A. B. Yehoshua, whose narrative world
is within the psyche, in the irrational and mythic, even beyond good and
evil).

The Border has a humorous dimension. A she-goat belonging to a
Yemenite Jew who lives close to the border strays into no-man's-land. After
stirring up the Israeli and Jordanian military, the goat (which has given
birth to two kids) is returned by the United Nations force. The animal
mocks the seriousness of war, but it also serves to extol the realities of birth
and life. The protagonist is somehow related to this incident, in his quest
for what is genuine and simple. He is attracted to the mysterious other
side, even though it carries an element of fear as well as unreality. He is
attracted to the Arabs and to the Jews who have come from Arab countries.
Besides, the division of Jerusalem into Israeli and Jordanian sectors (1948–
1967), with the border officially closed, is itself an unreality that leads one
to search for what is real and true.

One of the characters in the border area is an Israeli physician, Dr.
Danon, whose patients (before 1948) were Arabs who came from Silwan,
Ramalla, Bethlehem, Jericho, and Amman:

> They loved him, the Arabs, because he understood them, and because he
> loved them. How many physicians are there who were born in Hebron,
> even in the entire world? Now the border cuts between them and him. For
> seventeen years they have not had a physician to replace him, and he has
> no patients to replace them. But he is faithful. He has not moved to another
> part of the city, even though this neighborhood, which used to be one of
> the nicest in town, is a dilapidated slum in ruins, a border garbage-dump.
> He believes. He waits. He will be needed. He will be useful. (pp. 38–39)

Rafi Orlan talks to the Swedish UN officer, who tells him: "How long can
history be organized in hotel lobbies? You will have to venture outside, to
the crescent, the palm trees, the sands, the snakes." For Orlan it is all the
same mideastern landscape. The conversation is conducted in a swimming
pool, and the two have whiskey glasses in their hands. Orlan is in charge of
developing Jerusalem, and he wants to plant trees along the "border." An
irate Israeli, Dr. Hefetz, answers: "Our eastern border, sir, . . . is two
hundred kilometers east of the river Jordan, the Great Desert is our eastern
boundary. But if you refer to the armistice line . . . there we don't need a
green strip, we need a black strip of iron and a red strip of fire" (p. 156).
Ironically, Shamir himself will come to endorse this attitude.

Ishmael, the banished son of the biblical Abraham and Hagar, is the
progenitor of the Arabs. Shamir's book *My Life with Ishmael*,[13] published

soon after the Six-Day War, is his summation of his lifelong relations with Arabs, a combination of personal recollections and his political credo. Nurtured in the left-wing Mapam Party, Shamir here forsakes his former principles of universal brotherhood in favor of the nationalistic view that the Israeli claim to the land is stronger than the Arab claim. It was around this time that Shamir helped establish the Greater Land of Israel Movement, which urged the historical right of Jews to the undivided Israel of biblical times, a territory far more extensive than modern-day Israel. That unification is also rooted, for Shamir, in the land of pre-State times:

> I am trying to examine in all honesty the picture of Eretz Israel undivided, as I experienced it thirty years ago and as I experience it today. I am trying to distil from it all that is common to the many, all that is basic to the outlook of most of the Jews in Israel, including their government and their army leaders. It is quite obvious to me that the presence of Arabs in peace and mutual understanding is not inconsistent with the picture of Eretz Israel undivided. (p. 23)

That situation of Shamir's childhood and youth included close contact and friendship with Arabs:

> I try to recollect my encounters with Arabs.
> Throughout my childhood and my youth, in fact until the establishment of the State, the Arab was a natural part of the human landscape in which we lived. In Part I, I described in particular the constant accompaniment of the threat of Arab attack. Parallel to this, and somehow without being marred by it, our lives were also constantly accompanied by contacts and friendship with the Arabs, affection for them, and in many cases an attitude of romantic admiration. (p. 150)

Yet he is sufficiently candid to admit the element of condescension here:

> My life, the life of all who grew up in this country, is full of such moments and such experiences. I have already said elsewhere: the Arab lived in the Jewish consciousness as a symbol of naturalness, of deep-rootedness. He was the strong, objective element, existing for itself. Never and in no case could we doubt the stability of his presence around and among us. Our acquiescence to the proximity of the Arab needed no rationalization. It was as self-understood as acquiescence to the climate and mountains of Israel. This was the romantic approach, and no doubt I cling to it not only because it is bound up with the sweet memories of childhood and youth, but because it is the easy approach. (p. 154)

And he is also aware of the contrary fact: despite easy relations on the interpersonal level, there was continued violence. The book recounts the Arab attacks on the Jewish population in skirmishes, riots, and worse. In

1929 these were called "pogroms"; during the 1936–39 period, the designation varied from "disturbances" to "riots" to "bloody riots"—but the difference was only in terminology. Underneath, they were the ongoing Arab revolt, a national revolt—even the Great Revolt, as contemporary rhetoric still refers to it.

There are those who see the confrontation between Jews and Arabs in terms of classic tragedy, namely, as the clash between two contending parties, *each* with justice on its side (p. 73). It is a point of view held by writers such as Amos Oz.[14] But Shamir explicitly rejects this "justice against justice" view, since to him it asserts a self-contradictory proposition: that the Jewish claim that Israel *should* exist, and the Arab claim that Israel *should not* exist, both have objective justification (p. 74). It is an asserting of equilibrium where none can be. And to clinch this inequality of "justifications," Shamir points out that whereas there are Jews urging justice for the Arabs, there are no Arabs who demand equal justice for the Jews.

The spurious argument for equal claims is expressed as a clash between two national entities of equal status. To demolish this view, Shamir mounts a scathing attack against the notion of a Palestinian entity: the concept of a "Palestinian Arab nation" is a "historical bluff," he says. It was a concept picked up from Zionist nationalism. Not only is Palestinian nationalism a direct response to Zionism, says Shamir, but had there not been a Jewish state, the Arabs would have continued to fight among themselves for fifty years. A Palestinian state is what nobody wanted. What the "Palestinians" wanted, from 1918 onwards, was to be part of Syria (pp. 100–101). This amounts to saying, à la Voltaire, that for the sake of Arab motives, if there were no Israel "it would have been necessary to invent it."

Shamir therefore declares: "There will not be peace. Not in the foreseeable future" (p. 195). There will be peace only when the Arabs have come to see that they have no alternative. This is the message in the book's closing passage:

> They have not yet reconciled themselves to us. Their hearts are closed in hatred and their hands outstretched for slaughter.
> But they will have no alternative [but to realize] that this is it. Israel is here. The sons of Abraham, Isaac and Jacob are here in their Land. The unfinished war—will be finished: the unrecognized justice—will be recognized: the unheeded call—will be heeded.
> And [only then] the inevitable sequel will be peace. (p. 222)

In June 1987, on the twentieth anniversary of the Six-Day War, Shamir gave the interview cited above.[15] The interviewer reminded Shamir of his "There will be no peace" remark. What did he have to say about it now? In addition to preconditions such as the realization that losing a war to Israel would amount to an intolerable burden, etc., the Arabs would somehow have to accept Israel's legitimate existence. And however redundant and tautological this may seem, it is in some way to be foreseen in the created reality that is Israel. Shamir spoke of his dead brother Elik, and imagined showing him the country after almost forty years: the increase in population from a half million to four million, the phenomenal development of the country, etc.—all giving it a raison d'être which almost *compels* (wishfully) de facto recognition. Shamir concluded the interview by observing: "Those were the most beautiful years in Jewish history. . . . To be part of it, even the smallest cog, one cannot ask for more."

In discussing Yizhar and Shamir, we have taken the approach that what these writers are, in their view of themselves, can be seen in their respective protagonists. In addition to representing themselves indirectly through the personae of their respective heroes, Yizhar and Shamir also represent thereby (in a quite broad sense) their vision of the Israeli as they see him. Thus Nurith Gertz characterizes the writers of the Palmach generation as depicting a hero who sees his problems clearly, sees them as soluble and his goals as achievable.[16] This hero believes it possible to live in a meaningful way by harmonizing personal values with those of the collective social world. (In the fiction of the 1960s and after, the very term *hero* becomes ironic, in signifying someone apart.)

Where the Palmach hero sees the problematic relation to Arabs as soluble, Aharon (of Shamir's *Under the Sun*) sees his unambivalent relation to individual Arabs as non-problematic—which pushes that novel into the fiction of the 1920s and '30s, even though it was written in 1950. That is, the sense of deep commitment to the Zionist dream of co-existence was still intact in the 1920s and '30s. Aharon organizes the defense and the consequent attack, but with nothing like the self-questioning of the heroes in Yizhar's "The Grove on the Hill," "The Prisoner," or "Hirbet Hizah."

And yet the primary sense—in Israeli fiction where confrontation with the Arab is the core of the story—is that the victory, though it be just, is as often likely to be unjust also. The fairy-tale quality of the hero who harmonizes the personal and the collective aspects is not a part of contemporary experience. The implied reader can hardly achieve the willing suspension of disbelief knowing that there is blood being shed as he or she is reading the story. The concluding lines of *Under the Sun*, with the sense that blood, sand, and sun will persist as major presences in the life of the child, present us with Shamir's deep pessimism about the solubility of the problem. Reality has proven this somber meditation true, close to forty years after the novel was first published.

In a parallel manner, there is *He Walked through the Fields* to consider. The seemingly innocuous title is taken from a poem by Nathan Alterman, "The Third Mother." A loose translation reads: "My son is big and quiet / And here I sew him a shirt for the holiday / He walks in the fields / He will come back here / He carries in his heart a lead bullet." (Alterman had deeply affected the young writers of the Palmach generation.)

A different view is offered by Dan Miron, who says that the Shamir novels are loaded with a sense of tragedy and heroism. He also says that Shamir paved the way for the expansively romantic writing of his contemporaries.[17] Thus Shamir's 1948 protagonist is totally new to Hebrew letters: the native son who is "master" of the land; he "knows" the land in almost a biblical sense, as Miron says. He is the person who possesses the land "with his own hands."

Where the Yizhar character moves in his inner landscape, he accepts the will of the group, despite his inner (and silent) reservations. Shamir, on the other hand, is interested in the positive external social factors shaping his characters. The early protagonists of Shamir helped shape the persona of the young "sabra"—the native-born Israeli dedicated to the values of his Socialist youth movement, the kibbutz, the Haganah (the Jewish defense force prior to the establishment of the State), and the Palmach (the kibbutz-based crack units of the Haganah)—and, above all, are utterly removed from the Diaspora mentality of the very founders associated with the (pre-State) Land of Israel.

The 1948 War changed the very landscape of the old Land of Israel, just as it challenged its values. This is not to deny the element of nostalgia present in Palmach-generation writers and their protagonists. Yet that very nostalgia existed against the background of a land being overturned. The struggle, mental as much as physical, calling for fortitude and resourcefulness in the face of one's own death and the death of friends and family, and the inflicting of death on others—all served to create a new personal ontology beyond the expectations of the young men and women caught in a web of events, yet seeking to maintain their own autonomy.

8. AHARON MEGGED

Since the early 1970s, Aharon Megged, one of the prominent writers of fiction in Israel, has written a weekly column for the daily *Davar.* The column includes essays and articles in response to current events, and this polemical genre has been a central part of the cultural/political milieu from the very beginning of journalism in Palestine. Megged has collected some of his essays in a book titled *The Turbulent Zone.*[1] That is the publisher's English rendering of *Eizor HaRaash,* which would have been more accurately—and ominously—translated as *Earthquake Zone.* This expression is one of the many buzzwords that have entered the jargon since the Six-Day War, along with *eclipse, erosion,* and other such terms indicating a fundamental change in the original Zionist ardor.

Megged calls attention to the obvious polarization of Jewish society in Israel: i.e., between secular and ultra-orthodox Jews, between the Right and the Left, hawks and doves, and between the militant Gush Emunim and the conciliatory Peace Now movements. Earlier, one of the key terms used by the Socialist/Center leadership had been *havlagah* ("self-restraint," "moderation"). The weakening of the Center, and the subsequent polarization, has led to extremism and fanaticism, an entrenchment of attitudes that has "eroded" the moral fiber of society by weakening its elasticity and resilience. To Megged, the extremism of either side portends disaster, with Jewish intolerance not only of Arabs but also of the divergent views of other Jews. On the other hand, some factions of the extreme Left have expressed total endorsement of the Arab cause—but with a total repudiation of Israel's cause. As Megged observes, there is neurosis to be found in both the Right and the Left.

In Megged's view, the element of moral fiber in Hebrew literature since 1948 has found expression in the strong identification with the Arab uprooted from his land. But that identification, too, might have its neurotic side, he feels—the mark of a twisted Jewish sickness. And yet, along with writers such as A. B. Yehoshua, Ya'acov Shabtai, and others, Megged embraces this "sickness" and is even proud of it. History has fated the two nations to live in one land; and although Megged is fully committed to the Zionist ideals of Jewish settlement and defense, he feels that these must be supplemented by the ideals of co-existence, equality, and dialogue.

Megged's book concludes with a monologue—perhaps fictional, perhaps genuine—of a woman who is an ex-kibbutznik and ex-member of the Palmach. She admits that her sense of guilt toward the Arab was a part of her growing up in the 1940s, a guilt mixed with fear. Her father was killed by an Arab in 1947, on the border between Tel Aviv and Jaffa. Now, in the 1980s, she can identify neither with the "bleeding heart" tradition of "Hirbet Hizah" nor with the militancy whose victories have given Israel the inflated identity of a ruling power. As a result, she now feels a sense of estrangement—in contrast to the sense she felt, as a member of a kibbutz and of the Palmach, that she had a part in giving shape to national life. (Whether this is a real or a fictitious interview is secondary to the fact that her estrangement and loss of self-identity represent the feeling of Megged's own generation, perhaps even the basic *Zeitgeist*.) She concludes by saying that the Israelis need the Arabs more than the Arabs need the Israelis: the Arabs have been the link connecting the Jews to the land, the link "between us and our early history in the land." Thus the Arabs constituted a sense of power for the Jews: the early pioneers sensed it; the "Cana'anites" understood it. With the recent distance between Israeli and Arab, a source of strength has been lost to the Israeli, and the answer is to re-establish the link.

From its beginnings in the late 1940s, Megged's fiction has been marked by a strong moralistic tone, even to the extent of superimposing an intentionality, didacticism, and ideology. Often there will be a conflict of opposed moral attitudes. As a result, Megged will frequently resort to allegory, satire, parody, and irony as a way of putting distance between himself and the situations and characters he describes. Despite all this, however, there is a monistic and non-ambivalent dimension in his perception of fictional reality: the narrative itself is devoid of paradox. His major protagonist is essentially an antihero, a marginal figure—strange, bizarre, a fool—as in his 1959 novel *Fortunes of a Fool*.[2]

Characteristically, Megged sets up polarities of norms, values, and ways of life—and then examines the possibilities they offer. In the polarity of private versus public life, for example, his characters are never entirely free of society's demands, and they become marionettes manipulated by social forces.

Hebrew literature can be seen as divided between two orientations: Yizhar, for example, will make the land his basic emphasis; Megged, on the other hand, will be concerned with the nation above all else. Clearly, most Hebrew fiction will mix and combine these emphases. However that may be, the writers whose main emphasis is the land will give greater physical presence to the Arab, with both destructive and reconstructive effects on the land. On the other hand, writers whose main emphasis is the nation will link the Arab presence to Jewish history and Jewish fate as a nation.

Megged's moralistic stance in *Fortunes of a Fool*, and the stand-off between the individual and society, are concentrated in his chapter "The White

City" (pp. 220–74). Here, too, the stand-off between Arab and Jew constitutes but a part of the protagonist's moral excursions. The time is 1956, the Sinai Campaign, and the place is Gaza. The protagonist finds himself in the midst of battle. He is a part of the force that has begun to penetrate the enemy's formation. The ultimate aim is to break through entirely, into the besieged city. After a fierce battle, the city is taken. The protagonist suffers a sprained ankle, so that his triumphant entrance into the city is made comic by his lagging behind the rest. Prior to the war, he had considered suicide; now he acts the hero, but after entering the city he finds himself an outsider. The encounter with Arabs is an encounter with his own past, and childhood memories of an orchard. Jewish orchards had been cultivated by Arabs, who were (as the literature reminds us again and again) a part of the landscape:

He asked me if I knew the village of A. "Yes," I smiled, seeing in front of me a group of huts the color of red earth, hugging the shoulder of a hill like a nest of wasps, surrounded by crude fences of prickly pear bushes. He asked me if I knew Bergmann's orange grove. For a moment I was speechless. Within me rose the strong, intoxicating perfume of the orange blossoms, the sight of the dense dark-green foliage, the cool pools of shade around the tree trunks, the dampness of the earth during the hoeing, the irrigation canals with their ends blocked with wet, rotting sacks, the flies above the dump of rotten fruit, the well house marked with spots of lichen and containing empty boxes, rugs, packing materials with a smell of resin, a hill of sandstone on which blue beehives stood tilted on their sides in a field of wild yellow daisies with bees humming around them, the sound of the well being pumped in the great stillness of the afternoon. "Did you work there?" I asked. He didn't answer my question, but mentioned names—Rappaport, Zelkin, Schechtman, Abramski. This was a row of densely-located orange groves lying next to one another along the side of the road. "How is Mr. Yakub?" he asked in my own language. Then he said: "Weeds, right? A lot of weeds there." The people around us stood open-mouthed, as if watching a conjuring show, and waited for me to say something. I was stunned and couldn't say anything in reply, and after my silence became prolonged, they began throwing cries at me from all sides, like stones: "Zeligman!" "Marmorek!" "Tannenbaum!" "Yavne!" "Moskowitz!" Now the close-shaven man smiled a smile of victory. He unfolded his hands and showed me one of the fingers of his left hand, whose upper joint was missing. "That's from a hoe," he said, looking at me as if waiting for my reaction.

I wanted to shake his right hand, as a sign that we were friends, but at that moment the noise of a jeep was heard dashing from the military police, and at once the crowd scattered in all directions, like a flock of chickens among which a stone has been thrown. The jeep stopped with a screech of brakes, and one of the soldiers asked me if I hadn't heard the order forbidding fraternization with the local inhabitants. (pp. 235–36)

After this encounter, limping toward the center of the city, the protagonist muses: "I repeated to myself that I was the conqueror, the ruler of the city, but I felt no joy about this. There was a hot vapor over the sky, and this was like an ominous portent, like an eclipse of the sun" (p. 236).

He finally reaches the school which has been turned into a barracks. The euphoria of battle is gone, and there is no sense of victory for him. The mood is suggestive of a Dantean hell, of steps leading down to a pit from which there is no return.

On one hand, we can see Megged's protagonist as a native son, for whom the orchards, the dampness of the earth, the heavy foliage speak of land and soil. At the same time, and more intensely, he is afflicted with the collective memory of the Jew. In the midst of victory he foresees disaster: the restless sounds of night, a shot fired—all suggest an atmosphere of siege; the crowds in their sheltered houses could attack. The atmosphere of victory is undermined by the existential sense of being trapped in the school, with its blackboard, books, maps of the world.

His duty at the refugee camp is a further experience leading him to refrain from action: the distribution of rations, the poverty, the whistling of bullets, the dead girl. . . . There is a roll call of clans and villages, and rations are distributed according to place of origin. He decides to separate himself from the others, and he refrains from asserting himself as a conqueror; when asked to participate in a retaliatory action against the Fedayeen (whose main actions had, for years, been aimed at civilians), he declines.

We are thus presented with a moral dilemma similar to the one faced by the protagonist in Yizhar's short story "The Prisoner." Yizhar does not resolve the conflict, thereby involving the reader in a moral impasse, and asking us how we would act if we were faced with a similar predicament. But Megged's "bleeding heart" is not a free agent in the way that Yizhar's protagonist is. Megged's protagonist is closely tied to societal norms: his choice of action or inaction is motivated by social acceptance and the changing social climate.

In a short foreword to the English translation, Max Brod notes the influence of Kafka on the book: "Megged tells the story of a lonely outsider, which is really the story of the human conscience. The events take place in a society which has lost its sane criterion. Like Kafka's heroes, Megged's fool has lost his spiritual links with his environment; his life is also a cry of protest against a society which is losing its faith."

In confining our attention to one chapter of one book, as we have done here, we are faced with greater indeterminacy in interpreting its meaning and fixing the ambiguous messages sent by the text and the author. Can we relate to the experiences in "The White City" as those of yet another battle? Is the protagonist just another fool? What is the essence of the quest that is here sullied by immoral action? Is Megged saying that his protagonist merits his dire lot because he has tried to adapt to a society that negates everything he stands for? Is his refusal to commit atrocities a moral stance if that refusal leaves the dirty work to others? Is he culpable when he benefits from the wrongdoings of his comrades?

The allegorical mode of this novel can display the full range of reactions to war and its consequences. There is moral indignation on one hand, and the problem of choice on the other. And all this is coupled with problems of personal integrity in situations beyond the character's sphere of decision. He foresees his death, and while out on patrol he welcomes it. In existential fashion, is he embracing the indifference of reality, and is this a way out of a no-exit situation?

Since the form of the book is semi-allegorical, the protagonist will be accused by his comrades in a posthumous court. But the mixture of allegory and realism does not always work well. The description of the war and the city is realistic; the allegory is perhaps added on, to give the story a universal/moralistic configuration. The realistic story will present the protagonist as one who, despite moral vacillation vis-à-vis the Arabs, has paid with his life for what he believed in. There is the stand-off we mentioned between the individual and military authority. Yet Megged sees it as a way station in the spiritual odyssey of a man at odds with societal beliefs.

In a 1973 interview to mark the publication of two new books, Megged told the interviewer (the poetess Shin Shifra): "I think of myself as a realist, as an author who is in direct contact with reality—even when I go on an imaginary 'Journey to Nicaragua.' *Fortunes of a Fool* and *The Escape* are no less realistic for dealing with a world in which the frontiers of time and place are eradicated. Imagination and dreams are a reality as well, a spiritual reality. As I see it, a story by Kafka is realism" (p. 35).[3] The interviewer posed these questions: "Many of your characters voice severe criticism of Jewish life in the State of Israel. Do you sympathize with these indictments? Do you identify yourself with them?" Megged's extended reply included the following statements:

> I cannot identify either with the Establishment or with the anti-Establishment; I cannot identify with the tendency to negate whatever is being accomplished here or with the tendency to approve and concur. I live with ambivalence, and perhaps that is why I have been breaking down conventional literary structures in my recent novels. My ambivalent attitude extends even to the Jewish people. . . . And yet I am bound to this people by all the fibers of my being. I have nothing else. I have no homeland other than the Jewish people and its history, the history of Eretz Israel, my period in the kibbutz and the youth movement—all of it, taken together. (p. 41)

This ambivalence of his, then, may be taken as his personal characteristic—with regard to himself, to Israel, and to the Arab. As we have seen, in regard to his "fool," moral fortitude and the refusal to choose make for a very strange equation indeed. True, his protagonist lacks authenticity and the kernel of conviction. His refusal to bear responsibility is the negation of his freedom to choose. He embraces death because living presents a situation he cannot handle with integrity.

9. NATHAN SHAHAM

Nathan Shaham's fiction depicts something of the wide scope of Jewish relations to the Arab. In the early stories we see the Jewish reaction to the Arab riots of 1936–39. Later, as the Arab leaves his background position in the life of the Jewish population, he becomes a testing ground for the Jewish individual's moral fiber—especially in time of war, when existence itself is at stake. Time and again in the early literature we have expressions of Jewish love for the landscape, of which the Arab is an inescapable part, and that love is focused on the familiar fragrances of an Arab village. At the same time, the same Jewish protagonist, in his musings, will equate the Arab attacks with Russian pogroms against Jews.

This ambiguity, a mixture of the feelings of belonging and apprehension, becomes intensified, more complex, even conflicted. Thus in *Witness for the King*,[1] we meet with the native-born Israeli, a former member of the Palmach, now speaking after the Six-Day War:

> After the Six-Day War, I traveled in the Jordan Valley. Yellow and sad and wild and suffocating. But I felt that it belongs to me. Or better, I belong to it. I'm stating a fact. Look, I'm not talking about political arrangements. I had never been there before. You know how afraid we were to walk in those areas. Nevertheless, I belonged to this. Painfully. One can dream of richer landscapes. I felt I love this place like a poor sad child who has an illogical crazy mother. Motherland! Not to live, not to die. (p. 99)

Shaham's first collection of war stories, *The Gods Are Lazy*,[2] appeared in 1949. A motto to one of the stories reads: "All over the world the function of the scout is to discover the enemy; here his function is to discover the motherland." Indeed, in the writings of Shaham and his contemporaries, the war is a broad encounter with the land—and the individuation of many of the young men and women, as committed Zionists and as Israelis, is deeply affected by direct contact with the terrain.

Yet Shaham's protagonist is not always the bleeding-heart youth, the lonely romantic idealist found so often in the literature of the 1948 generation. Many of his characters are cynical; they experience the war directly, and are even maimed or killed in it. Despite all this, however, the awareness of moral dilemmas is inherent to the psychology of this generation—dilemmas about the cruelty of war and questions such as, "Why should I be moral?" On one hand, there is the young Palmachnik, "drunk with love of the land, acquiring each additional kilometer of the Eretz Israel landscape with his footsteps" (p. 69). On the other hand, this same young man, in love with the open spaces, is the one who will have to confront ethical dilemmas.

In the midst of the 1948 War, Shaham published a story that created an uproar. This was "They Were Seven," translated into English as "The Seven."[3] The narrator is accompanied by a comrade to the site of a battle, a battle in which he did not participate. The time of narration is a year after the battle, 1949, as the tale of the ridge is told: "Here, on this ridge Abbi had spent a bleak and heroic period of his life" (p. 87). Shaham employs a mixed narrative technique whereby the first-person narrator addresses the reader while the protagonist retells the story to the narrator. This allows for the "objective" voice of the narrator, who can describe the scene, and can introduce irony, while we readers are directly exposed to the voice of the protagonist.

The story tells of a dark period in the war: the enemy's superiority in numbers and armaments has been a source of despair for the Israelis, whose nerves are strained to the breaking point by the fear of defeat:

> There were forty-four of us left, isolated on the crest of this ridge, exposed to the enemy's counter-attacks, wrecked in spirit, browned off by the war, and haunted by a cursed obsession that whatever we kept on doing was just a muffled echo of a bygone epoch. In that state we were called upon to confront the horrors of a fierce, protracted nightmare. . . . (pp. 90–91)

Yet this is but an overture. A discovery of the body of one of the dead soldiers reveals that he was killed by a mine. An officer recalls that seven mines were planted on this very ridge. The man who planted them had been killed, and his map was destroyed. "We had no mine detector and . . . we knew that there was none at the base. Quite likely, there was none in the whole country at that time . . . forty-four young men grew old overnight. . . . Six more men would have to be killed for the dread of the mines to pass off" (p. 92).

Shaham thus creates the situation of an existential impasse, a test of man's moral sensibility when his life is at stake, and where his salvation is in the death of another. Even if the men could move, the ridge could not be given up, because of its strategic importance. The presence of the mines is spiritually devastating; the collegiality of the fighting unit has been shattered. Abbi and his lieutenant venture into the open area, trying to convince the soldiers who have barricaded themselves in their billets to come out; they refuse the order. Three men have escaped, one with a nervous breakdown, one killed by a mine. The distress grows; headquarters promises reinforcements to ease the situation. Eventually the men begin to walk the mined area, in something of a fatalistic mood. Forty-one men remain, with five mines left.

"That same day we were out on a patrol and took a prisoner. A cruel thought struck our minds. He was a young villager, about thirty, with a defiant, energetic cast of features that incited general antagonism. We took him to the grounds and ordered him to run. He ran out and back once, and nothing happened. We again ordered him to run, and he obeyed again. Nothing happened. The third time we insisted he run around in circles, but he refused. Running around like that to no purpose seemed like abuse to him, so he defied us and refused. At first we were astonished at his insolence, but then we beat him up until he spat blood. He was handsome, and his face depicted amazement and scorn. Suddenly he slipped away and began running down the hill slope. His strides were powerful, and none of us could catch up with him, but he was hit by our gunfire and collapsed and was lost sight of among the bushes. We thought we heard groaning, but we ignored it. To put an end to his miseries, we despatched another round to the spot where he had fallen. We didn't want his death, and since he hadn't been killed by a mine, I felt sorry for him. It was peculiar: when it came to our men who stepped on those mines, I was sorry for each one to the extent that I had or hadn't liked him in his lifetime, but not out of any vague sentiment for the ruin of glorious manhood. As for that stranger, who may or may not have been one of the enemy, I was sorry that he was not killed by those same mines whose explosion would have spelt relief to us; it seemed like a wasteful dying, senseless. . . . Have you guessed by now into what a strange morass of notions we had sunk?" (pp. 95–6)

"The next day we captured another prisoner. This time, an old, good-natured wag, who spun fantastic yarns about the enemy forces. It was I who had to 'deal' with him. I didn't beat him or order him to run, but loosened his shackles and treated him as I would my friend. The old man was overwhelmed, and it was all I could do to check his repeated efforts to kiss my hands. The degradation of those who surrender meekly is infinitely repulsive. He did whatever I told him, bringing water, marking tracks, doing odd jobs here and there all the while, under a guard which was quite unnecessary. He always came back to me like a dog to his kennel, and I welcomed him with a friendly smile, thanking him for the services rendered. I had never seen such affection before light up in a human face, such boundless affection and devotion. No one had ever been so fond of me. The outcome was that he kept on going and shuffling along the surface of the ridge until his feet found the mine. We showed true charity by contributing a bullet for his merciful release, and then we cremated his body." (p. 96)

This is not the end of the moral deterioration of the men. Reinforcements will be arriving. Should they be told of the danger of the mines? After some discussion it is decided not to inform the newcomers. "There was no escaping those mines, and ignorance would at least spare their nerves" (p. 97). A sense of conspiracy enters, drawing them together, although what they share is a base and ugly moral stance. The ensuing battle takes its toll. Two of the casualties are due to the mines.

The moral numbing is turned against the Israelis' compatriots. The reinforcements include a petite girl, a radio operator, who is serious and eager to be of help. With the coming of rain after a hot spell, she begins to prance around, filled with joy. She runs toward some trees. The area was never checked for mines.

> "I stared at this foppish dance and was beset by appalling phantoms. The dance of death, I thought. My eyes, transfixed with horror, followed the soles of her feet which, tripping here and there, seemed to be tapping the ground and testing it for mines. I saw the men watching her as if from an ambush. They had no compunction. I too was silent. I felt myself caught in a tense, fatiguing state of expectation of the inevitable. I stared mournfully at her slim, childish legs. Suddenly, I restrained my feelings and called her to the room, in tones that implied something urgent was required of her. Nobody could have convinced me it wasn't.
> "She ran towards me, coming, not to the door, but to the window." He again indicated the spot and looked intently in that direction. He then passed the three remaining fingers of his right hand across his brow, apparently trying to collect his thoughts, and added: "She hung onto the window sill and sang out: 'What is it?' I just managed to catch a glimpse of her small hands gripping the window—she was a short one, and her rain-washed hair; and a dewy droplet on her forehead was on the point of slipping into her eye-socket. . . . The explosion filled the room with smoke and heavy dust; and beneath the window, where no one had suspected, lay a very small corpse, scorched and footless, exposing forlorn naked parts in vain expectation of what would never be. . . ." (p. 101)

The Arab prisoners and the young radio operator are sacrificed to the frenzy of war—the force that strips one of humanity, in a mad desire to live and to overcome all odds. Abbi's missing arm, mutilated face, and glass eye are witness to the fact that he was the one to step on the seventh mine.

Shaham's fiction bears witness to the changing image of the Israeli, as reflected in the changing perspective of the Israeli/Arab relationship. This complex of reflections—images of images, like two facing mirrors—is compounded by the element of stereotype. In this regard, Shaham's novel *Witness for the King*[4] has a special significance, since stereotyping is its theme. It is set in the late 1960s, after the Six-Day War. Its protagonist is a professor of history, Benjamin Or, who returns to Israel after an extended stay at Oxford. His field of research is the period of the British Mandate in Palestine; and his special theory concerns the role of stereotypes in shaping the policies of the British, the Arabs, and the Jews. In addition there is a complex mixture of silence and speech, fidelity and perfidy, exposure and coverup—and these play a role, as well, in Or's private and professional life.

Or's reasons for returning to Israel are many, beginning with his nostalgic love of the land. With his close friend and alter-ego Porath, a novelist at work on a novel titled *Witness for the King,* the professor undertakes a trip to the Arab town of Tul-Karem. The trip evokes meditations in the two on the meaning of history. Porath muses: "Had we learned to live slowly, like the Arabs, we would not have become a foreign plant in the [soil of the] East." Professor Or continues Porath's line of thought, saying: "Had we learned to live slowly, like the Arabs, we would most probably have been a Jewish minority in southern Syria, and our daughters would have been belly-dancers in the exclusive nightclubs of Beirut" (p. 164).

Porath's adoption of Arab culture was a matter of conscious decision (rather than automatic acculturation). Through the power of will, he forced himself (as he says) to love olives, arak, Arab fables, and the afternoon nap. He cannot stand lamb, the sour yogurt known as labane, green olive oil, stories without beginning or end, Eastern exaggeration or anger. As they approached Tul-Karem, Porath had said (appreciatively) that he smelled the aroma of the Mandate. That is to say, Tul-Karem has not changed in decades, and the Arabs have (in their way) preserved the "old Eretz Israel." The two travelers enjoy seeing men leisurely smoking their water pipes, and after loading up on food they hurry back, afraid of terrorist activity (pp. 164–65).

A later visit to Jerusalem and the Old City (liberated in the Six-Day War) stirs excitement and emotion in Professor Or. He feels at home in the dusky alleyways, yet he is also a stranger; they attract and repel him, evoking the love and fear he experienced here in his childhood. His father had belonged to the Brit Shalom (Covenant of Peace) movement in the 1920s, endorsing its bi-national principle of two nationalities under one comprehensive government. That would mean equal rights for the two peoples and equal representation in the governing body. (The Arabs would have to give up the idea of Arab sovereignty, and the Jews for their part would have to do the same, thus rejecting Zionism.) The father, a physician, was threatened because of his beliefs, but he maintained them throughout his life. Unlike many of his colleagues he did not romanticize the Arabs, nor did he hate them. They were among his patients; he knew their mentality, their manners and customs. Yet his closest Arab friend was opposed to Brit Shalom, and said:

> When I listen to Ben-Gurion, or to Jabotinsky . . . even when they talk about the rights of Arabs, trying very hard to believe in what they say, I know exactly what they mean. I know that they would like us to leave, eventually. But when I listen to you I'm afraid. You are an honest man, and only an honest man can deceive me. (p. 122)

After a crude bomb was thrown into their garden, the father repudiated Zionism entirely. Hitler's rise to power silenced him completely.

The father's integrity is paralleled by the integrity of the old Palestinian statesman who is interviewed by Professor Or. The Palestinian says that the Arab revolt and strikes of the 1930s were successful: namely, the Arabs knew that Jewish immigration would deprive the Arabs of their independence (and he produces a 1920 article to show that they knew this at that time); and therefore the curtailing of Jewish immigration by British decree is proof of the Arabs' effectiveness. Professor Or is delighted with the interview, since it substantiates his theory of stereotypes as the bases of policy: the Arabs believed that London was subject to Jewish influence; the Jews believed that the British administration was anti-Semitic.

Throughout this study, we have discussed the question of how stereotypical or non-stereotypical a given depiction of the Arab is. However that may be, I contend that in the literature of the 1940s and '50s, the Israeli himself is portrayed in rather a stereotypical manner: his problems are those of the immediate present, and have their solution in the present; his moral dilemmas are regarded by him as entirely internal, as though the outer world had no bearing on them; the war literature is limited to the immediate range of action or inaction, so as to block out the broader universe; and in any case, problems of good and evil are too often faced by protagonists who are by nature non-contemplative, and thus not fitted to comprehend those problems in their true depth and complexity.

In "The Seven," the no-exit situation mocks the very values that are being confronted and challenged—the problem of survival makes it impossible to continue adhering to those values, let alone to live by them. In *Witness for the King*, a corresponding challenge is raised, but in a historical perspective: the historian/protagonist is in search of a formula that will unlock the mystery of the repeated pattern of war and unrest in the Middle East, and such a formula would be the only way he could come to terms with the otherwise irresolvable situation.

As a result of all this, Shaham's fiction reflects a change in the way the Arab is depicted. That change is connected to the possibility of historical insight and perspective. Thus *Witness for the King* perceives the Arab not only in personal terms but also as a part of a historical process that has its origins in the early pre-State days. Many writers of the 1948 generation were interested in the pre-State era; some even went back to the beginning of Jewish immigration in the 1880s. We see, therefore, a transition from the total involvement in the experience of the 1948 War to a new historical awareness, including the history of the land, and inevitably the presence of the Arab.

In Yizhar's *Days of Ziklag* and "Hirbet Hizah," Shamir's *He Walked through the Fields*, and Shaham's "The Seven," we are given war literature that was written while the war was still raging, or soon afterward. In the work now to be discussed we have literature about the same war, with some of the immediacy of having been written on the spot, but actually written some three decades later. One may wonder, offhand, whether the advantage of the added decades has provided the author with a hindsight she might not otherwise have enjoyed. However that may be, in writing in her own voice she touches upon problems that have plagued the ethos of her generation.

Netiva Ben-Yehuda was born in Palestine to the "Mayflower Generation" of the Second Aliyah; thus she came from Ashkenazic European stock, and through her father, one of the most influential educators of his time (he should not be confused with the lexicographer Eliezer Ben-Yehuda), she belonged to the educational/political establishment.

Netiva Ben-Yehuda's *1948—Between Calendars* is a first-person narrative based upon the writer's experiences in the 1948 War.[5] The story is told in one continuous breath, an attempt to capture the experience through spoken (non-literary) language. Thus the book is a continuous monologue, combining "big" events and everyday minutiae, with no attempt to "beautify" event or style. The narrator is a nineteen-year-old girl who is an officer in the Palmach and has seen military and paramilitary action. After months of Arab sabotage of Jewish transport and Jewish settlements in the Galilee, the Palmach is to attack a bus of the Arab forces. As the bus approaches, she sees women and children in it. She tries to tell herself that she is seeing "the enemy"—and in her mind she sees some of the evils perpetrated by the Arabs (their torture of a girlfriend of hers; the massacre and mutilation of thirty-five Palmachniks near Gush Etzion). "This time we'll show them, once and for all, that this is not the riots of 1936, and not like the Holocaust" (pp. 149–50). The target is an Arab sapper who is on the bus. A battle ensues; the Palmach is victorious.

Despite her commitment to Zionism, the incident is traumatic and leads her to question her beliefs. In a letter to her father, she tells him that when he reads the account in the newspapers, he must not rejoice in the victory, he must not be proud of her. She has killed, she has murdered. She says: " 'Enemy' is now a ridiculous word for me. When you are involved in murder, the enemies turn out to be people, suddenly" (p. 171). And can we be sure that every one of the persons killed was an enemy? True, they too killed without discrimination; her best friends are dead now, and in regard to one of them, at least, she is "a thousand percent sure" that he was an enemy to no one.

She goes on to say that she is no longer sure about the slogan (attributed to Joseph Trumpeldor, who was killed in 1921 defending a Galilee settlement) "It is good to die for our country." One thing that she is sure about is that "it is not good to kill for our country." In any case, we must rethink what we have been doing—and above all we must not be proud (pp. 171–72). Later she says how much her generation had admired Arabs and even imitated their ways. They were brave, and superior in arms and numbers—and now they ran away in terror (p. 175–76).

Ben-Yehuda's second book, *Through the Binding Ropes*,[6] is a further attempt to "set the record straight." As in her earlier book, the message is double-edged: the Israeli Jew is no longer a sheep led to the slaughter, as the Diaspora Jew was: "It's not only a thing between us and the Arabs. It is to prove to the whole world that we are no longer the Jews they thought we were, especially after the Holocaust." Thus we saw an awareness of change in the Jew's image of the Arab ("they ran away in terror"), but (in this book) an awareness of the Arab's part in the Jew's changing self-image ("we are no longer the Jews they thought we were").

With this there is an awareness of the unique love/hate ambivalence. Billy, an American in the Palmach, says: "You, you're sentimental about your enemies. I never saw the like of it. With us, it would never be this way. You're sorry for them! They slaughter you—and you, you don't merely pity them, you love them! Where in the world do you see anything like this? They hate you, and you go on loving them. Shit!" (p. 98)

This is also a book about the loss of faith. The topic is introduced through the motif of the Binding of Isaac (*Akeda*), a theme that was introduced by Yizhar and then became central in Yehoshua, Oz, and others. Ben-Yehuda recasts the story in her sardonic/sarcastic tone. The sacrifice of Isaac is a parable for Zionism, but the story is always told by the "Abrahams"—and it is *their* faith, not that of the "Isaacs," that is being "tested." The "Abrahams" were the Founding Fathers, the thinkers and dreamers who spoke directly to God. It is they who are supposedly on trial, and are paying the heaviest price. The "Isaacs" are extras, "the son of . . ." And to extend the metaphor, the modern-day Isaacs, willing to die in order to demonstrate their *elders'* faith, are not saved at the last moment, nor is there a ram in the thicket to be sacrificed in their place. This, then, is the story of one such "Isaac," who tells what it was like to be there, on the sacrificial altar, in 1948, and how things looked "through the binding ropes."

10. THE CANA'ANITE MOVEMENT
Yonatan Ratosh and Others

Why should the territory that is now Israel be identified with *any* ethnic source? Couldn't its residents identify themselves with the language and soil alone, and bypass Zionism's claims and aspirations? Couldn't these residents seek a new secular nationality that would disavow all ties to Diaspora Judaism and its redemptive hopes in Palestine?

The Cana'anite movement[1] is composed of people who answer these questions in a way that is entirely their own: they seek to renounce all ties to Judaism and to Zionism. In their view, Zionism is a nineteenth-century European ideology serving the needs of European Jewry alone, and having no sound basis for a claim to the land. Judaism, too, in its biblical basis, makes a claim that is questionable indeed, as they see it. In returning figuratively, to a "pre-biblical" basis, these people are called "Cana'anites." The name was given to the group, in a semi-derogatory fashion, by the poet Avraham Shlonsky. Although the group was formed in the 1940s, its roots go farther back. It consisted of writers, poets, and intellectuals whose main program was the recognition of the "Hebrew" nation and Hebrew identity, as totally separated from Jewish identity. The conception of a "Land of the Hebrews" was an attempt to suspend the Jewish or Muslim historical claims to the land, and to establish the dominion of ethnic groups who were the (so-called) original inhabitants. The Cana'anites regarded themselves as "Hebrews" rather than Jews.

The most shocking element of the program was the demand for a total separation from Jewish history and the Jewish heritage, along with the goal of creating a native culture devoid of a Jewish component. The ultimate aim of the movement was the eventual creation of a new pluralistic national entity comprising all the various peoples of the area, and totally disassociated from Judaism and Jewish history.

In a famous story by Haim Hazaz, "The Sermon,"[2] written in 1942 by a man who was unquestionably a Zionist, the faltering protagonist declares: "I am opposed to Jewish history" (p. 273), "Zionism and Judaism are not at all the same," and "Zionism begins with the wreckage of Judaism" (p. 283). Although the Cana'anites felt that Zionism has not been successful in transforming an immigrant society into a national/territorial entity, the Cana'anite movement did acquire some of its utopian character from the utopian ideas of Zionism.

The primary ideologue, motivating power, and intellectual force behind the movement was Yonatan Ratosh (1908–1981). He was brought up in a Hebrew-speaking household in Warsaw, and came to Palestine in 1921.

Despite its marginality and its small number of followers, the Cana'anite movement was a significant cultural, political, and literary phenomenon. Perhaps the most serious consideration of the movement came from the eminent literary critic and philosopher Baruch Kurzweil.[3] He perceived it as a dangerous phenomenon that would lead to the final breach between Israel and the Diaspora, and between Israel and its Jewish heritage—and these are precisely the goals the movement hoped to achieve. Kurzweil also traced the movement's roots to the religious skepticism of the *Haskalah* ("Enlightenment") of the eighteenth and nineteenth centuries. Thus the denial of Jewish values and the break with Jewish continuity created a vacuum that allowed vague mythic concepts to emerge as components of a political program. The "rediscovery" of a Semitic East does not, however, provide a full system of values that can serve as the foundation of society; at most it can lead to a Levantization of life and the impoverishment of cultural and spiritual values, Kurzweil felt.

The divisive nature of Ratosh's perception can be seen in his view that Hebrew literature is to be the creation of Hebrews in the land of the Hebrews. Thus, literature written in Hebrew in the Diaspora is Jewish literature. In the 1930s, Ratosh was active in right-wing underground organizations; eventually he founded a group called "The Young Hebrews." One of his closest followers was the poet/novelist Aharon Amir, who continues to endorse Ratosh's ideas to this day. It is significant that the movement had its own right and left wings, and not all members were staunch followers of Ratosh. Some past members advocated rapprochement with Palestinian Arabs. Ratosh himself did not advocate a federation of the two nations. Rather, his neo-romantic vision saw a political solution in the assimilation of the Arab nation into the Hebrew nation—and he held to this utopian/messianic view to the end of his life.

The Holocaust, followed by the mass immigration to Israel from Europe and the Islamic countries in the late 1940s and early 1950s, strengthened the "Jewish" character of Israel. The almost constant wars, as well as the demographic and political changes, created a climate in which the Cana'anite movement could hardly attract new members. In an extended interview with Ehud Ben-Ezer in 1970, Ratosh was asked why the Arabs should agree to the establishing of a non-denominational, non-ethnic political entity.[4] Ratosh answered by advocating the integration of Arabs, Druse, and Maronite Christians into Israeli institutions, including the Israel Defense Forces.

Ratosh had a unique eschatology, foreseeing three wars: the first, to be fought in Israel, would be between national/secular and denominational/theocratic forces; the second, over the wider area he called the "Euphrates

Country," would be fought between the new Hebrew nation and the forces of Pan-Arabism; and the third would be waged against the forces of imperialism from without. The war of liberation of the Hebrew Nations and the Euphrates Country would be a liberation from foreign imperialism, Pan-Arabism, Zionism, and Judaism. (For him, "Pan-Arabism" was synonymous with "Palestinianism"—and in this spirit he rejected the idea of a separate "Palestinian Entity.")

In a last interview shortly before his death, Ratosh was asked by the poet Natan Zach[5] if he saw Israel as "a people that lives by the sword." In a chiding tone, Ratosh retorted that he didn't know what world Zach was living in. As for himself, he had lived through two world wars and others; in his lifetime, entire empires had collapsed, and there had been widespread genocide, as early as the massacre of Armenians. He therefore rephrased the question: Is Israel a state that, without the sword, would not continue to exist, and whose people would be massacred? Fighting, like love and death, is a natural and inseparable part of life itself, he said.

The primary literary position of Ratosh was as a poet. One critic has stated that Ratosh is considered by many to be the greatest Hebrew poet of our time.[6] The assertion has been roundly contested. In the age of Uri Zvi Greenberg, Natan Alterman, and Avraham Shlonsky, it is an assertion that is hard to sustain. The critic does speak of Ratosh as a war poet, one who celebrated war—presumably because he did not believe in human evolutionism, but held that historical change is produced by force. This is clearly an element that remained a part of his political thinking, even from the days of his early "revisionist" right-wing Zionism, which he repudiated once he conceived of the Cana'anite ideology. The poetry of Ratosh also attempted a "pre-biblical" style, involving the incorporation of Ugaritic myths and ancient Cana'anite ritual.

I conducted personal interviews with two prominent writers who commented on the issues Ratosh raised. The first was with Benjamin Tammuz in Tel Aviv, on January 1, 1987. Recalling the Stalin-Landower debate—where Stalin said that there would be no place for Jews as a nation in the Soviet Union of the future, since a nation must have a language, a territory, and an economic interest, and the Jews have none of these—Tammuz said that the Cana'anites had correctly diagnosed the Israeli predicament: the more rooted in Israel its Hebrew-speaking people become, the wider the gap becomes between them and the Diaspora, and he felt that this gap could not be bridged because Diaspora Jewry does not constitute a nation. Thus Tammuz said that the Cana'anite movement had correctly emphasized the eventual gap between the Hebrew nation and the Diaspora. (Ben-Gurion, Tammuz said, acted like a Cana'anite in this regard, even though he disliked the Cana'anites immensely.) The Cana'anites, in Tammuz's view, were totally wrong, however, in assuming that the Druse, the Maronite Christians, and the Arabs would agree to become part of a Hebrew-speaking nation.

My other interview was with Aharon Amir in Tel Aviv, on July 29, 1987. Amir sees a part of the materialization of the Cana'anite movement in the writings of Israeli Arab writers such as Anton Shammas and Na'im Araidi. Shammas is a Christian Arab born in a village in the Galilee, and Araidi is a Druse—and the fact that both write in Hebrew supports the Cana'anite dream of a shared language in Hebrew. Amir sees this happening as a natural process. Like other newcomers in the past, the Israeli Arab will accept an Israeli identity on the road toward a Hebrew national entity. Amir does not perceive neighboring Arab nations as a problem. And despite the existence of powerful historical forces, the symptoms of the "Israelization" of the Arab portend a basic change. On the other hand, one cannot overlook the "Arabization" or "Levantization" of Israeli society—but that is a different issue entirely.

For his part, Anton Shammas, in a recent article,[7] stated that Zionism, as a national movement, had completed its task with the establishment of the State of Israel. Whoever lives within the Green Line boundaries and is an Israeli citizen should be defined as "Israeli." He concluded with the ambiguous question: "Ought we to wait, with Levantine patience, for the first Jew who will declare, hoping that others will follow, 'Zionism is dead. Long live the Israeli nation.'?" And he added, enigmatically, "Happy is the believer."

In the same issue in which the above appeared, Boas Evron addressed the topic of Israeli identity: Who is an Israeli? The real state has not yet been created, he argued, namely, a state after the West European model, devoid of any religious or ethnic definition. And therefore, he agrees with the thesis of Ratosh, who rejected the claim that the raison d'être of Israel is Zionism.

I would like to conclude this discussion of the Cana'anite movement by referring to Moshe Dayan and his "pre-biblical" interests. Clearly, Dayan was in no way associated with the Cana'anites. He was a controversial figure in his own right, although he symbolized for Israeli society the Israeli-born "Zabar." His love of the land and his deep ties to it and its past were materialized in his vast collection of archeological artifacts: among the more than a thousand articles, few belonged to the ancient Jewish era. He purchased and exhumed Cana'anite objects of the fourth millennium B.C.E. And unlike Ratosh, Amir, and Tammuz, all of whom were born in eastern Europe and underwent a change of name and of heart, Dayan was a native son who, in his colorful personality, tried to disclose the life of the inhabitants of the land of six thousand years ago.

The following is from the epilogue to his autobiography:[8]

After seven years in the Defense Ministry, I returned to civilian life. The nights were undisturbed by the telephone, and there was no dashing to the office in the morning. I spent my first free day out of government at Nahal Beersheba, a wadi in the Negev desert. That year we had enjoyed a very wet winter. . . .

It was now early summer, the water had vanished, but not its impact. I drove along the edge of the winding Beersheba wadi, and at one of the bends I saw what I had hoped to find. Glinting in the sunlight were several white stones embedded in the middle of the north wall of the gully. They were oddly out of place.

Six thousand years ago, this area was inhabited by people who existed by hunting and pasture. They lived in caves burrowed in the hillside, with narrow openings to make them easier to defend. The interior of the cave would be broad and comparatively high. A strip of floor skirting the walls would be paved with stones, usually smooth pebbles taken from the gully, to serve, probably with a covering of animal skins, as sleeping pallets. . . .

I attached a rope to the bumper of my jeep and clambered over the side, letting myself down the steep cliff toward the white stones. I crawled inside and started exploring. In one corner I noted a depression in the ground surrounded by small rocks. This was the hearth, its fires used for cooking, for warmth, and for lighting the dwelling. Scattered among the ashes which covered the floor were potsherds, part of a milk churn, a cup, and the bottom section of a soot-laden cooking pot. Beneath the ashes, on the surface of the floor itself, were flint objects, mostly broken blades. I also found an ax head with an oblique edge fashioned from a large pebble. The inhabitants must have taken the rest of their vessels and implements with them when they left the cave, driven out by drought or enemies, and wandered to another territory.

As I tried to learn more about this ancient cave community and recapture their daily pattern of living, the quiet within was occasionally shattered by the ultra-modern sounds of jet fighters roaring overhead. I examined the animal bones left over from their last meal, saw the fingerprints of the potters on the vessels they had molded. These cave dwellers had lived here some two thousand years before our Patriarch Abraham. They could neither read nor write, but they occasionally drew and painted on rock and stone and decorated their pottery with deep-red stripes. This was their home, the center of their lives. From there they would go out to hunt in the Negev and in the Sinai desert, and they were familiar with every wadi, every hill, every fold in the ground. This was their land, their birthplace, and they must have loved it. When they were attacked, they fought for it. And now here was I, at the end of a rope, having crawled through an opening in a cliffside across their threshold and inside their home. It was an extraordinary sensation. I crouched by the ancient hearth. It was as though the fire had only just died down, and I did not need to close my eyes to conjure up the woman of the house bending over to spark its embers into flame as she prepared the meal for her family. My family.

PART THREE

WRITERS
OF THE STATEHOOD
GENERATION—
1960s–1980s

CULTURAL BACKGROUND

The Israeli writers of the 1960s, '70s, and after belong to what is often called the Generation of Statehood. Despite the short time span between this generation and that of 1948, the difference between them is vast. Writers of the 1948 generation were involved in the values and the concerns of the Jewish settlement of pre-State days: they were immersed in the fight against the British, and in conducting the illegal immigration of Jewish refugees into Palestine. Their values continued to be those of *halutziut*—the "pioneering spirit" that had shaped their lives from the earliest times. Zionism, Socialism, and humanism continued to be their life-affirming ideologies, and these entered into the shaping of the national identity.

Beginning in the early 1960s, a totally different spirit pervades Israeli literature. For one thing, the new literature is strongly influenced by Kafka and existentialist fiction. (The more immediate source of that influence was S. Y. Agnon.) In addition, the new writers expand on a motif that had been introduced by Yizhar in "Hirbet Hizah"—namely, the reversal of roles in Arab-Jewish relations. Now it is the Arab who is the victim, the uprooted native son whose plight is in essence "Jewish," and who has in some ways taken on some of the age-old aspects of the Jewish identity. Writers such as A. B. Yehoshua, Amos Oz, and David Grossman will show how, as a result of this process, the Arab has become a part of the Israeli psyche and thus a part of the Israeli malaise. This has led to a general atmosphere of indeterminacy in Israeli fiction since the 1960s, reflecting something of the complexity of Israeli cultural life, where the ongoing conflict has by now taken on the aspect of "right versus right." And if we take the word *right* in both of its major senses (i.e., moral justification and political claim), we can begin to appreciate something of the many-sided ambiguity in Israeli fiction featuring the Arab since the 1960s.

The terms that are heard most frequently of late—*crisis of conscience, spiritual malaise, moral vertigo, state of siege,* and *existence in the shadow of war*—come from those most closely associated with the Establishment (Zionist/ Labor Party/Ashkenazi/secular). These phrases do not necessarily represent the feelings of the orthodox (on the one hand) or the non-Ashkenazi (on the other), segments of the population that came into their own politically and economically in the 1970s and '80s. The phrases reflect elements of alienation, self-criticism, and self-doubt, and these elements have found their way into the writings of the Statehood Generation.

Here, a number of complex questions present themselves. How are these self-critical elements, which are clearly reflective of a changed political outlook, also related to changes in the literary portrayal of the Arab? If the self-critical elements are destructive, why is this destructiveness directed against the national "self" and not against the Arab? Is the Israeli incapable of bearing with victory? Is the more positive valuation of the Arab (in Israeli literature) linked to a corresponding devaluation of the Israeli (in his own literature)? In more mystical terms, is the Israeli's self-denigration (if that is what it is) an unconscious attempt to evade the repeated pattern of the *Akeda* (the sacrifice of the young as testimony to the faith of the old)? Or is all this a part of a broader self-laceration and self-hate that have been a part of the Jewish psyche (as literary presence) for over a century?

We have already qualified the self-critical phrases by observing that they do not reflect the entire spectrum of social-political-religious outlooks. The self-questioning belongs mainly to the left-center orientation. The volunteers who make up the special units of the Israel Defense Force come from strongly nationalist/religious groups where such self-questioning does not go on. (And the greater part of immigration to Israel in the 1980s has been of those people of strongly nationalist/religious orientation.) If this is the population that swept the conservative Likkud coalition into power in 1977, can we continue to speak of a uniform ideological outlook—or of a "spiritual malaise" infecting the Israeli people throughout?

Clearly, the self-questioning concerns moral issues, and it is carried on in a moral dimension. No one would say that to be a Swede or a Dane has any special moral implications. To be Israeli, however, does carry moral implications with it—and that is reflected in the literature of the Statehood Generation. Beyond the boundaries of fiction, a series of talks with kibbutz members who took an active part in the Six-Day War appeared in 1967, and set much of the self-questioning in motion.[1] The young men had been thrown into situations beyond their control, situations involving acts of killing and destruction, the sight of pain and of their friends being killed in their presence—situations for which their prior values had not prepared them. Their shattering experiences had called into question the firm ideals of their upbringing. "Defense" now called for acts of offense; the concept of "purity of arms" was challenged by a new reality. Israel's short history is studded with dates—1948, 1956, 1967, 1973, 1982—referring to wars; and the self-criticism has gained in depth and momentum in the literature that has followed each war, to the point of what has been called a "crisis of values" *(mashber arahim)*.

This leads us to an interpretive problem: Must every work of literature be regarded as the symptomology of a society in crisis? Must we posit a directly reactive relation between the political situation and contemporary fiction? Paul Ricoeur has spoken of the "archeological" and the "teleological" approaches to reading a text. The "archeological" approach regards the text as a verbal covering, behind which (or underneath which) the *one* true meaning is hidden. The "teleological" approach will relate to the text as an end in itself (a telos). Neither of these approaches, taken alone, will be satisfactory for our purposes in this study. Indeed, the texts are self-sufficient structures; at the same time, however, they are reflective of their cultural milieu. That wider milieu does not deposit hidden sediments of "meaning" that are yet to be excavated out of the literature—in "nuggets" of meaning that exclude all other deposits. On the other hand, the text will not be an end in itself to the extent of having no relation to the ambient world.

The fiction of the Statehood Generation is modernistic in essence: a major concern of its members has been the art of fiction and its intricacies. The merely mimetic reflection of reality or of states of mind as such no longer interests them. The flow of emotion still noticeable in the fiction of Yizhar gives way to a more elliptic, ambivalent, and multivalenced fiction. The implied message (the "excavated nugget") is no longer to be stated in terms of liberal humanism. And for the first time in Israeli literature, the reader, the protagonist, and the implied author do not necessarily share the same palette of reactions.

11. A. B. YEHOSHUA

In present-day Israel, the incessant political and military conflicts have forced the writer, of whatever persuasion, to define and redefine his relation to the land and its past, to Judaism and its heritage, to Israelis and Arabs—and to himself and his craft. In a talk at Brandeis University in March of 1985, A. B. Yehoshua addressed the topic of "The Writer in Israeli Society." He pointed to a central phenomenon characterizing not only Israeli sociopolitical life but the writer's situation as well. He referred to the "crumbling of the center," a dissolution of the erstwhile solidarity of Israeli national experience.

For some eighty years, writers had related (in their individual ways, and directly or indirectly) to an assumed "center" consisting of a Zionist/Labor orientation. With the political reversal of the 1970s, however, and with what was to become the continuing Israeli involvement in Lebanon, some former certainties weakened—and this had its effect on Israeli writing. The "crumbling of the center" amounted to the deterioration of a national focus, and Yehoshua saw this reflected not only in the weakening of the Labor coalition, but also in the failure of the Likkud bloc to establish a new "center." Apparently, the era of leaders who were "larger than life" had come to an end. As a result, Yehoshua felt, writers have been experiencing a need to create new "centers" of their own. Yehoshua's fiction demonstrates the supreme difficulty of the task.

The central fact in modern Israeli life is, and has been, the ongoing Arab-Israeli conflict, and as an underlying condition of existence, it has constituted the persistent "topic" of Israeli writing (in more or less overt forms). Israel's involvement in Lebanon, however, has transformed the "given" of war into a political issue. As a result, works of literature, too, have become polarized along political lines—and instead of reflecting the overall situation in its complexity, they have come to express one political orientation or another. Although he has been emphatic in his opposition, Yehoshua confessed his inability to incorporate the war into his fictional work.

He illustrated the effect on Israeli writers by reference to two of his own works: "Early in the Summer of 1970" (a novella written in 1971) and *The Lover* (a novel, 1977). During the period known as the War of Attrition, from 1967 to the early 1970s, the "old father" (in "Early in the Summer of 1970") would have reacted to a given situation in predictable ways (here Yehoshua recalled his own father-in-law). Today, the old man's attitudes

125

would no longer be predictable (whether relating to the Arabs, to the ongoing conflict, to internal politics, or whatever). One could not even *guess* what his opinions might be, and the possibilities abound.

This has had a direct impact on the writing of fiction. Yehoshua said that a fictional character similar to the original "old father" could be created today only as a deliberate caricature. The effect goes even deeper, he emphasized, to the writer's very ability to portray his subject. Today, he said, he would have extreme difficulty in portraying an Israeli Arab, a difficulty he did not experience in creating Na'im in *The Lover.* Acknowledging the baffling array of possible combinations of political, familial, academic, and intellectual allegiances, Yehoshua admitted his inability to gauge with any certainty the individual views even of a young Israeli Arab who had been his student for some years, at Haifa University. Above all, we can see (as Yehoshua does) a shift away from the older traditional issues that were the staples of Israeli writing: themes such as assimilation, the return of Jews to their homeland, the definition of a national identity, etc. These are no longer central to Israeli writing.

There is little question but that the ongoing Arab-Israeli conflict has been the engine of these changes. What we shall explore is the variety of ways in which the conflict has generated the content for a new and viable literature. That process has arisen from the persistent and self-conscious engagement of the Israeli writer, typically addressing that perennial topic through the years: "The Writer in Israeli Society." Yehoshua is by no means unique in his thoroughgoing involvement in the issues that beset Israel—and these include not only the current ones but also the broadest questions regarding the existential situation in which the Israeli sees himself. Like so many other fine writers, Yehoshua is too intelligent to fall into the facile dualism of "right" and "wrong." Indeed, he has titled a collection of his essays *Between Right and Right.* This approach may be seen, then, as a possible new opening for Israeli literature, in something like a tragic awareness of the contemporary scene.

A. B. Yehoshua was born in 1936 to an established Sephardic family that had lived in Jerusalem for five generations. His father, Yaacov Yehoshua, himself a Hebrew writer, died in 1983; his work revolved around the Sephardic community in Jerusalem, and he treated its life and folklore with a sense of closeness and warmth. Yehoshua's mother came to Jerusalem from Morocco in 1930.

In his own work, A. B. Yehoshua makes no mention of his past, and does not even give it an indirect presence. He has never been identified as a Sephardic writer. And yet, the contact that Sephardic writers, past and present, have had with the Arab problem is of considerable significance. Even the Sephardic Jews of the Balkans and other Mediterranean areas (whose language is Ladino, a Hebraic version of Spanish) were closer to the

Arab, directly or indirectly, than were the East European Jews, to whom the Arab was totally foreign. In the light, therefore, of the Yehoshua family's contact with Arabs, the younger Yehoshua's self-alienation from his immediate past in his fiction is of critical import. That is, he has not (so far) made his childhood experience the direct subject matter of his narrative. As a result of the self-alienation, his fictional characters are not autobiographical.[1] It would seem, moreover, that from the beginning of Yehoshua's writing, the relation between the protagonist and the surrounding world has been in question, if we try to take the author's description of that world as representing reality.

By 1975, Yehoshua had published two collections of stories in Hebrew, *The Death of the Old Man* and *Facing the Forests,* as well as the novella "Early in the Summer of 1970." In the summer of 1975, he was interviewed by Menahem Perry and Nissim Kalderon,[2] who asked to what extent Yehoshua's latest writing included more realistically identifiable elements. He answered: "I still cannot face reality and be satisfied with a spontaneous absorption of the gushing stream. I always must search for the intellectual side, the symbolic, to try and perceive reality as representing a general idea. I have never managed to overcome this inclination, and I don't know if I ever will."

The interviewers pointed to the crucial issue facing Yehoshua as a writer *engagé:* "Would it be correct to say that your recent stories involve a certain need to break the dividing line between your activity as a writer within the story and your other activities?" He answered:

> I certainly feel the need . . . to connect the reality I live and the reality I try to present in literary form. I am not talking about the political side, which is the most marginal. . . . Lately, I have been aware of a certain alienation, within me, from the reality around me. Accordingly, it seems that the alienation of my protagonists was not merely a fashionable pose, but something corresponding to an inner problematic feeling within me. . . . There are writers who try to bear witness . . . to a certain place, a certain era, certain characters. I am not one of those writers. I am still basically interested in the naked human situation. Time and place strengthen the experience, they are functional to a certain extent, but they are not autonomous.

Later in the interview, he remarked that the writers of his generation have felt a certain discomfort regarding the work of writers of the 1948 generation. He polarized the difference between the generations by suggesting that the 1948 writers bore the yoke of systematic moral values, while his own writings have escaped that yoke and are "beyond good and evil."

Asked if his turn toward the center of Israeli political reality would affect his future protagonists, Yehoshua answered that his protagonists might still be alienated, perhaps because the Israeli political reality is more changeable and problematic than it once was. In "Facing the Forests," for example, the watchman confronts a stable reality, serene and clear, and tries, through his own failure, to bring about the "failure" of that reality and to reveal its weak spot. In Israeli literature, the depiction of war may be unavoidable, he said, yet the writer must try to evade it, and not make it the "leading vehicle" of a story.

What can we conclude so far from all this? The 1948 generation of Israeli writers were blessed with a sense of the rightness of Israel's claim and the certainty of ultimate victory. Their connection to the Jewish past served to strengthen that feeling. For the generation of A. B. Yehoshua, however, no such certainty is forthcoming. Instead, he and the writers of his generation have become increasingly aware of the complexity of Israel's claim; the surely dubious justification of the present by linking it to the past; the ambiguity of Israel's situation in light of the Arab counterclaim; and the consequent ambiguity of the position of the individual Israeli. A situation of this sort has, in the history of other nations, worked its way into rich and vital literatures (e.g., that of Ireland in the early years of this century). Yehoshua's elaborate recognition of the ambivalence of the claims and counterclaims, in *Between Right and Right,* is one result.[3]

What we may now consider is the way Yehoshua's sense of ambiguity has affected his fiction. His style has always been terse and carefully fashioned. The main sources for his world of allusion are the Hebrew language and the Bible. The biblical myths are part of his upbringing (although he does not link them to his upbringing in his fiction). Even more prominent as an influence, however, is the Israeli landscape, which almost serves as a protagonist in his fiction. And for Yehoshua that landscape is connected to war:

> War has deepened the sense of landscape, has brought its details to the fore, and has personalized it. The concept "a place where our blood ran" intermeshes landscape with political ideas. Love and fear, a desire to flee and a desire to establish contact, are powerfully fused in the Israeli's relationship to landscape.[4]

In his fiction, it is space more than time that is given weight and importance. Sometimes the spaces he depicts are metonyms of temporality—an abandoned village, a distant forest planted at a certain time, the desert with its biblical and modern allusions. The human protagonist in Yehoshua is an individual moving through space, changing location as his self-realization emerges. We have noted that for Yehoshua the landscape is connected to war, and this is where the process of self-realization is manifested. What the writer seeks to show is the insidious way that war can become the chief motivating factor for individuals—individually deployed in space but not in time—so that it becomes both the problem and its solution, an utterly frightening proposition for Yehoshua.

In "The Last Commander" he gives us an anti-war story about the senselessness of pursuing the fight for its own sake.[5] The story has apocalyptic overtones, on one hand, and the inverted archetype of the creation of the universe, on the other. This early work has three elements that will characterize his writings into the 1980s. First, the reality described seems quite ordinary, except that the ordinary is essentially extraordinary because the causal element is missing in the flow of events. Second, Yehoshua inverts biblical myths, thus making the implausible plausible in a modern fictional milieu. Third, a certain quest exists, concomitantly with a sense of deep malaise.

The story is about the fatigue and the embracing of sleep-cum-death by a generation saturated and satiated with war. Maneuvers are under way, as a reprise of the preceding war (a bloody one) and as inevitable rehearsal for the coming one. There is a dimension of allegory in the fact that the dark figure Yagnon (whose name, ironically, has the etymological root GNN, "to defend"), who is the deputy commander, falls asleep; he represents inertia; and chaos reigns for seven days. These are seven days of the undoing of Creation, that act which created order, names, meanings, goals, and the projection to the future. They are seven blissful days of the men's total return to the primitive desire to be objects rather than men and soldiers. Then there are seven more days, wherein the new (and last) commander, symbolized by light, restores the world. But after his departure, it is obvious that Yagnon and his men will return to chaotic disorder once more, and to a Sartrean *mauvaise foi*. Thus, "The Last Commander" is more than an anti-war story; it is a story of the anti-rational tendency in all things human. This theme will receive further development in "Facing the Forests"—i.e., that history is dialectical, and destruction and rebirth are its inevitable aspects.

"Facing the Forests" is a landmark work in the relation toward the Arab in modern Hebrew literature.[6] Yet it is comparable in impact to the works of an earlier generation: Yizhar's "The Prisoner" and "Hirbet Hizah" and Shenhar's "The Tamarisk." There is also a closer comparison to be made between "The Tamarisk" and "Facing the Forests"—in plot and protagonists, despite the great difference in world outlook. Both stories depict an Arab and a Jew; in both stories the two protagonists are strongly connected to the land. In "The Tamarisk" the two are killed—the Jew by the Arab, and the Arab by another Arab; the blood of both seeps into the roots of the tamarisk. As in Yizhar and Yehoshua, the landscape (for Shenhar) is the meeting ground for man and his true purpose. All the writers mentioned, along with Amos Oz and Benjamin Tammuz, introduce the problem of the true ownership of the land. To Shenhar, the real deed to the land is in Genesis. Yizhar, who is essentially *a*political as a writer, presents the conflicting claims. But in Yehoshua's writing, there is greater uncertainty about the right to the land.

Whatever their differences, however, these writers are united in rejecting as alien the western ways others have brought: they do not want to reproduce the Jewish Diaspora in the land of Israel. Thus they reflect the view of the earlier Cana'anite movement that began in pre–1948 days: namely, that the connection to the land supersedes all Jewish history.

The sense of connection to the land brings with it the biblical suggestion of native sons fighting over a contested birthright; it also suggests that Man (on either side) inevitably brings destruction to the land. In "Facing the Forests," the Arab burns the forest. All this has the purpose of enabling us to see the Arab-Israeli conflict in emblematic terms: man as destroyer, man's presence as catastrophic.

The basic theme of this study, that the image of the Arab in Israeli literature is closely tied to the self-definition of the Israeli, is abundantly demonstrated in the 1963 novella "Facing the Forests." The story is apparently simple in structure, though baffling in meaning: its Israeli protagonist is an "eternal student"—a man in his thirties who has been residing in Jerusalem. (The time is the late 1950s or early '60s.) He is alienated, is spiritually uprooted, has not completed his studies, and is living an unstructured life. His friends (whose wives he beds) decide that solitude will encourage him to finish his studies: they decide on a thesis topic for him (the Crusades from the aspect of the Church); and they secure a source of income for him, getting him a six-month appointment as fire-watcher in one of the forests south of Jerusalem. The place is desolate except for an Arab (whose tongue has been cut out) and his daughter. On the day before the job is over, the Arab burns the forest completely—with the tacit consent of the Israeli protagonist, or at least with his knowledge—and afterwards the Israeli (who is unnamed) returns to Jerusalem.

If the story is read solely on the literal level, it can be seen to portray the erratic behavior of a strange young man; and the element of willful self-destructiveness can be understood if we assume that we are reading a psychological novella. Self-hatred and self-destructiveness are bona fide themes in Yehoshua's early work and in modern literature in general, and therefore one ought not to rule out this interpretive approach to the work.

The young man fails to emulate the two "father" prototypes (his own father and the man in charge of the Department of Forestry), and he therefore takes as his model the mute Arab. With the burning of the forest, the Israeli is transformed—from someone who did not know that there are forests in Israel to an individual with a past, from a cipher out of touch with his world to a person with a cultural memory. It is his "memory" that now is his claim to ownership. On the other hand, the forest had been planted on the ruins of the Arab's village, and this accounts for his act of arson. Yet the burning of the forest is the culmination of the Israeli's "education"; it is his initiation to the status of native son, and it gives him a claim to the land. Tragically, it is not hatred but rather a deepened understanding which lets the Israeli await the fire. The language of the two men is that of fire, war, destruction; struggle is their only area of contact. Yet the Arab has been the Israeli's teacher, teaching him the secret of clinging to the soil. Indirectly, it suggests that the Diaspora is no longer a solution: it is *this* land that must be built up, and the forest cannot be moved to another place.

All these themes, perennial in the writings of Yehoshua, emerge from a literal reading. But there are other themes here, and a "deeper" reading will expose them. For one thing, the novella can be read as a metaphor for the "Israeli situation," a metaphor whereby the forest is the land (and emphatically not the state), and the two figures represent two successive stages in the struggle for ownership of the land. But these two readings, the literal and the symbolic, can function simultaneously. Their combination, indeed, will create a metaphor in and of itself.

The opening sentence reads: "Another winter lost in fog" (p. 131). This sets the Israeli protagonist against the background of his inactivity and inertia. Rootless and jobless, he is a parasite living off others. (At what point, we may ask, does the protagonist become a symbol of Israel?) His eyesight is defective; but here there are also metaphoric overtones: his poor vision relates to his faulty self-perception, and to his blurred view of the land he inhabits. His friends, who pity and/or envy him, arrange for his removal to the solitary job; his disdain for order and routine threatens their petit-bourgeois feelings. Told that there might be a job as a fire-watcher in a forest, he responds, myopically, "What forests? Since when do we have forests in this country?" (p. 133) The man in charge of the Department of Forestry is a living symbol of the country's founding fathers. The job interview is hostile, even disastrous. When the protagonist repeats his question, sarcastically, as to whether there are forests in this country, the old director responds by asking the candidate whether he knows what is happening in this country at all (p. 135). Perhaps he needs a stronger pair of glasses.

The Crusade theme (i.e., his thesis topic) is significant; in certain Arab quarters, Israelis are perceived as modern-day Crusaders.[7] That is, they are seen as intruders from the West who have come east and are a temporary nuisance. In another reading the fire-watcher, with his western background, is implicitly opposed to the role he will eventually adopt, after being transformed from a rootless individual into a person with a cultural memory. He will undergo a metamorphosis. (For example, he will neglect his research, and he will study the forest as his "text.") At the outset, he relates to this adventure as one more of the kind he has experienced and dismissed: it "will go the way of all others and be drowned in somnolence" (p. 136). On the way to the forest (and his awakening), he loses his sense of

direction (symbolically). In answer to his question about food arrange-
ments, he is told that the Arab will take care of everything—an ironic
foreshadowing of future events. Upon arrival, he situates himself on the
second floor of the observation building, facing the forest. He is equipped
with a telephone, binoculars, and a sheet of instructions, all symbols of
western civilization, and all to be consumed by the eventual fire, along
with his books and clothes (his spiritual and physical coverings).

At the beginning of his six-month stay, the Israeli relies mainly on his
binoculars. Eventually he adjusts his eyes to see the forest. Yet he relates to
the forest externally (unlike the Arab, who does not "face" the forest but is
within it). His scholarly demeanor puzzles the Arab and his young daughter. His relation to the Arab is supercilious. Noting that the Arab is mute,
he speculates, "His tongue was cut out during the war. By one of them or
one of us? Does it matter?" (p. 140)

For writers of the 1948 generation, the cut tongue would have served as
the basis for an entire story. But that is (as we observed) because that
generation was concerned with war, and with suffering, from the standpoint of good and evil. Yehoshua is beyond this, and questions of right and
wrong are no longer pertinent. Rather, the choice, for him, is between right
and right—in both senses of the word.

The Israeli protagonist in "Facing the Forests" is fascinated by fire and by
the possibility of it. Clearly, fire is basic to the story—in the sense of
limitation and inevitability. The presence of the two men, the Israeli and
the Arab, must bring the fire about.

The image of the father is of central importance in Yehoshua's fiction. He
frequently represents authority, but in most cases he is not a model for
emulation. The flight from authority is often a flight from the models that
had been established by the founding fathers of Israel, for whom Zionism
and social justice were elementary doctrine. The perennial predicament,
however, has been that the sons cannot follow in the footsteps of the
fathers, yet have no other models to follow. The cruel irony is that the land
was built by idealists who were not native sons; their offspring, the native
sons, are no longer builders and have lost whatever idealism they may have
had. Thus, in the fiction of Yehoshua and Amos Oz, the image presented
by the father is often pathetic: he is either a tyrant who sacrifices his son on
the altar of his ideals, or (as in many of Yehoshua's stories) he is a man who
has lost direction altogether. But in general the image of the father represents the impotence of the old generation. In "Facing the Forests" the father
of the protagonist presents just such a figure. As he does not manage to
create meaningful contact with his son, so he fails in his contact with the
Arab. Yehoshua has this revealing passage (the prose is in a non-temporal
present):

> In the evening the father tries to become friendly with the Arab and his
> child. A few words of Arabic have stuck in his memory from the days of

his youth, and he will seize any occasion to fill them with meaning. But his pronunciation is unintelligible to the Arab, who only nods his head dully. (p. 144)

Ironically, the eventual contact, superficial though it remains, will be between the two offspring, not between the father and the Arab. In the six months, the Arab girl will blossom into womanhood and take her place as fire-watcher, while the older generation remains unchanged and uncomprehending. The Israeli father, for example, cannot understand why his son, in dealing with the Crusades, does not write of the Jewish aspect, the mass suicides for the sake of the Sanctification of the Name of God. On the other hand, the son's apathy toward the Arab ("By one of them or one of us? Does it matter?") is counterbalanced by the father's inquisitiveness and apprehension:

> During the last days of his visit the father occupies himself with the mute Arab. A host of questions bubbles up in him. Who is the man? Where is he from? Who cut his tongue out? Why? Look, he [the father] has seen hatred in the man's eyes. A creature like that may set the forest on fire yet some day. Why not? (p. 144)

Yet despite his curiosity, the Israeli father (like the son) is described as blind, as having lost his bearings. When the father leaves, he mistakenly waves goodbye to the forest—foreshadowing its inevitable doom.

At one point, following the instruction sheet, the Israeli goes into the forest on his own, thus overcoming the need for the binoculars that distort reality and keep it at a distance. This is his first step toward becoming a son of the land. Like the biblical Abraham, he takes possession of the land by walking in it. This is the beginning of the Israeli's initiation, as the result of which he will be closer to the Arab, yet closer to sensing danger:

> Suddenly he hears voices. He wavers, stops, then sees the little clearing in the wood. The Arab is seated on a pile of rocks, his hoe by his side. The child is talking to him excitedly, describing something with animated gestures. The scout tiptoes nearer, as lightly as his bulk will permit. They are instantly aware of him, sniff his alien being and fall silent. The Arab jumps up, stands by his hoe as though hiding something. He faces them, wordless. It is the Sabbath eve today, isn't it, and there is a yearning in his heart. He stands and stares, for all the world like a supervisor bothered by some obscure triviality. The soft breeze caresses his eyes. If he did not fear for his standing with them he would hum them a little tune, perhaps. He smiles absently, his eyes stray slowly and he withdraws; with as much dignity as he can muster.
>
> The two remain behind, petrified. The child's joy has shriveled halfway through her interrupted story, the Arab starts weeding the thorns at his feet. But the scout has retreated already, gone forth into the empire. He has been wandering in the woods for all of an hour now and is still making new discoveries. (p. 147)

His initiation is slow. At first, there is nothing he can relate to. "There is nothing here, not even some archeology for amateurs" (p. 149). (Again, we might read all this as intended symbolically.) The forest is a novelty for the Israeli, whereas the Arab and his daughter can disappear and reappear in the forest, thereby demonstrating their mastery of it. The occasional hikers, appearing from afar "like a procession of Crusaders" (p. 151), try to draw his attention to the existence of an Arab village nearby. In an authoritative way, he declares that there is no village there, the map must be wrong. But later he realizes that the forest was indeed planted over the ruins of an Arab village, and that the Arab belonged to it. (On the occasion of one of the ceremonies for donors to the Jewish National Fund, the Israeli questions the director about it.) He awakens the Arab and whispers the name of the village in his ear. "The Arab listens and suddenly he understands. An expression of surprise, of wonder and eagerness suffuses all his wrinkles. He jumps up, stands there in his hairy nakedness and flings up a heavy arm in the direction of the window, pointing fervently, hopelessly, at the forest" (p. 153).

As the Israeli becomes more involved in the question, he neglects his research. "For the past few weeks . . . he has been devoting his zeal to one single sheet of paper . . . a map. A map of the area. . . . What interests him in particular is the village buried beneath the trees. . . . His curiosity is of a strictly scientific nature" (p. 157). His "historical" awareness changes the mutual relation between himself and the Arab. As a disinterested "scholar" observing the forest through binoculars, he posed no danger. But as a native son, someone who is interested in the past, he can be seen as having a possessive interest. The Arab has become suspicious.

The Israeli's next encounter with the Arab and the girl, in the middle of the forest, is different. "How light his footstep has grown during the long summer months" (p. 158). His appearing startles them. The forest is no longer an alien territory to him. He intensifies his search—and discovers small tins of kerosene, covered by the girl's discarded dress.

He receives a visit from his aging mistress. Like the other visits—from his father, the hikers, others—this one only points up the temporality of his tenure of the forest. The old generation planted it over the ruined village, and now asks its sons to protect it; he will have to find a reason of his own for being there. The visitors have no true claim to the forest; only the two who watch have a right to it, because theirs is the responsibility for it. But the Israeli's "right" will therefore be over when his job as fire-watcher is finished. Temporality is the negative element throughout. Time tells us only what we do not have. Thus, for example, the humiliated mistress, with her high heels, points up the change between her lover of the past and what he is in the present. Now he is a fire-watcher; he does not remove his binoculars throughout her stay and their lovemaking, and he excuses himself in the middle to scan the forest. She is the last visitor to what is the exclusive domain of the two fire-watchers; her visit and departure mark his break with a shabby and senseless past. The two fire-watchers are the only reality:

> Together, in silence, they return to the forest, their empire, theirs alone. The fire-watcher strides ahead and the Arab tramples on his footsteps. A few clouds, a light breeze. Moonlight pours over the branches and makes them transparent. He leads the Arab over roads that are the same roads always. Barefoot he walks, the Arab, and so still. Round and round he is led, roundabout and to his hideout, amid chiseled stones and silence. The Arab's steps falter. His footfalls lag, die and come alive again. A deathly cold grips the fire-watcher's heart, his hands freeze. He kneels on the rustling earth. Who will give him back all the empty hours? The forest is dark and empty. No one is there. Not one campfire. Just now, when he would dip his hands in fire, warm them a little. He heaps up some brown needles, takes a match, lights it, and the match goes out at once. He takes another and cups his hands around it, strikes, and this one too flares up and dies. The air is damp and traitorous. He rises. The Arab watches him, a gleam of lunatic hope in his eyes. Softly the fire-watcher walks around the pile of stones to the sorry little hideout, picks up a tin of clear liquid and empties it over the heap of pine needles, tosses in a burning match and leaps up with the surging flame—singed, happy. At last he, too, is lit up a little. Stunned, the Arab goes down on his knees. The fire-watcher spreads his palms over the flame and the Arab does likewise. Their bodies press in on the fire, which has already reached its highest pitch. He might leave the flame now and go and bathe in the sea. Time, time wasting here among the trees, will do his work for him. He muses, his mind distracted. The fire shows signs of languishing, little by little it dies at his feet. The Arab's face takes on a look of bitter disappointment. The bonfire fades. Last sparks are stamped out meticulously. Thus far it was only a lesson. (p. 163)

How should we interpret the beginning of the understanding which will culminate in the burning of the forest? Should we see it as a moral outcry of the Israeli who, through a deep sense of justice, feels that the burning of the forest will atone for the destruction of the village? Or rather as the tacit act of a disturbed individual who, after suspending all social norms, sees himself as the master of the forest and as therefore having the right to burn it? (Is he, as some critics have suggested, suffering from personal tensions that find their outlet in his mute consent to the arson?)

At the beginning of the story, his dreams consisted of "a yellow waste, where a few stunted trees may spring up in a moment of grace, and a naked woman" (p. 131). These reveal his emptiness and aridity—to be replaced by his obsessiveness and a wordless covenant between the two men:

> The idea has taken hold in his dim consciousness that he is being called insistently to an encounter at the edge of the forest, at its other end. But

when he plunges out of the forest and arrives there, whether it be at night or at noon or in the early dawn, he finds nothing but a yellow waste, a strange valley, a kind of cursed dream. And he will stand there for a long time, facing the empty treeless silence and feeling that the encounter is taking place, is being successful even though it happens wordlessly. He has spent a whole spring and a long summer never once properly sleeping, and what wonder is it if these last days should be like a trance. (p. 164)

Once he realizes that he can risk staying among the trees, and not merely facing them, he relates to the young girl in a new way: he places her in his seat, and teaches her the Hebrew word for "fire"—*esh*. Here, this is suggestively connected to the word for "woman," *isha*, to symbolize the fact that the girl has become a woman. Her father chains her to the chair to curb her restlessness. With this, the two men are somehow drawn closer to one another—even though the Israeli (as we saw) begins to pose a threat with his growing interest in the land. Something of an ambivalent "dialogue" arises between the two:

He can therefore afford to stay among the trees, not facing them. In order to soothe his conscience he sits the girl in his chair. It has taken less than a minute to teach her the Hebrew word for "fire." How she has grown up during his stay here! She is like a noble mare now with marvelous eyes. Unexpectedly her limbs have ripened, her filth become a woman's smell. At first her old father had been forced to chain her to the chair, or she would have escaped. Yes, the old Arab has grown very attached to the negligent fire-watcher, follows him wherever he goes. Ever since the night when the two of them hugged the little bonfire the Arab, too, has grown languid. He has abandoned his eternal hoe. The grass is turning yellow under his feet, the thistles multiply. The fire-watcher will be lying on the ground and see the dusky face thrusting at him through the branches. As a rule he ignores the Arab, continues lying with his eyes on the sky. But sometimes he calms him and the man comes and kneels by his side, his heavy eyes wild with terror and hope. Perhaps he too will fail to convey anything and it will all remain dark.

The fire-watcher talks to him therefore, quietly, reasonably, in a positive didactic manner. He tells him about the Crusades, and the other bends his head and absorbs the hard, alien words as one absorbing a melody. He tells him about the fervor, about the cruelty, about Jews committing suicide, about the Children's Crusade; things he has picked up from the books, the unfounded theories he has framed himself. His voice is warm, alive with imagination. The Arab listens with mounting tension and is filled with hate. When they return at twilight, lit by a soft autumnal glow, the fire-watcher will lead the Arab to the tree-engulfed house and will linger for a moment. Then the Arab explains something with hurried, confused gestures, squirming his severed tongue, tossing his head. He wishes to say that this is his house and that there used to be a village here as well and that they have simply hidden it all, buried it in the big forest. (pp. 165–66)

With this unspoken dialogue, some degree of openness is created, although it is immediately limited:

> The fire-watcher looks on at this pantomime and his heart fills with joy. What is it that arouses such passion in the Arab? Apparently his wives had been murdered here as well. A dark affair, no doubt. Gradually he moves away, pretending not to understand. Did there used to be a village here? He sees nothing but trees.
>   More and more the Arab clings to him. They sit here, the three of them like a family, in the room on the second floor. (p. 166)

(They no longer occupy separate floors; the distinction between the watcher and the laborer is erased; the Arab, like the Jew, is in charge of the forest.)

Once again, the temporal element is destructive, and the instrument of time is the fire, devastating space (and ownership). "Time, time wasting here among the trees, will do his work for him" (p. 163). Or, in my own more exact translation: "What the will cannot accomplish time will do—the idle time cast amongst the trees."

There is, then, an insinuation of the horrifying idea that the only dialogue possible is through fire (i.e., war). "He is happy. Where is the Arab now? The Arab speaks to him out of the fire, wishes to say everything, everything and at once. Will he understand?" (p. 168) The fire, therefore, turns apprehension into reality. While his mistress was there, he had said: "I am still awaiting the conflagration" (p. 162). Now, amid the fire, "The earth is casting its shackles" (p. 169).

Indirectly, the idea of fire is connected to every danger the Jew can fear in the Diaspora. Every destruction of land meant a move (provided it was only land and property, not people, that were destroyed). Since it is a deep-seated dread, it distorts reality. "For a moment it seems as though the forest had never burnt down but had simply pulled up its roots and gone off on a journey, far off on a journey, far off to the sea, for instance, which has suddenly come into view" (p. 169).

What survived the fire? And what was consumed? As we saw, the fire consumed all his "false" temporal props—books and clothes, binoculars, the telephone—all connected with western culture. What survived were the things connected with the region: memory, history. Although in the subsequent investigation the Arab is implicated, "there is a gratified expression in his eyes now, a sense of achievement" (p. 173). Finally, it is the Israeli who is blamed.

He appears to have lost everything. He has not completed his thesis (he hardly began it), and he returns to the city, in his long beard and tattered clothes, apparently poorer than when he left. But this is a superficial reading. In actuality he has gained what the Arab had: memory, roots in a land that usually rejects what is new and what is hurtful to it. The Arab has given him a sense of belonging to the land, even if fire is its fatal reality. In its growth and destruction, the land is the meeting place of all its histories; its true owners are they who build and destroy it. In the process, its nakedness is revealed—along with the nakedness of the Israeli who has lost his western trappings. The fire is the power that creates history, giving the Israeli and the Arab a joint memory and a joint claim to the land.

> He returns to Jerusalem:
> At night, in some shabby hotel room, he is free to have a proper sleep, to sleep free from obligations for the first time, just sleep without any further dimensions. Except that he will not fall asleep, will only go on drowsing. Green forests will spring up before his troubled eyes. He may yet smart with sorrow and yearning, may feel constricted because he is shut in by four walls, not three.
> And so it will be the day after, and perhaps all the days to come. The solitude has proved a success. True, his notes have burned along with the books, but if anyone thinks that he does not remember—he does. (p. 174)

This novella has been given numerous interpretations, and apparently an "anti-Zionist" as well as a "Zionist" reading seems possible. If the fire-watcher is seen as complicitous in the burning of the forest, then that would suggest anti-Zionist sentiment on his part, possibly as the result of guilt regarding the wrong that was done to the Arab in the story. We may also see the fire-watcher as a "modern" existential figure, thrown into a situation he cannot change. His quenching the fire will not alter the fact that the land is contested by two opposed parties. Moreover, his "modernity" is reflected in the destructiveness extending from all sorts of appropriate forces: anomie, alienation, the "spiritual malaise" that is so widely discussed of late. Thus, had Yehoshua written a story in which the uprooted Israeli protagonist prevents the fire and becomes a national hero, it would have seemed entirely out of place for its time, and more appropriate to the Hebrew fiction in Palestine between the two world wars.

There is an even deeper consideration at work here: namely, the suggestion that in order for the uprooted Israeli to become a native son, he must shed the trappings of western tradition. Yet that means the rejection of classical Zionism, which was formulated in Europe in the wake of European nationalisms. In the story, the father represents the Jewish consciousness; the man in charge of afforestation stands for the pioneering ethic. The young protagonist cannot follow in their footsteps, since the Arab is not an obvious part of *their* ideological frame of reference; and for parallel reasons he cannot adopt a Zionism that does not acknowledge the voice of the Arab.

Tragically, the Israeli discovers a new basis for Zionism in the burned soil, a Zionism born of fire and war, and perceived with all its tragic ramifications in the reality of the land and its people. Thus we can see the underlying theme of the novella to be a lesson in history—the living history of the land, a place where the "text" is inscribed in the soil, and where the destructiveness of repeated struggles has led only to the undoing of aspirations. The two watchmen speak to one another through fire; this is the only language that creates the native sons, as well as the memory that unites and divides them.

An extremely challenging interpretation of the story has been offered by Mordechai Shalev.[8] Not only is Yehoshua's underlying theme to be found in the younger generation's rejection of the ideology of the forefathers (as I have suggested); Shalev goes further to see that rejection as a war of the younger generation against the Jews. For this war, there are two accomplices: the Arab, and the Christian history apprehended in the protagonist's historical research. The burning of Jews at the stake during the Crusades is replicated by the burning of the forest. The "war" against the founding fathers is thus a new crusade.

What is of the utmost importance to Shalev is not the spiritual malaise of the Israeli, or the destructiveness that is taken to be a reaction to the injustice done to the Arab. What is important is a point Shalev was the first to make, but which has been echoed many times since: namely, that the Arab has become a part of the Israeli in this story, a part of his psychological functioning. The Arab is the "native son" the Israeli wants to be. The two have the same problem: both are oppressed, and both lack a voice. The village is not merely an Arab village; rather, it represents the past against which the Israeli protagonist is struggling, insofar as it represents the idealized agrarian existence that had been envisaged in the Zionist dream as the symbol of a national mission.

For Shalev the story's climax is in the emergence of the village from the ruins of the burned forest: what it leads to is not the Arab's return to his village but the return of the Israeli protagonist to his village. The guilt he feels is not in regard to the Arab but in regard to himself for having left the land for an academic career; and the guilt toward the Arab is but a projection of the more basic guilt, namely, guilt regarding his own existence as an existence that no longer embraces a mission.

Moreover, the Arab and his village represent the past; and the Israeli's complicity in the fire is a destructive act not against the Arab but against the Jew (i.e., the founding fathers). The destructive act "restores" the land to its true character as wasteland. The forest which the older man had tried to create is but a symbol of pagan idolatry. In this act, the character of the son is forged and strengthened; he now has a mission. But since the Arab and the Israeli have become "one," the Arab is a monstrous reflection of the Israeli "sabra"—in his animosity toward the fathers, and in his yearning to recover the real nature of the land by means of a violent struggle with them. The Zionist fathers have failed to transmit a sustained normative system.

In an informal symposium held at Tel Aviv University in May 1985, Yehoshua said that upon rereading the story he was quite proud of it, not for its artistic merits but for the fact that he had dealt with the problem of Palestinian suppression as early as 1962, when he wrote the story. He went on to say that he does not see eye to eye with his friends of the left because of the self-hate he finds in them: he said that he sees in some of them a variation of his protagonist in "Facing the Forests," willing to burn the forest only to discover the skeleton of the village. His protagonist is the destructive power of self-hate, ready to rebel against the establishment and destroy its infrastructure, but without helping the Arab.

Yehoshua admitted that he had not conceived of an Arab in the story when he began to write it. Although it now seems almost too "tailored" to the Arab-Israeli tension, this was not the original aim. He also felt, however, that his Israeli could not burn the forest because it would not be "in character" for an Israeli to do that (given the strongly ingrained feelings Israelis have for afforestation as a national project). For this reason, among others, he had to introduce the Arab into the story. As to the Arab's being mute, Yehoshua felt that if he let him talk, it would strike a false note. Yet the tongueless Arab could function in the story.

Yehoshua's *The Lover*[9] is significant not only for being his first novel (after an impressive output of short stories, plays, and novellas), but also for being the first major novel in modern Israeli literature wherein an Arab is portrayed in fully rounded and realistic fashion. There is perhaps a lesser difficulty in deriving a thematic "meaning" from a work such as "Facing the Forests," where everything is cast in symbolic terms that will convey a symbolic "message." In *The Lover*, where the story is presented entirely in realistic terms, the symbolic message will be harder to extract. Set in Israel immediately after the 1973 war, the novel is structured as a series of monologues by six characters, each of whom relates the events from his or her viewpoint; the constant cross-reference between the characters enables the reader to create an additional point of view by combining the monologues.

The characters are Adam, a well-to-do garage owner; Asya, his wife, who is a history teacher in a high school; Dafi, their teenage daughter; Na'im, an Arab boy of fourteen who works in Adam's garage; Veducha, a ninety-three-year-old Sephardic woman; and Gabriel, her grandson. After a sojourn abroad for ten years, Gabriel returns to claim his inheritance; he becomes Asya's lover, is conscripted into the army during the October War, and subsequently deserts to join an ultra-orthodox Jewish group. The search for the "lover" is what motivates Adam and activates the other characters.

In earlier works of Yehoshua, as we saw, the image of the father is typically tarnished: fathers indirectly transfer the legacy of Judaism and Zionism to their sons, and send them to war. In *The Lover,* the interrelation is more complex: Adam's five-year-old son died in a road accident some years earlier; as a consequence, Adam has been unconsciously seeking a lover for his wife, and a son for himself. Gabriel fulfills the role of the first; he is a weakling, an uprooted intellectual with a history of mental disturbance. Na'im fulfills the role of the second; he reminds Adam and Dafi of the dead boy. Dafi is attracted to him, and the novel concludes with Na'im and Dafi making passionate love.

Both lovers, Na'im and Gabriel, are marginal characters, although they come to occupy the center of this affluent Israeli family whose three members are incomplete and in constant search of completion. Each one touches the one he or she loves through others. This sort of indirection is manifested at numerous points of irony and parody. Na'im, the Arab boy, recites the poetry of Bialik by heart, especially poems of great national Jewish fervor, Jewish martyrdom, and persecution. In himself, Na'im depicts the emptiness of the young Arab generation, attracted to the city, movies, clothes, girls. He is caught between two tidal waves: the transition from the traditional Arab village to the city; and being indirectly involved in the Palestinian cause (one of his brothers is the head of a terrorist unit, and is killed).

Among other things, this novel is something of a *Bildungsroman* of two young people: the rebellious Dafi and the reserved Na'im. Their pent-up energy and lack of direction draw them to one another. The novel is also significant in that the Arab is given a voice, a quest (he would like to continue his studies), and a fulfillment in experience and maturity. Once again, two typical phenomena we encountered earlier recur: first, the fact that the self-definition of the Israeli is made up of the totality of his fears and desires; second, the fact that that self-definition is bound up with irrational, foreign, and even hostile components.

On the surface, it seems that Yehoshua for the first time has produced a realistic story that takes place in definite locales (Haifa and Jerusalem) and a definite time (the short period before and after the October War of 1973). The characters, too, appear altogether believable. Yet the story also has elements that attempt to go beyond "believability" (in the sense of what is typical) and approach uniqueness. Na'im, in his fascination with Adam's family, infiltrates it, is given the key to the apartment, and becomes Dafi's lover with Adam's tacit consent. The same holds true for Adam vis-à-vis Asya and Gabriel. Adam is attracted by the latter's honesty as well as his

1947 Morris auto. Gabriel has been abroad in order to avoid what we have called the Israeli malaise. Deserting the army, he joins (without conviction) the ultra-orthodox group, whose members are not conscripted: thus he is in Jerusalem (where he was born to a noble Sephardic family) and yet is "outside" Israel. He chooses to live within the walls as a way of being outside the unpredictable Israeli situation (because belonging entails danger). With a past of mental illness, he attempts to save his sanity by regressing to the orthodoxy that lives outside time, in its own airless bubble.

In a Hebrew article entitled "The Shadow That Hovers over Us,"[10] the critic Gershon Shaked points to a typical fatigue and impotence in Adam, while Na'im eagerly tries to enter the Israeli world and understand it from within. Shaked also points to the element of self-destructiveness: the Israeli loss of a raison d'être, while the potential enemy acquires a cause. As we have seen, the element of self-destructiveness is an ongoing theme in Yehoshua's fiction: in "The Last Commander" it is manifested in allegorical terms involving Israelis alone; but in "Facing the Forests" and *The Lover*, it involves the Arab as its means of realization.

The Lover can be seen as spanning the duration of Jewish settlement in Palestine—from 1881, the year Veducha was born, to 1973–74, the year of her death. Symbolically, she is Mother Earth and guardian to the three men who touch her life: Adam, her grandson Gabriel, and Na'im, whom she houses and upon whom she becomes dependent. Essentially, it is a novel about freedom and dependence. Love, responsibility, commitment, the past—all spell dependence, while aloneness spells freedom and the right to be. Veducha feels an affinity to Na'im: both despise the food of European Jews; her death coincides with the discovery of her grandson in orthodox Jerusalem and the sexual encounter of Dafi and Na'im. Seen, again, in historical terms, she represents the basic foundation of Jewish presence; Asya's parents (introduced indirectly) represent the wave of immigration of the 1920s; and Adam and Asya are of the generation of 1948, while Dafi and Na'im belong to the post–1967 era. Gabriel is essentially the indeterminate Wandering Jew.

The Arab-Israeli conflict is the ubiquitous concern of the novel's characters. Na'im's brother, the member of the terrorist group, hates Jews and blames them for his not being accepted to the university. When Asya refers to Na'im as an "unfortunate Arab," Dafi's reaction is: "So what if he was an Arab, and why was he unfortunate all of a sudden? Not because he was an Arab. Just like that . . . even if he was a Jew, and what's the difference?" (p. 164) In his first visit to Adam's house, Na'im's sense is that "they really know nothing about us" (p. 165). He speaks Hebrew, and quotes Hebrew poetry (as we saw). But when he quotes, "We are heroes, the last generation to bondage and the first to deliverance" (p. 168), there are ominous undertones emanating from the ironic situation.

Dafi, too, is concerned with the Arab-Israeli problem, and she confronts Na'im, asking him, "Do you hate us very much?" "Hate who?" he asks. "Us, the Israelis," she replies. He answers, "We are Israelis too." When she says: "No . . . I mean Jews," he answers: "Not so much now" (pp. 185–86). At the beginning of the novel, Na'im sees the Israelis relating to the Arabs as if the latter were shadows. Yet he is attracted to the Jews, although he knows that a mutual distrust exists.

Adam's workers are almost all Arabs. He entrusts his business to them, and he muses: "It's a real art, you don't appreciate it, to live this kind of double life among us, to live our world and to live its opposite" (p. 150). To Adam, Na'im is like an adopted son. He is equally indispensable to Veducha, who thinks of him "like the little grandson that I once had years ago . . . there's a light in the house again. . . . I talk to him in Arabic to make him feel at home, but he answers in Hebrew, that's how far they've infiltrated us" (pp. 208–209).

Na'im and Dafi talk politics, and grow closer to one another, despite the unseen barrier. Na'im's immersion in Israeli existence contains serious as well as ridiculous elements; his attraction to action movies carries the danger of a loss of identity. In one of his dreams he answers a question by saying, "I'm a Jew as well" (p. 228). Eventually, Na'im is no longer identified as an Arab. "They didn't realize I was an Arab, nobody does these days, not the Jews anyway. Only the Arabs are still not quite sure about me. Has something about me changed? Am I not exactly myself any longer?" (p. 242)

To Na'im, the sense of freedom is welcome, although foreign. He enjoys his new independence, where father or uncle no longer plays a role—but he has a feeling of having been forgotten by one and all. He no longer belongs to the Arab milieu, and he is as yet outside the Israeli milieu.

It is possible to distinguish two periods, and eventually two modes, in the Hebrew narrative written in the Land of Israel since the end of the nineteenth century. One mode is clearly realistic, and deals with such specific problems as land settlement, land recovery, water shortage, friction with the Turkish and Arab population, etc. These problems were portrayed in the traditional narrative form based on verisimilitude and proximity to reality. At best, these were complex narratives depicting the Jewish newcomers in the struggle for survival; at worst, these stories were episodic, using two-dimensional characters and offering simplistic ideological solutions.

The second mode—symbolic, meta-realistic, ironic—has prevailed in Hebrew writing in the Land of Israel over the last eighty years. The forefathers of this complex mode are Brenner and Agnon. The orientation of the first mode is external, spatial; the orientation of the second is internal, temporal. The second mode will involve a synoptic view of time, and therefore will utilize symbol and metaphor, which can escape the limits of realistic description. This distinction between the realistic and the symbolic modes has persisted to the present day, and any one writer can embrace both, as we have seen in the case of Yehoshua.

The early fiction of Yehoshua was also influenced profoundly by the tales of Franz Kafka. Yehoshua was fascinated by the possibility of creating modern fantasy; he wrote realistic tales set in landscapes of remote vistas. Dostoevsky provided the example of psychological writing built on contrast and paradox. Above all, what typifies Yehoshua and his generation is the depiction of conflict and alienation. The final product is marked by irony and the absence of identification with a fixed ideology; on the contrary, Yehoshua and his generation are marked by ambiguity and uncertainty in theme and treatment—and for this, there is ample use of symbolism, allegory, and fantasy. Naturally, this creates for the reader problems of interpretation that do not arise in reading the work of writers in the realistic mode, or writers of an earlier generation in general.

There is also a difference between the generations in regard to education and early experience. Yehoshua and his generation were not sent into battle at an early age. They attended universities, were open to the world of literature and philosophy, and were influenced by forces as diverse as French existentialism and the poetry of Eliot and Auden. With this, we must not overlook the social changes that took place in Israel in its first decades of statehood: changes in values and population, the flux of immigration from post-Holocaust Europe and from Arabic-speaking countries—and this served to shatter the ideological infrastructure that had been established and reinforced between two world wars, an infrastructure with its foundations in Zionism and Socialism.

One remarkable feature about Yehoshua is the pattern of development of his fiction. He began by adopting a meta-realistic mode of narration, emphasizing the fluidity between the story and its meaning. He himself speaks of this as his "allegorical" period—and here his debt to Kafka, Agnon, and existentialist thought is indisputable. But in time he came to neglect the tales, anti-tales, open fables—where the impossible becomes possible—and came closer to a realistic mode. And yet, even in his realistic mode, horror becomes almost commonplace—which only serves to increase the horror. Along with this, there are elements that have been prevalent throughout his work: the elements of destruction and disintegration.

These literary elements obviously have their source in historical experience: World War II and the Holocaust; the wars Israel has endured since 1948; the friction between Arabs and Jews from the days of the Ottoman Empire, through the British Mandate—all this and more has been distilled, in various ways, to find expression as destruction and disintegration at different levels and in varying modes of narration. In Yehoshua's work these themes are given different degrees of force and focus, from the early writings of a more surrealistic nature, wherein causality is suspended, to the recent work, where the realistic mode is very much in evidence.

Yehoshua is also adept at the art of ironic inversion—inverting not only the basic myths and archetypes, and the expectations of the reader, but also the conventional values of Israeli society (as in "The Last Commander"). Together with such inversions there is the element of indeterminacy, the swift changes in the state of mind of the Israeli protagonist, in the oscillation from a siege mentality to the euphoria of victory. The alteration in mood between 1967 and 1973, for example, has served to erode what were fictional certainties, to the point where the reader's willing suspension of disbelief is severely taxed.

All the features I have mentioned have a direct bearing on the Israeli portrayal of the Arab. But perhaps the most fundamental feature in that portrayal will be the author's general relation to his protagonist. The Yehoshua protagonist typically is a lonely individual—in the long tradition of the uprooted one who inhabits Hebrew literature since the 1880s and re-emerges in the 1960s. This model was suspended in the work of the 1948 generation, with its emphasis on the collective voice, to give way once more to the individual character who places the societal code in abeyance. Thus, instead of the collective voice, Yehoshua's generation emphasizes the personal viewpoint, with its moral indignation at society, and anarchic tendencies that can challenge the national consensus.

In addition to all this, literature can reconstitute the Arab-Israeli conflict in terms of myths and archetypes, or see that conflict as reflecting the deeper primordial struggle between man and man. There is a strong mythic element in "The Last Commander" and "Facing the Forests," and these narratives gain much of their strength from their mythic tonality. Perhaps the ultimate extension of that approach is for literature to see the Arab-Israeli conflict in fatalistic terms. Then the reader is made to wonder to what extent that contest has already been decided, i.e., to what extent the fate of Israel has been determined by cyclical patterns of history, so that the present protagonists are seen as mere pawns in an ancient game.

Many of the interpretations of Yehoshua that have emphasized the elements of destructiveness, disintegration, insanity, and violence have failed to give sufficient attention to the biblical substructure of his fiction. Other interpretations have seen the Binding of Isaac as a basic theme. Yet Yehoshua inverts that story: fathers willingly sacrifice their sons, with no need of a divine command to do so (so there is no need of the Kierkegaardian "suspension of the ethical" at the behest of an unquestionable authority). Rather, the sons were sacrificed for the ultimate materialization of the values of the preceding generation, the Founding Fathers of the State of Israel. This, then, is the implicit viewpoint some critics have found in Yehoshua's fiction. More recently, however, Yehoshua has explicitly re-

jected the cogency of the myth itself, in its applicability to the present-day
Israeli situation. Thus, in *Between Right and Right*, he says:

> Often attempts have been made to apply to the Israeli situation the
> greatest and most important Jewish myth: the *Akeda*, the binding of Isaac.
> Despite the many attempts of this sort, and despite the fact that art and
> literature have used metaphors borrowed from this myth, I believe that
> basically it is irrelevant to the true feeling of Israeli reality. The fathers have
> not sent their sons to death in the name of some idea. First of all, the
> fathers themselves went to fight a war, the justice of which they thor-
> oughly clarified to themselves, and the sons followed the fathers of their
> own free will, not on behalf of anybody else. Here the situation was in no
> way that of an all-knowing, believing father sending his passive son off to
> slaughter. The myth of the *Akeda* was much more applicable to the acts of
> martyrdom, of sanctification of the Name, performed in the *Golah* in the
> Middle Ages. There the model of the myth was applicable; here it is
> essentially irrelevant. (pp. 173–74)

Nevertheless, the *Akeda* theme is ineluctably present throughout
Yehoshua's fiction—not only in "The Last Commander," "Facing the For-
ests," and *The Lover*, as we have seen, but also in his novella "Early in the
Summer of 1970."

Beyond this, Yehoshua sees the present situation of Israeli society as
emblematic of a deeper state of affairs besetting man in the latter part of this
century. Siege, strife, and war are therefore seen as in no way local conditions but as part of a broader twentieth-century neurosis. The myth that
human nature is perfectible has been roundly challenged by the history of
our time. And Yehoshua has been influenced by Dostoyevsky, and later
existentialist writers, to question the idea that men naturally seek goodness
and happiness.

Is the Israeli situation, then, a malady with no cure? Is it immersed in
inescapable self-deceit? Should the Israeli forsake all ideals for mere subsistence, as in "The Last Commander"? Ideals are usually expressed in
"texts"—the Bible, codes of law, implicit social conventions, etc. In "Facing
the Forests," the protagonist renounces all "texts" and is left (symbolically)
with nothing more than a map of the land. But can this new "text" fail us,
as the old "text" has? The theme of the failure of the "text" has been
prevalent in Hebrew literature for the last two centuries: e.g., Enlightenment writers rejected the Talmud as the source of man's spiritual suste-
nance; in contemporary Israeli literature, the Zionist/Socialist ideals are the
rejected "text." (Thus the theme of the Binding of Isaac, with faith attached
to the *suspension* of ethical/social values, is so much more tragic in
Yehoshua than it might otherwise be: it is a secular sacrifice, sending sons
to their death during a spiritual eclipse when all justification is lacking, and

ideological certainty has given way to what is fortuitous, senseless, absurd.)

Why does Yehoshua choose the symbolic, the allegorical, the surrealistic as a mode of expression? Why does he write inverted anti-fables about states of alienation? Is it a form of escapism? Is he like Moshe Smilansky, who, at the turn of the century (in the harsh days of the Second Aliyah), preferred to write folk tales about the life of Arab nomads rather than face the dire reality of the encounter of European settlers with the land of Israel? Although the question could be academic, in view of Yehoshua's realistic turn since the late 1970s there is little doubt that the realistic mode—whether practiced by Yehoshua or the writers of his generation or the 1948 generation—cannot be adequate to address the complexities of the present situation, its ironies and paradoxes.

Clearly, Yehoshua's fiction has a tragic sense about it, an awareness of the unrelieved tension between appearance and the ideal, between "is" and "ought," seeming and being. His recourse is irony—yet it is an irony not of language or tone but of situation: in "Facing the Forests" the voice of the mute is heard. In a traditional tale, the irony may be dissolved when the truths are revealed, in a tension "between right and right," the Israeli's and the Arab's, that of the Fathers and that of the Sons.

In the 1985 symposium, Yehoshua said that the realistic way in which the Arab was depicted in the fiction of the 1970s is no longer feasible in the 1980s—namely, portraying an Arab as an independently credible character such as Na'im in *The Lover*. A character must be capable of being depicted with humor on the part of the author, at least in principle, and this is no longer possible with an Arab character in Israeli fiction. In a conversation in July 1987, Yehoshua amplified this concept, telling me that in fiction involving Arab-Israeli relations two things are taboo: sex and humor. With Na'im, Yehoshua broke the taboo on sex between Arabs and Israelis in a conclusive way (even though there is an ambiguous sexual "encounter" in Amos Oz's 1963 story "Nomad and Viper"). As for humor, Yehoshua pointed out that for him humor does not mean comedy; there is humor to be found in Kafka's darkest stories, he said. As he sees it, the mixture of guilt and anger (vis-à-vis the Arab) makes it impossible to depict an Arab in an easy and believable way, and it neutralizes all humor. Na'im, a creature of the 1970s, not the '80s, was conceived by Yehoshua in sympathy and humor, as he worked on his novel in the Bodleian Library during his sabbatical. Perhaps that is why Na'im is himself a sympathetic character. In the 1980s, it seems that Israeli society is no longer a model for emulation by Arabs. For all these reasons, Yehoshua said it is unlikely that he would include another Arab in his fiction in the foreseeable future.

12. AMOS OZ

Amos Oz is a contemporary of A. B. Yehoshua. In Yehoshua's fiction, as we have seen, it is the Arab's social and political existence (within Israeli society) that is taken up, to be treated in either a realistic or a symbolic fashion. The emphasis, therefore, is on what can be depicted in terms of external elements. In the work of Oz, on the other hand, the Arab's sociopolitical existence is internalized in the Israeli, and the Arab becomes the focus of libidinal dreams and fantasies. The fact that the image of the Arab can be made to serve this purpose in Israeli literature is itself a sociopolitical phenomenon—a phenomenon whose significance we can only begin to glimpse at present. Nor can we say conclusively whether this is healthy or pathological, constructive or destructive in the complex of Jewish-Arab relations in Israel. However that may be, the psychological phenomenon is there, and it has engendered a distinct literary approach, with its own problems and aesthetic ambiguities.

As a result of the characteristic ambiguities implicit in this approach, the literary work itself is marked by a deep-seated indeterminacy in content and treatment. The American critic Robert Alter, writing in 1969, had this to say about Amos Oz's novel *My Michael* and the rest of his oeuvre to date:

> What should be noted is the peculiar double edge of his whole literary enterprise. In one sense, it can legitimately be conceived as a document, and a very troubling one, of Israel's state of siege; but at the same time, paradoxically, it bears witness to the complete freedom of consciousness of the Israeli writer, who does not feel compelled to treat the conflict with the Arabs in a context of political "responsibility" but may reshape it into an image of human existence quite beyond politics.[1]

What this tells us is the truism that in literature, a sociopolitical issue can be recast in non-political terms. And yet politics and literature are inevitably intertwined in Israel, and there is no way to evade the political implications in even a supposedly "non-political" literary treatment. It is crucial to bear this in mind when dealing with writers such as Yehoshua and Oz, who have definite ideas concerning the Arab-Israeli situation in Israel and who have taken a decided political stand not necessarily associated with one political faction or another.

In their political writings, Yehoshua and Oz make two points which have a direct bearing on their literary work: the first is their commitment to Zionism, and the ardent belief that the State of Israel is the only true homeland for the Jewish people; the second is their shared perception that the Arab-Israeli conflict vis-à-vis the Land of Israel, is a conflict not between right and wrong but between right and right. Thus the comparable legitimacy of claims on both sides points to a tragic stand-off which defies a solution that could be satisfactory to both sides. With this in mind, they have called for reason and moderation—and the ambient extremism on both sides makes their moderating voice sound all the louder.

Oz expressed his credo in an article that appeared a few months after the 1967 war.[2] Acknowledging his allegiance to Judaism and Zionism, he states:

> I am a Zionist because I will not and cannot exist as a splinter of a symbol in the consciousness of others. Not as the symbol of the shrewd, gifted vampire, and not as the symbol of the sympathetic victim who deserves compensation and atonement. Therefore, there is no place for me in the world other than in the country of the Jews. That does not make me circumvent my responsibility as a Jew, but it saves me from the nightmare of being a symbol in the mind of strangers day and night. (p. 10)

At the same time, he makes a sharp distinction between the Jewish people and the land, and that stance is all the more problematic in the light of Oz's active membership in the Peace Now movement:

> I do not regard myself as a Jew merely by virtue of "race" or as a "Hebrew" merely because I have been born in the land of Canaan. I *choose* to be a Jew. As a Jew, I would not and cannot live anywhere but in a Jewish state. The Jewish State could only come into being in the Land of Israel. That is as far as my Zionism goes. (p. 12)

There are those who would say this is far indeed, and as a viewpoint it carries the seeds of confrontation despite its moderating stance. For that very reason the tragic clash is all the more apparent:

> As I see it the confrontation between the people that returns to Zion and the Arab inhabitants of the country is not like a Western film or a saga, but like a tragedy. Tragedy is not a conflict between "light" and "darkness," between justice and crime. It is a clash between total justice and total justice, even though one should not seek the simplification of symmetry in it. And as in all tragedies, there is no hope of a jubilating conciliation based on a clever compromise formula. The choice is one between a blood-bath and a sad, disappointing compromise, more in the way of accepting the situation by force of necessity than of the sudden break-through of mutual understanding. (p. 15)

The outlook for a resolution of this tragic conflict is inevitably fraught with hurt and harm, and this view will have its implications for his fiction. According to Oz:

> I am not one of those who hold the fatalistic view that there is no other way out of the tragedy than the ultimate defeat of one side in blood and fire. On the other hand, I do not share the melodramatic vision of the two reconciled sides embracing each other as soon as the magic geopolitical formula is found. The best we can expect, in the usual way of tragic situations between individuals and peoples, is a process of adaptation and psychological acceptance accompanied by a slow, agonizing awakening to reality, burdened with bitterness and deprivation, with shattered dreams and suspicions and reservations which, in the way of human wounds, heal slowly and leave permanent scars. (p. 19)

Thus neither a nationalistic romanticism nor dreams of political grandeur or mythic renewal will solve the problem. Rather, what is called for (in Oz's view) is a Zionism that "faces facts"—namely, the equal validity of the conflicting claims.

How political, then, is Oz's fiction? Certainly it is not political in the narrow sense of ideology and indoctrination. Rather, it is concerned with the far-reaching malaise in Israeli society, a malaise shaped by many factors, not the least of which is the Arab presence.

Oz was born in Jerusalem in 1939, four months before the outbreak of World War II. Both parents could be said to have belonged to the class of genteel and cultivated East European Jews. His father was a librarian and scholar with a command of fifteen languages. Amos Oz's Jerusalem childhood left an indelible impression on him and seems to have continued to haunt him. The attitude of his family was right-wing nationalist, and he went to a school that inspired him with dreams of the glory of ancient Israel. In a short autobiographical article, he says, "My childhood in Jerusalem rendered me an expert in comparative fanaticism," and he speaks of that Jerusalem itself as "a lunatic town flooded with conflicting dreams, a vague confederation of communities, peoples, faiths, ideologies and hopes."[3] It is a world filled with messianic dreamers, Arab nationalists who called the Jews "children of death," Christians who sought to be born again, and Jews from all corners of the world.

In 1952, Oz's mother committed suicide. A year later, at the age of fourteen, he joined Kibbutz Hulda and was later accepted to full membership. The contrast with his Jerusalem childhood was stark. He recalls writing biblical poems about blood and fire, and vengeance upon Israel's enemies. In the kibbutz, he attended classes in Socialism, and he believed in the possibility of improving human nature by political means. He admits that he still holds to the collectivist-egalitarian principles, "though with a certain sadness and a mild smile" which make him reject Socialist panaceas for the world or for Israeli politics.

Yet there is a clear dichotomy between Oz's strong political involvement and his highly individualistic and subjectivist fiction reaching to psychological extremes: "And so I wrote about the haunting shadows, about yearnings, fears, hatreds, nightmares, messianic aspirations, longings for the absolute." This approach of his has remained virtually unchanged since the early 1960s. Thus his fiction seems to belie the moderation he adopts as a public figure and political critic. His characters are captivated by fear and desire, they are mired in the irrational—and their tragedy is that they themselves lack a tragic sense. The founding fathers in the kibbutz, for example, are blind to the nature of the Arab presence, and this can be taken as emblematic of the national malaise.

It can be said that Oz exorcises his psychological and political ghosts in his fiction, but he also combines those ghosts and thereby gives them added strength. Thus the Arab is to be found not only in the political arena (as the enemy) but as an extension of the Israeli. In his autobiographical sketch, Oz speaks of himself as "the conjuror of evil spirits." In view of all this, and of the way the self-definition of the Israeli Jew must incorporate his relation to the Israeli Arab, the psychological internalization I noted earlier is altogether inevitable. It is almost as though the face of the Arab has become a part of the persona of the Israeli Jew, a second covering to the mask—and irremovable.

Two of Oz's works of the 1960s, the 1963 story "Nomad and Viper" and the 1968 novel *My Michael*, illustrate these themes. The starting point of our discussion of "Nomad and Viper" is the observation made earlier, namely, that the Arab is no longer a passive character, a predictable entity. Rather, in the work of Yehoshua and Oz, the Arab acquires an operative function in the plot. In "Nomad and Viper" he is the dark stranger posing a danger to the organized world. That organized world is represented by the kibbutz, which is encircled by the wilderness. It would seem, therefore, as though the Arab has remained a stereotype here; but as we shall see, Oz overcomes the stereotype by activating it. If anything, Oz parodies Israeli society, its myths and heroes, and that requires him to give the social stereotypes his full (if ironic) attention.

Among his main targets in the collection of stories titled *Where the Jackals Howl* are the founding fathers of the kibbutz and their Socialist Zionism. They are portrayed in an array of characters, from the innocent and naive to the arrogant and fanatic. As in Yehoshua, these individuals are occasionally represented as those who "bind" their children (as in Abraham and Isaac) to the altar of their ideals. The typical hero in the writings of the 1948 generation is here replaced by the anti-hero, for whom nothing is as clear-cut as it was to his predecessors: alienation, angst, and rootlessness are coupled with a deep sense of *mauvaise foi;* and collective certainty has given way to individual doubt.

"Nomad and Viper"[4] is a story about the kibbutz and the Bedouins who surround it, sporadically pilfering from it and thus bringing a new and strange tone to its characteristic ethos. It is also a story of a young kibbutz woman, Geula, who has an ambiguous encounter with a Bedouin, is bitten by a snake, and dies. The encounter between man and woman is filled with mutual attraction and dark desires, but also with a mixture of fact and fancy, the uncertainties of guilt and innocence embedded in wild accusations. In its outlines the story is based on an old fabula: the dark (and inferior) stranger who rapes the vulnerable white woman. Oz takes this fabula to a high point of mythic archetype, then gives it an ironic inversion challenging the reader's expectations. In doing so, he takes these primordial motifs and plants them amid Israeli reality, as a mark of its schizoid existence, where evil besieges the characters from within and objective uncertainty besets them from without.

The dark Bedouin is a mixture of shrewdness and innocence. His intentions are never quite clear, but the meeting with Geula in the orchard has the potential of a sexual encounter. The very landscape is loaded with erotic allusions, thereby enhancing the tale's epic quality, but also providing a stage for the irrational powers in the human psyche to come forth. The traditional fabula would see her as the victim of the dark power; here she is the initiator of the encounter, and is eventually shocked by her own desires when she fantasizes a rape. In herself she is the anti-heroine, short of figure, with an acned face and excessive perspiration. She is presented in an ironic tone as being poetic and sensitive, but she is a woman in heat. She despises her body, yet entertains the idea of corrupting the young Bedouin, who, until this moment, is virginally innocent. They smoke a cigarette, and this is their sexual rite. After the first cigarette, she asks for another—an indication of her desire to prolong the encounter and bring it to a climax. The young Bedouin cannot fulfill her wishes. Geula is shocked by the revelation of her desires; she leaves and then is bitten by the snake. By activating the suppressed desires of the "civilized" Geula, Oz shows her death to be the consummation of her dream wish and rape fantasy.

Rape occurs on various symbolic levels in the story: the Bedouins "rape" the kibbutz by entering it and stealing, although this cannot be confirmed (while the Bedouin's "rape" of Geula does not reach consummation); the snake "rapes" Geula (and here is another inversion of a traditional motif, in that the temptress/Eve is not lured by the snake but is lured into a sexual act with "Adam"); there is a "rape" in the retaliation taken by the young people of the kibbutz against the marauding Bedouins (although the action does not occur in the story but is only alluded to at the very end). As Geula is lying on the grass after having been bitten, the young people (who shun words) are seen preparing their retaliation.

The only "real" action of the story is that of the snake. It is an account borrowed from the realm of the mythic, except that the serpent here does not speak but bites, and the woman is not its accomplice but its victim. Oz's story is a multi-layered system, reworking traditional archetypes. That is one of the interpretive keys to the story. Another key is to divide the story into the characters' text and the reader's text. The reader's text reflects the Israeli condition (or malaise, in Oz's view); the reader can identify the Israeli setting, and can easily identify the characters who seem to lead a typical Israeli existence, so that the reader's text is highly probabilistic and "realistic." The characters' text, on the other hand, contains mythopoeic elements, such as the Arab who is seen by the female protagonist as projecting an atmosphere of erotic attraction and repulsion.

Although Oz overcomes the stereotyped presentation of the Arab, at least to the extent of giving him a real presence, he does not yet give him a substantial voice (much of his speech is paraphrased, and when he does speak it is in response to Geula); thus the story retains some of the stereotyping qualities. We pointed to the fact that as the image of the Jew had served as the dark figure in the Christian/European subconscious, so the Arab (as a stereotype) serves that purpose in the Jewish/Israeli subconscious. Something of this is suggested in the passage that introduces the Bedouins:

> Dark, sinuous, and wiry, the desert tribesmen trickled along the dirt paths, and with them came their emaciated flocks. They meandered along gullies hidden from town dwellers' eyes. A persistent stream pressed northward, circling the scattered settlements, staring wide-eyed at the sights of the settled land. The dark flocks spread into the fields of golden stubble, tearing and chewing with strong, vengeful teeth. The nomads' bearing was stealthy and subdued; they shrank from watchful eyes. They took pains to avoid encounters. They tried to conceal their presence. (p. 21)

The omnipresent narrator places emphasis on their wiliness, and it would seem that that voice of stereotyping is also part of the story. This, too, is a key to interpreting the story: a stereotyping of a "stranger" or "foreigner" (be he Jew, Arab, or whatever) usually expresses itself in terms that reflect some element of fear. In "Nomad and Viper" the narrator does just this, as when he says that the singing of the Bedouins can be heard at night: their voices "penetrate to the gardens and pathways of the kibbutz and charge our night with an uneasy heaviness" (p. 23). The image of "penetration" here suggests another "rape" or a sense of fear expressed in erotic terms. Oz continues on this erotic plane, and this leads to a question about the identity of the narrating voice: Is it the omnipresent author? the "we" of the kibbutz? the younger generation of those who are eager to take action against the Bedouins? Or is it a definite person in the story (namely,

Geula's erstwhile boyfriend)? Depending on what answer we give, the characterization of the Arab might itself be seen as "characterized" and as an integral part of the plot—or else as an attempt at value-neutral objectivity (although that is unlikely, given the highly "pointed" nature of the characterizations).

Two encounters occur in the story. The first is between the elders of the Bedouin tribe, the kibbutz leaders, and Etkin, the kibbutz secretary, discussing the thieving of the younger Arabs. The nomads are offered coffee prepared by Geula. The Bedouin leader offers platitudes and a mild reprimand of the young people in his tribe. Etkin attempts to speak Arabic, although the Arab speaks Hebrew. Once again Oz mocks the founding fathers of the kibbutz—as a movement—for continuing to believe in the Socialist ideology of the brotherhood of man. Etkin's suggestion of mutual visits between the children of the kibbutz and of the Bedouin encampment is not even acknowledged. The young people of the kibbutz are entirely dissatisfied with the ineffectual way the police have dealt with the Arab marauders, and an urgent meeting is scheduled for discussion of the matter.

The second and more fateful encounter is between Geula and the Arab. A tension has been building up; the night is "damp and hot and close." As Geula (an "old maid") seeks solitude, Oz creates a series of possibilities for further encounters between the two groups—possibilities which do not materialize but which lead the story to its climax in Geula's death. Oz's way of inverting the reader's expectations is to make the Arab "invader" the vulnerable target, and Geula the initiator of aggression. Again she is compared to a beast in heat as she tramples the earth with her bare feet. She sees an abandoned bottle on the ground and kicks it; it does not break. She tries a number of stones, and eventually she smashes it. Her nerves quiver with excitement as she walks decisively toward the orchard. Her actions are loaded with sexuality barely repressed. (Drinking from an irrigation pipe, she lets the water pour over her face and neck and into her shirt. She picks a plum and crushes it; she picks another and rubs it against her cheek so that she is splattered with juice.)

At first, their encounter is silent: she is unaware of the Arab's presence, and only his movement draws her attention. He asks her for the time of day. She tells him. She is hot and perspiring. He is "repulsively handsome" in her eyes. He offers her a cigarette. "She ran the cigarette through her fingers, slowly, dreamily, ironing out the creases, straightening it, and only then did she put it to her lips" (p. 31). She sucks in the flame he offers, then closes her eyes. She becomes aware that as they are smoking, the black goats are attacking the trees. She says, "What are you doing here, anyway? Stealing?" (p. 32) Blinking nervously with his blind eye, he protests that stealing is forbidden by Allah. She answers with irony, quoting the commandments that forbid coveting and adultery. He is baffled by her verbal barrage. He praises her beauty, and he tells her (in his broken Hebrew) that he has had no girl, and he is still "small."

As a goat is devouring some of the foliage, the Arab leaps forward, seizes the animal, lets out a terrifying scream, and flings it to the ground. As he turns back to Geula, a shudder runs down her back; she asks for another cigarette. He picks up a stone to throw at the goat; she restrains his hand. This act of touching, which she initiates, goes beyond the bounds of permissible behavior. She stands over him and begins to mock him for still being "small." He is frightened, begins to pray, and hides himself among his goats.

What has happened between the two? Was there any physical contact (other than the touching of hands)? Has a rape occurred? We do not know with any certainty. It would have been consistent with Oz's method of inversion to have had Geula rape the Arab. Yet there is a built-in ambiguity in the fact that the narrator speaks at times as the omniscient author, and at other times as one of the characters and first-person narrator (with a limited point of view). That ambiguity has positive literary value in the way it enhances the ambiguity of the characters and their situation.

What is significant is that Geula behaves as though she *has* been raped—a reaction brought on by her having been rejected by the Arab goatherd. She opens her mouth to scream, but no sound comes out; she begins to run home in panic, as though she is being pursued. She has been humiliated—close enough to being raped—and she does believe that rape is what the Arab intended and attempted. She considers herself lucky to have escaped, and she even imagines that she had to fight to do so. As she washes herself, she feels it would be a good thing if the young men of the kibbutz were to go to the Bedouin camp: "Yes, let the boys go right away tonight to their camp and smash their black bones because of what they did to me" (p. 35). The "experience" of attempted rape is real enough to make her start crying again, and she vomits into the shrubbery.

At the kibbutz meeting, the young men are after revenge for the Arabs' thievery; they ridicule Etkin's notion that the feud is as old as civilization, going back to Cain and Abel, the original herdsman and the tiller of the soil. The narrator seeks to restrain them, reminding them that there has been no rape or murder. (They are as yet unaware of what has happened to Geula.) Etkin is shocked by the likelihood of eventual publicity about a kibbutz acting as a lynch mob against Arabs. The young people leave the meeting.

In her room, Geula is full of forgiveness as she relives the incident. She remembers the broken bottle she had smashed earlier; apparently there was a viper living in it, and Geula has been bitten. It felt like a sliver of glass. In the earlier version of the story, her encounter with the viper is described in sexual terms, and her feelings afterward are distinctly post-coital: as the venom spreads through her bloodstream, she shivers in pleasure. She listens to the sweet wave of intoxication . . . in total yielding. The 1975 version has excised this passage, and that later version is the basis of the English translation:

> And the living thing slithering among the slivers of glass among the clods of earth was a snake, perhaps a venomous snake, perhaps a viper. It stuck out a forked tongue, and its triangular head was cold and erect. . . . A thorn in her flesh, perhaps a sliver of glass. She was very tired. And the pain was vague, almost pleasant. A distant ringing in her ears. To sleep now. (p. 38)

As the story ends she is at peace. She sees the young men of the kibbutz carrying sticks, on their way to even the score with the Bedouins. In death, "her fingers caressed the dust, and her face was very calm and almost beautiful."

In the novel, *My Michael*,[5] the chief protagonist is a young woman who feels that her life is being consumed by her child and her husband—the child a model of pure reason, and the husband a patient and mediocre man. Hannah Gonen would prefer to feature in her own "text," as it were, not in the text constituting the typical and mundane reality of a young couple facing life in a small apartment and the struggle of completing a doctorate (Michael's). She prefers fantasy to sympathy, even prefers sickness to health, and she creates an imaginary world for herself, in which she can reign. The materials for creating that world involve dreams and even hallucinations, bringing her near to breakdown. She retreats to books she once read (Jules Verne, James Fenimore Cooper), and to the childhood memories of the Arab twins who were her friends during the time of the British Mandate (the early 1940s) in Jerusalem. These dreams and memories have heavily erotic undertones: she is the princess being abducted, humiliated, almost raped by virile men; she wanted to have been born a boy, and she rejects her femininity.

She grows up to be an attractive young woman, studying literature at the Hebrew University in Jerusalem, and working in a kindergarten to support herself. Yet the reality she cherishes is that of her inner world.

Thus far, it would seem that this is to be read as a psychological novel. The "surface" text is the realistic portrayal of a young couple living in Jerusalem in the 1950s; the "deep" text is Hannah's world of dreams and fantasies, the world of a neurotic woman torn between the wish for love and the wish for death (and Oz's richly allusive language creates pictorial equivalents for her states of mind from a limited catalogue of a few childhood memories and adventure stories).

Another "depth" reading is that of Gershon Shaked.[6] Here it is the psychological novel that is the "surface" text. The "deep" text here consists of the irrational archetype gnawing at the heart of Israeli society and at its most idealistic offshoot, the kibbutz. For Shaked, it is the Arab twins (who move from Hannah's childhood into her adult dreams) who constitute the archetypal motif with which she attacks her outer world, yet finds herself besieged. This is indirectly confirmed by the way Hannah sees Jerusalem. (Shaked regards Jerusalem as a major presence in the novel.) The personification of the city as a "wounded woman," its description as surrounded by Arab villages and neighborhoods—all this points to a heroine/city at bay, attacked by winds, dreams, strangers who threaten her from within and from without. The city is the extension of the woman; the two are one soul—and the Sinai War and Hannah's orgiastic hallucinations coincide. Moreover, the Arab twins are explosives that have the potentiality of fictional detonation, the aim of Oz (like that of Yehoshua) being to attack the fortress that is institutionalized Israeli culture.

The Arab twins have a pronounced presence in the novel by way of Hannah's fantasies. They have names—Halil and Aziz—but (as with the Arab in "Nomad and Viper") they are not given a substantial "voice." Undoubtedly, this is Hannah's way of exerting some control in a dream fabric wherein she loses control. Along with Hannah's childhood desire to be male, she had a wish to dominate the boys, though not necessarily as a male: "I was a princess and they were my bodyguard, I was a conqueror and they my officers. . . . I ruled over the twins. It was a cold pleasure, so remote" (p. 9).

As an adult, she continues to reside in the city; the twins fled during the 1948 War. Her desire to recapture her past is paralleled by the fantasy of the twins' desire to return, all representing the Israeli phobic fear of Arab return. The fear is diluted, in Hannah, by the fantasy of her domination, retrojected back to her childhood games. "When I was a child I used to play a game I called 'Princess of the City.' The twins acted the part of submissive subjects. Sometimes I made them act rebellious subjects, and then I would humble them relentlessly. It was an exquisite thrill" (p. 18). The theme is carried forward, indirectly, into adult life, where we see Michael's complete submission to Hannah—although this results in her contempt. Indeed, she fantasizes about the Arab twins because (we might say) their submission is as a game only, never real. In her fantasy they grow, in years and in virility, and the projected shift from her domination to her submission functions in two ways: as a concretization of the fear of Arab return, and as a contrast to Michael's own desire to please her.

The twins now live in her stream of consciousness, where they shed all semblance of realism. Their former submissiveness as children now gives way to their manly forcefulness. She dreams of being in the Arab market in Jericho, carried by two men and thrown violently into a dark cellar. The twins now mock her. They are

a pair of strong gray wolves. . . . Aziz drew out of the folds of his robe a long, glinting knife. There was a gleam in his eyes. He sank down on all fours. His eyes were blazing. The whites of his eyes were dirty and bloodshot. I retreated and pressed my back against the cellar wall. The wall was filthy. A sticky, putrid moisture soaked through my clothes and touched my skin. With my last strength I screamed. (p. 47)

The dream occurs two nights before her wedding, and we could all too easily interpret it in Freudian terms. (Her landlady, who heard her cry out, tells her the next morning that if a girl cries out in her sleep two nights before her marriage, "that is surely a sign of some great trouble." Perhaps Oz is thereby circumventing the Freudian interpretation by mocking it as folk wisdom.)

Later on she feels that Jerusalem, despite its apparent calm, is being slowly surrounded by powers that menace and embrace her: "Even within the walls [there] are whispering pines. Sinister things are plotting by the blind light of dawn. Plotting as if I were not here to hear them. . . . They know that I am here awake and trembling. They are conspiring as if I were not here. Their target is me" (p. 93). The link is now complete between city and woman, with the Arab threatening both. The faces of the threatening Arabs are those of Halil and Aziz:

> Dreams.
>   Hard things plot against me every night. The twins practice throwing hand grenades before dawn among the ravines of the Judean Desert southeast of Jericho. Their twin bodies move in unison. Submachine guns on their shoulders. Worn commando uniforms stained with grease. A blue vein stands out on Halil's forehead. Aziz uncurls and throws. The dry shimmer of the explosion. The hills echo and re-echo, the Dead Sea glows pale behind them like a lake of burning oil. (p. 105)

To be superficially Freudian, again, we can point to the combination of sexuality and violence, Eros and Thanatos, in all this. The ravines, the valleys, all are sources of attack and rape—and all are joined by the wind that unravels the city (p. 119). As Hannah comes closer to derangement, she dreams not only of tanks but of warships entering the city, compounded by military conspiracies instigated by the Arab twins (pp. 198–199). Once again, the betrayal and rebellion are aimed at the princess and the city. Vile forces take over, raping and pillaging. The fall of the dream city culminates in the portrayal of the twins as two assassins, reaching out to her, and with leering, lecherous eyes (pp. 200–201). In her waking hours, her identification with the city is reinforced by the oncoming Sinai War (1957). While the lives of other people are powerfully affected, Hannah continues to function as wife and mother, though living in her private world.

In the Hebrew edition of the novel, Oz noted the date of completion as May 1967. Arab Jerusalem was recaptured by the Israel Defense Forces in

June, at which time it was reunited with western Jerusalem. Hannah's dream war is closer in essence to the 1948 War, when Jerusalem was divided. In another dream (pp. 211f.), Aziz is fighting with Yehuda Gottlieb—the prize is Hannah. (Yehuda is the biblical kingdom of Judah; *Gottlieb* means, in German, "beloved of God.") They fight viciously but soundlessly and inconclusively. The vision ends with a scene of rain, evoking the mountains of Moab, the Dead Sea, the engulfing deserts. The twins are seen again in commando uniforms and are armed with machine guns. There is a fantasy of a lurking man, lying in wait:

> Let him come live and snarling hurl me to the ground and thrust into my body he will growl and I shriek in reply in a rapture of horror and magic of horror and thrill I will scream burn and suck like a vampire a madly whirling drunken ship in the night will I be when he comes at me, singing and seething and floating I will be flooded I will be a foam-flecked mare gliding through the night in the rain the torrents will rush down to flood Jerusalem and the sky will come low, clouds touching the earth and the wild wind will ravage the city. (pp. 214–15)

At the novel's end, Hannah is emotionally unchanged. A certain calm has set in; she is pregnant; she is bemused by a woman colleague who covets Michael. She is also pregnant with more words, more dreams. The twins are there at the end, and she now dreams of setting them free.

We can, of course, raise all sorts of problems of interpretation in this first-person narrative, problems having to do with the voice of the narrator, the voice of the author, and their interrelation. Having entered a nearly deranged mind, however, our suspension of disbelief must be total, since the protagonist herself dissolves the line between "reality" and fantasy. There are some traditional elements here (the aggressive male; the seductive female), but these have been utterly transformed, as we have seen, to the point where the male aggression is distorted by the symbolization provided by the female's unconscious; and the female psyche and its seductiveness are diffused to the extreme of total identification with a city.

Taking the protagonist at her word, then, we must wonder whether Jerusalem is not the true heroine of this story. One way to deal with such a question would be to examine the author's own identification with the city. After the Six-Day War, in June 1967, a series of recordings was made of talks with kibbutz members who had been in the fighting.[7] Amos Oz was among those interviewed, and he recalled that re-entering east Jerusalem (which he had not seen since 1948) was a shock, since he had only the dimmest memories of it, and had since woven it into a fictional entity. He recalled being in Jerusalem when it was under siege, in 1948, and he was a boy of nine: "It was then that I first saw a dead man: a shell fired from the

Arab Legion's gun batteries on Nebi Samuel hit a pious Jew and tore his stomach apart" (p. 237).

His sense of the city of his childhood is expressed as follows (and we should note the sense of foreboding and danger in the string of Arabic names of the surrounding villages):

> A city surrounded at night by the sound of foreign bells, foreign odors, distant views. A ring of hostile villages surrounded the city on three sides: Sha'afat, Wadi Jos, Issawia, Silwan, Azaria, Tsur Bachr, Bet Tsafafa. It seemed as if they had only to clench their hand and Jerusalem would be crushed within their fist. On a winter night you could sense the evil intent that flowed from them toward the city.
>
> There was fear too in Jerusalem. An inner fear that must never be expressed in words, never called by name. It grew, solidified and crystallized in the twisting alleyways and desolate lanes. (p. 238)

The echoes of Hannah's words here are too obvious to need pointing out. The following passage makes the connection even more explicit:

> Jerusalem was often the background for nightmares and dreams of terror. I no longer live in Jerusalem, but in my dreams I am hers and she does not relinquish her hold on me. I would see us both surrounded by enemies. The enemy in my dreams came not only from east, north and south, but completely surrounded us. I saw Jerusalem falling into the hands of her enemies. Destroyed, pillaged and burned, as in the stories of my childhood, as in the Bible, as in the tales of the destruction of the Temple. And I too, with no way of escape, with no place to hide, was trapped in the Jerusalem of my dreams. (p. 239)

And in passages such as the following, the actual language of Hannah appears in Oz's own voice:

> In my childhood dreams it was Arabs who wore uniforms and carried machine-guns, Arabs who came to my street in Jerusalem to kill me. (p. 241)

In the light of all this, it is not far-fetched to imagine Oz saying about Hannah what Flaubert said about Emma Bovary: "Madame Bovary, c'est moi!"—except that Oz explicitly (but playfully) denied such a connection.[8] The best that we can conclude in regarding *My Michael* as a psychological and/or symbolist work is that it presents a case not of an "either/or" but of "both . . . and. . . ."

Amos Oz's portrayal of the Arab (and of his other protagonists) emanates from his characteristic world view and his unique aesthetic. His typical protagonist is a solitary, even solipsistic, individual, encircled by what he or she sees as hostile presences. Not only does this adversarial relation energize the motivations of his characters, it also colors his depiction of them. Thus there exists a connection between the inner self and the surrounding world, echoed in what might be seen as the individual's state of being. (This holds true not only for Oz's characters but also, as we have seen, for the writer himself.) The connection is manifested as an unhealthy tension between the individual and the world of everyday reality, accompanied by characteristic dissatisfaction and frustration (even, as we saw in Hannah, close to the point of derangement). Indeed, we have attempted to show that it is the psycho-sexual component in Geula and Hannah that shapes their relation to the Arab. In addition, that tension will also be manifested in ambiguities in their relations to social institutions such as the kibbutz and the family. And for Oz this is materialized in the way the attraction to the irrational seems to undo the world of order.

Although Oz cannot be regarded as a determinist, it is nevertheless true that the situation in which he plants his characters brings them deterministically to an extremity of humiliation, even tragedy. A similar extremity characterizes the confrontation of Arab and Israeli in his works—manifested (as we saw) as the erotic attraction between the Israeli woman and the Arab male. This compounded extremity is carried over, in turn, to Oz's language, with its convoluted style marked by metaphor, ellipsis, and hyperbole. It may or may not be true that Oz chose his complex style as a direct reflection of the complexity of Israeli-Arab relationships; nonetheless, the two—style and life—do complement each other. This is why the connective tissue of his narrative is analogy, linked to the one constant element of inconstancy: i.e., the constant deviation from the reader's expectations. In creating his structures of analogy, Oz's aim is to unsettle the narrative world of his reader. The tone of irony, satire, parody—all aim at leaving the reader in a state of doubt and unease, with a heightened awareness of the inconsistencies between text and experience.

Oz's depiction of the Arab has a mythic core, and this has two sides to it: first, the actuality of Arab presence in contemporary Israeli society; second, the erotic element that infiltrates the dreams and waking fantasies of Oz's women. We pointed to the autobiographical dimension in all this, but we also indicated the ambiguity of that link. Each narrative of his is rooted in reality, while serving as a metaphor of reality—their interplay enabling him to link reality to fantasy, reversing all ground rules of mimesis and giving his narrative a baroque richness.

Ultimately, Oz's fascination with the Arab comes down to a tension between rationality and the irrational, and it is in the service of this tension that his irony, metaphor, elevated style, and the other characteristic components of his aesthetic are employed. The element of the irrational, too, underlies his criticism of Israeli society, the kibbutz, and the ideals of Socialist Zionism—as though digging beneath them ironically, to undermine their solidity and stability.

We can say, therefore, that Oz uses the image of the Arab as a symbolic weapon against Israeli complacency, as when he has the Bedouin marauders encroach upon kibbutz lands (in "Nomad and Viper"), and he points with fear to the Arab villages surrounding Jerusalem (in *My Michael*). In each case, the Arab serves as a tangible "boundary," and thus a living presence, in Israeli society. Of course, it is possible to regard Oz's women as self-enclosed individuals who are motivated by nothing but their frustrated sexuality; but that would be to overlook Oz's way of relating to them as living symbols of the irrational and aggressive nature of Israeli society. For a corresponding reason, Oz's Arabs could be seen as individuals who happen to be hostile to Israeli women; but that would be to overlook Oz's way of relating to them as loci and embodiments of the Israeli's fears and fantasies.

In all this, the main target of Oz's indirect criticism is the totality of values upheld by the older generation: the Israeli male (in his intellectualism embracing secular Tolstoyanism, egalitarianism, Socialism, and Zionism) is suddenly portrayed as impotent and emasculated (with the implied impotence of his values); this is set in contrast to the virile Arab, so that sexuality is used here as social symbolism and (as we pointed out) the figure of the Arab is the weapon of social criticism. It is the Arab who, directly and indirectly, places traditional Israeli values in doubt, just as he directly endangers Israeli security on a daily basis. The resulting insecurity is therefore as spiritual as it is military or political. This connection is made possible by Oz's way of seeing a parallel between the outer and inner worlds: the external threat is matched by psychic disorientation of the Israeli individual—not because the Arab has directly caused that disorientation, but because the Israeli has made the Arab the focus of his own (the Israeli's) instability. The external threat to the Israeli has been made the fulcrum of inner imbalance, the point around which his imbalance turns.

But to the extent that the image of the Arab is "used" by Oz as a (say) "weapon of criticism," a "focus of eroticism," or whatever, the Arab is not given a voice of his own, as a *character*. Here Oz can be seen as arch-manipulator, activating the Arab protagonist to suit his own (Oz's) critical intentions vis-à-vis Israeli society. Yet to the extent that the critical function of his Arab protagonist is preset by Oz, the Arab cannot function in the literary sense with the full range of a character's causal indeterminacy and "self-directedness."

Oz seeks to overcome this limitation by giving his narrative an epic breadth. He strikes a sharp contrast with the naive realism of the writers of the 1948 generation, concerned as they were with their immediate world; for Oz, the power of his narrative relies on analogy, pointing beyond the immediate to a more universal range of meaning, beyond the boundaries of Israel. In this respect, he is closer to the writers preceding the 1948 generation, writers such as Brenner and Agnon, who struggled to push their narratives beyond the limited range of immediate connotation. Like Dostoevsky, who was the inspiration behind Brenner, Oz in part embraces the realistic/psychological novel. And like Dostoevsky, he is fascinated by evil, madness, and the irrational as components of everyday existence. Like Dostoevsky, further, Oz seeks to go beyond the confines of the simplistically psychological, with its causal explanation of motives moored in the commonplace; rather, he seeks to reach for something like an existential level of understanding. This is where the Arab protagonist can justly function by way of symbol, analogy, and metaphor, letting the reader *infer* the presence of evil, deception, and self-deceit rather than depicting them as literally there. The Israeli protagonist functions in a corresponding way for Oz, by way of symbol, analogy, and metaphor. Thus Geula's rape fantasy is made real and concrete by the symbolic agency of the broken bottle, the sliver in the flesh, and the slow death. Geula's wish to taste temptation was answered tragically; her Eros was her Thanatos.

In consequence of the emphasis on symbol and analogy (rather than the mechanically causal way of looking at events), there must be a dichotomy between reality and appearance. Thus Oz's world is one of trembling uncertainty, with a twofold effect—shattering the erstwhile certainties retained by his characters, and challenging the firm values and expectations of the reader. This could have an unintended and opposite effect. In "Nomad and Viper" the symbolic embodiment of evil in natural phenomena can serve to restrict the power and scope of the story. It is all too easy for a reader to fall back on a Manichean dualism between cosmic good and cosmic evil, especially when we see Oz's characters in conflicts imposed upon them by external factors in the world. Indeed, one of the ways Oz emphasizes the factor of existential uncertainty is to point to the external as a source of human events: e.g., the Bedouins, their episodic thievery, etc.

Accordingly, we can say that by pointing to the externally contingent as the source of events, Oz is drawing away from the internally introspective as such a source. And when he does point to inner sources, these are invariably accompanied by self-deceit as well as the shattering of the protagonist's normative world. The outside world is destabilized by the irrational, the incalculable, the unpredictable; the inner world is shaken by the mad dialectic of love and death.

What is the place of the Arab protagonist in this scheme? For Oz, the Arab is a part of the "external," the phenomena of nature; he is not a character with an inner life, an interior source of motive and action. Oz's technique of "telling" rather than "showing"—and, indeed, a mode of "telling" associated with an interfering author (as in "Nomad and Viper," where an experience is depicted by an omnipresent author as well as a first-person narrator)—mars the credibility of the text. But it also precludes the possibility of our entering the inner life of more than the one protagonist. The result is twofold: first, the inner life of the Arab must remain closed to us; second, the main protagonists (Geula and Hannah Gonen) begin and end in a state of self-deceit involving fantasy and neurosis. The characters whose inner lives are partially opened to us are themselves blind to their true desires. This too is a result of Oz's "telling" technique, and in the light of this we can see his characters ending in what we would regard as a foregone conclusion. Oz's reality and his aesthetic can be said to condition each other reciprocally. But for the very reason that enables him to enter into the inner life of his Israeli characters, he remains outside the inner life of his Arabs.

We have been suggesting a mythic, metarealistic reading of Oz's fiction. Quite deliberately, he creates a unique universe for his characters. But despite the realistic markers of time and place, it is not his aim to reproduce the surrounding world in realistic terms. Characteristically, his protagonists feel themselves to be surrounded by hostile forces: *Somewhere Else* (1966), *My Michael* (1968), *Touch the Water, Touch the Wind* (1973), *Perfect Peace* (1982)—all point to the external threat of war. The internal threats are sexual and erotic. Oz's innovation is to translate these threats, outer and inner, into each other's terms. As we saw, the outer threat of Arab hostilities is reworked into the erotic language of inner yearnings.

Thus the outer becomes the metaphor of the inner, and vice versa. But here we are led to raise a methodological question: Is he portraying the outer world as a way of entering into personal human frailty? Or is he probing the unconscious as a way of exposing the outer "Israeli condition"? Perhaps the most balanced approach is the open-ended reading which makes room for the mythic, whereby sexuality and war serve as images of one another, as reciprocal analogues. And then there is his ironic tone, often directed mercilessly at his characters, that obviates the tragic dimension. Thus his title *Perfect Peace* may seem reassuring—until we realize that the phrase is taken from the mourner's prayer, the Kaddish.

In the 1980s, the Arab is not the central character he was earlier, and we have seen something of Yehoshua's reasons for the change. In Oz, too, the Arab's centrality has diminished—although here the reasons remain hidden and obscure. With the passing of the founding fathers, the young protagonist in Oz's fiction must shape himself in his own image. He might be drawn to the desert in search of himself, but he eventually returns to the kibbutz (as in *Perfect Peace*) or to the family estate (as in *Black Box* [1986]). The earlier gulf between external heroic deeds and dark inner passions is now softened, becoming almost elegiac. Similarly, the earlier gulf between the messianic zeal of the founding fathers and the dwindling enthusiasm of the younger generation to continue along the path of Socialism and Zionism has itself diminished—but this has also led toward a radicalization of the Right, in whose camp the messianic zeal is now to be seen. Oz's fiction has thus undergone a mellowing, and the burning issues now merely smolder. And what has become of the Arab as protagonist in Oz's fiction? In *Perfect Peace*, the Arab presence is nothing more than a ruined Arab village, close to the kibbutz—a constant presence but little more than a reminder of childhood memories for the kibbutz members.

In 1982, Oz produced a book of interviews with a broad spectrum of people, representing the widest range of classes, affiliations, and views.[9] He sought the extremes of political orientation, and gave all too little attention to the views of moderates. For those who were drawn from the extremes, it was clear that there *is* a solution to the problem of the Jewish state, and (further) the solution admits of no compromise. As one of the leaders of the Peace Now movement, Oz is deeply committed to compromise. And if the extremes are taken as the prevailing mood, the Peace Now program appears to be the only sensible possibility. The book is therefore flawed—because the extremes are not the prevailing mood, nor is the Peace Now program the only viable alternative.

The Arab-Israeli problem is central to the book. The most extreme Israeli view is expressed by one "Z"—the only individual not named, and therefore thought by many to be Oz's fabrication. Z is not hesitant to express the most virulent jingoism. He blames what he calls "the Hirbet Hizah complex" for the failure of the 1948 War to finish the "dirty work" of Zionism. (The phrase "the Hirbet Hizah complex" does not appear in the English translation; see p. 96.) Toward the end of the "interview" Z says: "I'll wipe out the Arab villages and you can hold protest demonstrations and write epitaphs. You'll be the family's honor and I'll be the stain on the family's honor. Be my guest. Is it a deal?" (The passage in Hebrew reads, "I'll wipe out Hirbet Hizah. . . .")

In the autumn of 1982, Oz visited Ramallah, the West Bank Arab city, and conducted an interview there, something that would hardly be possible in 1989:

> Now Abu-Azmi mutters something to himself. His voice rasps like an old machine that has a hard time starting. He sways in his chair, grunts, and finally speaks his piece, casually breaking our grammatical agreement to use only the third person plural; in good Hebrew and a hoarse voice tinged with sadness, he says, "You took everything from us. How can you sleep at night? Don't you fear God? You took everything! But we were wrong, too. Guilty. You know, it used to be that our people would kill Jews for nothing. For no reason! Now we've got our punishment. You've been punished by God, too. Write in the Israeli newspaper: What was is over. Finished. Everyone wants to live on the land. All the Jews and Arabs want

to live. Write that the land doesn't belong to the Jews or to the Arabs. The land is God's. Whoever finds favor in His eyes will receive His land. God alone decides. And whoever does evil will pay the price: God will pass over him and forget him. And write in the Israeli newspaper that Abu-Azmi sends his regards to Mr. Cohen—that's a good man." (p. 84)

At one point, Oz quotes his own credo:

"For a month, for a year, or for a whole generation we will have to sit as occupiers in places that touch our hearts with their history," I wrote in the daily newspaper *Davar* only two months after the Six-Day War. "And we must remember: as occupiers, because there is no alternative. And as a pressure tactic to hasten peace. Not as saviors or liberators. Only in the twilight of myths can one speak of the liberation of a land struggling under a foreign yoke. Land is not enslaved and there is no such thing as a liberation of lands. There are enslaved people, and the word 'liberation' applies only to human beings. We have not liberated Hebron and Ramallah and El-Arish, nor have we redeemed their inhabitants. We have conquered them and we are going to rule over them only until our peace is secured." (p. 120)

13. BENJAMIN TAMMUZ

Benjamin Tammuz is old enough to have been included among the writers of the 1948 generation in this study. Born in 1919, he made his first appearance as a writer in the mid-1940s, and he was one of the leading members of the Cana'anite movement even earlier. (He gave up the family name of Kammerstein; "Tammuz" is the name of a Cana'anite deity, and became the name of one of the Hebrew months.) He belongs with the writers of the later generation because the powerfully individualistic tone of his stories effectively removes him from the earlier group, which always placed a strong emphasis on the collective "we."

His first thin volume of short stories, *Sands of Gold* (1950), contains pieces that express a romantic yearning for a land where one can experience a solitary encounter between heaven and earth, as an epiphany, and this lyrical tone will persist in his fiction, as a hedge against the ills of urbanization. At the same time, Tammuz has been a satirist, criticizing Israeli society from the sources of his own urbanity. (He studied in Paris in the 1950s, worked as a sculptor and as an editor, and served as Israel's cultural attaché in London from 1971 to 1977.)

In a conversation with Tammuz in Tel Aviv in January 1987, I asked him to talk about the image of the Arab in his fiction. He said that his starting point was autobiographical. Having come from Russia with his parents when he was five, he lived in an Arab border area between Tel Aviv and Jaffa, where his mother rendered medical services to the people in the neighborhood. In 1929 the Arab riots broke out, and these were traumatic for him. He had Arab friends, and during the unrest in 1937 he would go into Jaffa with them, speaking Arabic. Throughout his childhood, he felt that his activities with his Arab friends were of the category of the "forbidden." When he was twenty, and as part of his service in the British army, he lived with a Bedouin tribe in the Sinai. He was adopted by a sheikh, but the 1948 War brought an end to his close friendships with Arabs. He still sees the possibility of personal contact with Arabs, and he rejects the sense both of superiority and of pity toward them.

Tammuz sees a profound fallacy in Zionism, which he regards as a constellation of hopes without a substantial basis; he sees a widening gap between Israel and the Jews of the Diaspora, a gap that is becoming unbridgeable. Despite the Cana'anite rejection of both Zionism and Judaism, however, Tammuz felt a great respect for Judaism while he was in Paris, since it takes considerable heroism, he says, to be a Jew among

Gentiles. He joined the Cana'anites out of a desire to belong. "My family could not assimilate in Palestine. They spoke Russian, they read Russian, they could not adjust themselves to the Hebrew language."

Tammuz's relation to the Arab is marked by ambivalence: fascination and fear; the loss of childhood landscapes in the 1948 War, amounting to a loss of a part of oneself. Yet the Arab has been a constant presence in Tammuz's fiction for over thirty years. Some of that ambivalence can be seen in his 1964 story "The Swimming Race."[1] This is a rich and intricate story combining the realities of the pre-State days and the 1948 War. It is told from the point of view of the narrator, who witnesses the three-sided encounter between land, Jew, and Arab.

The first part, depicting events in the life of a young child, exudes nostalgia for the tender pre-war days. The child and his mother have been invited to stay at the summer home of a noble Arab woman who had been cured by the mother. Entering the courtyard, they are met by the tranquility and gracious charm of cultivated Arab life. But here the child/narrator, now become an adult, interposes:

> You don't see such courtyards any more. And if you should happen to come to a place where there once was such a courtyard, you will only find a scene of wartime destruction: heaps of rubble and rafters, with cobwebs trying to impart an air of antiquity to what only yesterday still breathed and laughed. (pp. 115–16)

This passage foretells the tragic reality that will ensue toward the end of the story.

The Jewish mother has lost a husband, and earlier a home in Europe; she has no summer home but lives in a rented apartment. The old Arab woman tries to reassure her: "That's because you are newcomers, immigrants. . . . But with the help of God you'll thrive and build yourselves houses. You're hard-working people and your hands are blessed" (p. 117).

The boy and Nahida, the old woman's granddaughter, have a touching juvenile conversation about God. There is a lovely light supper:

> We had supper out on the veranda. We were served large dishes of fried potatoes, sliced aubergine in tomato sauce and diced salted cheese, and a bowl of pomegranate and watermelon. There was a heap of hot *pitas* in the center of the table. (p. 119)

Nahida's uncle, Abdul-Karim, wears the traditional Arab headdress and attends the College of the Mufti, in Jerusalem. He gently mocks the boy. There is a swimming race between the two, and Abdul-Karim wins. The competition shifts to the category of general knowledge, and this time the boy proclaims himself the winner, on the question of who discovered America. This first part of the story ends in a tone of foreboding:

> "He beat me in America," Abdul-Karim said, "but I beat him *right here*, in the pool."
>
> "You wait till I'm grown up and then I'll beat you right here in the pool," I told him.
>
> Nahida seemed about to nod her agreement, but thought better of it and looked at her uncle to see what he was going to answer to that.
>
> "If he ever manages to beat me here in the pool," Abdul-Karim said, "it will be very bad indeed. It will be bad for you too, Nahida. Bad for all of us."
>
> We didn't get his meaning and I wanted to tell him to cut out his philosophizing; but I didn't know how to say that in Arabic, so I kept quiet.
>
> Later we went hunting rabbits in the orange grove. (p. 123)

Tammuz has assured me that this first part of the story is an exact account of a childhood experience he had. The second and third parts, his experience as a young man in the 1940s and then 1948, are fictionalized additions.

The narrator's yearning for that enchanted land, mingled with a presentiment of coming trouble, leads him (in the second part) to an Arab home in the village of Ein Karem, near Jerusalem. He is vacationing, and he rents a room for two weeks. Despite the difference in time and place, the room evokes the earlier experience:

> There was a deep stillness all around, pervaded by the familiar smells of frying oil, mint leaves, black coffee, rosewater and cardamom seeds. I felt my face break into a smile as my ears strained to catch a sound that was missing in order to complete a dim, distant memory.
>
> Suddenly I heard a tap turned on in the kitchen and the sound of gushing water made me hold my breath: water gushing from a pipe into a pool!
>
> I got up and went out to the yard. There was no pool, not even orange trees; but there was something about the apple and plum trees, some quality of strangeness peculiar to an Arab homestead. It was obvious that the courtyard had not evolved all at once, that each generation had added something of its own. One man had planted the apple tree by the water tap, another the mulberry tree near the dog kennel, and in time the garden had sprouted up to tell its masters' life stories. I stood listening, my fantasy peopling the courtyard with Nahida and her grandmother, with Abdul-Karim, with the horse-cab that would suddenly draw to a halt outside the gate. . . . (pp. 125–126)

In the evening the narrator dines with the family: "The food that was served was no more than a continuation of that faraway supper in the orange grove. At that moment I realized what I had come for" (p. 126). The memories of that visit are reawakened in a synesthetic way: "It was then that I knew that I had been waiting all these years for just this moment, that I would relive our story at the house in the orange grove" (p. 127).

In the 1948 War there is an encounter that is irrevocably tragic and inevitable. After an abortive attack on an Arab stronghold in the dunes of Jaffa, the Israelis expect a retaliatory attack. Some of the Arabs have escaped to a nearby orange grove—the scene of the visit to the old Arab woman twenty years earlier. There is heavy fire coming from the house, and a bloody battle ensues. Eventually, the defense weakens, and a charge of high explosives causes the Arab defenders to surrender.

The narrator is not surprised when he sees Abdul-Karim: "He seemed to have expected this, too, though that was something I had never dared to imagine." The narrator expresses the wish to talk to Abdul-Karim alone.

> "You're the victors," he said. "We do as we're told."
> "As long as I haven't beaten you in the pool," I told him, "there's no telling who is the victor." (p. 130)

As Abdul-Karim is taken to the orange grove with the other Arab prisoners, the narrator takes a dip in the pool. A gun goes off accidentally, and Abdul-Karim is killed.

> I went over to Abdul-Karim's body and turned it over. He looked as though he had seen me swimming in the pool a few moments ago. His was not the expression of a man who had lost. There, in the courtyard, it was I, all of us, who were the losers. (p. 130)

Tammuz's fiction oscillates between Jewish morality and primal Cana'anite notions: war as the way of becoming master of the land. At the same time there is the romanticization of the land in an unperturbed time. Tammuz thus bemoans the passing of the way of life in the pre-State days—prior to the waves of mass immigration in the 1950s.

We have noted the frequent reference to the Binding of Isaac (*Akeda*) as a theme in modern Hebrew literature. Another biblical theme found with some frequency is that of Jacob's struggle with the angel, in Genesis 32. Tammuz's protagonist in the novel *Ya'akov*[2] is Ya'akov Angelson, an unsubtle allusion to the biblical Jacob. The book is a *Bildungsroman* about a young man born to immigrant parents who nevertheless wants to be a native son to the new landscape. Moshe Shamir opened his book *With His Own Hands* with the now-famous sentence "Elik was born of the sea." Tammuz's opening sentence is "Ya'akov was not born here."

Tammuz's Cana'anitism can be seen in the way his protagonist is in search of the biblical, and prebiblical, origins of the local population. Thus Ya'akov and his friend Arik are certain that the poor Arab villagers, the fellahin, are the true Hebrews of old, those who were not sent into exile in Babylonia in 586 B.C.E., but survived as a remnant in ancient Judah. The two therefore perceive the Arab villagers as their brethren, their own flesh and blood—a notion to which the Arabs must be reawakened. The Arabs might resist the idea, and the initial encounter with them might be fierce; but the second meeting, the two are sure, will be an embrace of brothers, "heart to heart, from now to eternity, never to be parted again" (p. 41).

Throughout his fiction, Tammuz has made use of the biblical theme of strife between two brothers as an almost mythic element: Jacob and Esau. But the problem in our own time is to determine who the contenders will be. Ya'akov and Arik join the Cana'anite movement, thereby delivering themselves of the "old" generation of Jewish leaders. Deliberating on what they themselves are to be, they decide: "Jews we won't be. Arabs, naturally not. And neither English nor Turkish. What then? Hebrew" (p. 35). They will belong to the Hebrew Nation. Training themselves in the tradition of the biblical heroes, they walk from Tel Aviv to the Judean desert, there to wrestle with a bush. For them, this act is symbolic and meaningful.

The book is studded with visions and epiphanies. One of these occurs after Italian planes bomb Tel Aviv in June 1941. Ya'akov is driven east; he walks into Ramle. He encounters an elderly Arab who is trying to force a young woman, pushing her and kicking her cruelly. Ya'akov attacks the attacker, and then the young woman attacks Ya'akov, throwing stones at him. Tammuz suggests that this encounter has a meaning beyond its realistic implications: "At that particular time I did not understand what happened to me in that courtyard there, and who the man was that I left prostrate on the ground" (p. 94).

Again and again, the Tammuz protagonist yearns for the east, almost envying the indigenous Arab son his village and landscape. At the same time, he yearns for the west, for exile, the state of an outsider. The biblical Jacob was a cunning individual who wrung a blessing from the angel with whom he wrestled. The blessing was: "Thy name shall be called no more Jacob, but Israel [i.e., he who strives with God]; for thou hast striven with God and with men, and hast prevailed" (Genesis 32:29). But the blessing has carried a curse with it. Throughout Jewish history, there has been a repetition of this motif: the tainted blessing. The modern Ya'akov in effect wants to release the angel from his commitment to the blessing suffused with a curse: In order to shed the "Jewish fate," in order to shed the Diaspora mentality and gain a chance for a different future, he wants to reject the blessing, the naming of Jacob as Israel-the-contender-against-God.

Ya'akov senses that these emblematic elements have been scored into his own personality. As he sees it, Jacob's encounter with the angel is the last national event. The biblical story encompasses the encounter, the victory, the blessing—but also the struggle, the defeat, the curse. If a single link could be torn from the chain, the entire thing would be nullified. Ya'akov desires to encounter the angel again, to cancel the contract, to wipe the slate clean.

There are repeated encounters in Tammuz's fiction, always physical, and at one point (wrestling with an Egyptian soldier), Ya'akov feels a "deep mysterious contact" with his "national past" (p. 108). Are these to be regarded as two men who are vying with one another for one woman, the land? After a dream, he says: "Did I really wrestle with an angel? In effect I wrestled with my brother. One might say I wrestled with my brother within me, with myself" (p. 119).

What is to be the basis for genuine encounter? What basis is to replace nineteenth-century European Zionism? In this and other books, Tammuz points to the land as the only possible basis, the only solution. Only the land would provide a basis free of historical Jewish memory; yet the presence of the brother-enemy on the same land has spelled tragedy for both.

In a 1973 article, Tammuz recast some of these ideas in the form of a theoretical discussion.[3] He speaks of three "encounters with the angel," and he arranges these in a dialectical pattern. In the first, we have the direct contact of Jacob and the angel, at the mythic/personal level. It is at the second encounter that this takes on its more problematic dimension: here it becomes mythic content for the religion of a people, protracted over its entire span of history. Thus, the first direct encounter is negated in the second; but moreover, history itself shatters and belies the absolute nature of that content, because Jewish *history* contradicts the notion of a "chosen people" or Jacob's blessing. The second encounter is still characterized by "intimacy" (between Jews and their God); but the Jew will also have to "vindicate" his contrary fate. Thus, if history belies the Jews' chosenness as a people, perhaps it is because God is "concealing" Himself and allowing the Holocaust to happen for reasons that are unfathomable to us, etc.

That process of vindication has also found its way into Hebrew literature: Israeli writers, for the most part, had ceased to accept the earlier "intimacy" with God, as religious conviction gave way to a nationalist consciousness— and therefore the earlier sort of "vindication" of Jewish fate was no longer needed, once the phrase "our God" was replaced by the phrase "our national destiny."

The process of vindication also spawned the Cana'anite movement, which Tammuz sees as the expression of Jewish "self-hate" and Jewish anti-Semitism. Jews in Israel acquired deep feelings of guilt: for allowing themselves to suffer persecution for two thousand years and during the Holocaust; for returning to the land of their forefathers despite the loss of their ancient faith; for expelling the Muslim villager from his land. These expressions of guilt have led to agonizing questions: Are we turning into a Levantine society? Are we becoming a chauvinistic society? And in literature, as Tammuz points out, the self-doubt reached its climax in Yizhar's "The Prisoner" and "Hirbet Hizah."

For Tammuz, the dawn of the third encounter is on the horizon. Different from the original encounter in Genesis, and no longer the vision of a "chosen people," this last encounter occurs in the individual psyche, where the "wrestling" is internalized and issues in the Israeli malaise and the psychoanalyst's couch. Thus the last encounter is initiated not by the angel or God but by ourselves, Tammuz says. Yet the last encounter will retain many of the previous elements in an attenuated form: "It will be a fusion of skepticism with the tradition and the memorabilia of the Faith; with Israeli literature being just one element in the process" (p. 59). Literature will thus have the impossible task of merging the first two encounters, but in a new semantics.

This third encounter will determine the destiny of the Israelis, Tammuz says. Only if the theological idiom of Genesis 32 can be realized in a new and demythologized language will Israel survive.

In *Ya'akov,* we saw Tammuz returning to the motif of fratricide: "In effect, I wrestled with my brother." The Bible revolves around this theme as one of its most basic archetypes: Cain and Abel, Isaac and Ishmael, Jacob and Esau. Tammuz's 1972 novella *The Orchard,*[4] is a modern retelling of the classic feud. With the two "brothers" a Jew and an Arab, the implications are direct, immediate, and inescapable. The time span extends from the beginning of Jewish settlement in Palestine, during the period of the Ottoman Empire, to present-day Israel. The modern protagonists are Daniel, a Jewish idealist who has come to work the land and make a meaningful existence for himself, and his half-brother Obadiah-Abdullah, born to a Jewish father and a Muslim mother. The setting is Eretz Israel, the "orchard."

Interwoven into the story of the brothers is another archetypal model, the Oedipal triangle of father-mother-son. The father is Daniel, the mother an Earth Mother who appears in the image of the moon goddess and bears the name Luna. Married to Daniel, she has a long-standing love affair with his brother, so that we do not know who fathered her son. Eventually, the son kills his uncle/father Obadiah-Abdullah, and becomes Luna's lover as well.

For the forty years of the narrated tale, Luna does not change, does not age, does not speak. Like the land, she has an *a*historical nature. In her lunar aspect, she is herself the history of the two contending brothers, each of whom claims to own the land, to own Luna. She is ageless, ever-present. She is married to Daniel, the Jew from the West, but he has owned her more in his conception than in reality. She comes closest to being an archetype—mute and immutable, she transcends all, outlasts all.

One basic source of the Earth Mother motif is the kabbalistic *Zohar.* Here she appears as the image of the divine radiance—*Shekhinah*—emanating from God's presence. Her image is essentially spiritual, although she is connected to the Land (*Eretz*) and Soil (*Adamah*), and yearns for Israel's return. One of the many faces of the *Shekhinah* is that of the compassionate mother who is a source of love, grace, and pity, especially to the people Israel, which stems from her and expects her help. In one version, she goes into the Diaspora in order to aid her exiled sons; in another, God leaves her in territorial Israel as a guarantee of His covenant with the nation and as an assurance of its eventual redemption; in yet another version, she herself is exiled following the destruction of the Temple; and in still another version, she has been abducted by the powers of evil, thus explaining the Diaspora. In all these versions, she is directly connected to Israel's fate.

Uncertainties abound in *The Orchard*. Is Luna Jewish or non-Jewish? Is her son the offspring of Daniel or Obadiah? Is Obadiah a Muslim or a half-Jew? The 1948 War polarizes attitudes, and facilitates self-definition. Obadiah emerges as an Arab officer; but his son/nephew identifies with the Jewish cause and he kills Obadiah. The bloodshed challenges Daniel's claims, and introduces self-doubt:

> What can I see?
> You see that the orchard serves as a cover and a hiding place for all sorts of things that have no justice in them, said Daniel.
> Justice? I repeated the word like an echo. I was alarmed and agitated.
> Yes, no justice in them, he repeated his words firmly. I came to the land of my fathers so that I could live a life of justice and honesty, and look, what have I done? I have made a dark orchard, a sanctuary for wrong-doers. I murdered my brother in the orchard. . . .
> Perhaps we ought to thin it out a little, said Daniel softly, as if revealing a secret. Perhaps we ought to pull out a few trees, so they won't be able to hide there, so that it'll be possible to see from one end to the other. So it'll be clearer. Things will clear up a little.
> Thin it out? Pull up trees?
> Perhaps burn it, Daniel whispered. If we burn it, bare trunks will remain, and it will be possible to see from one end to the other, and everything will be completely transparent and clear again. (p. 84)

A sense of guilt haunts Daniel: "He began seeing the ghost of Obadiah wandering among the trees, and he would pursue this ghost, running over clumps and begging it for forgiveness" (p. 86). Again and again in Israeli fiction from the 1940s on, there is the theme of the return of the land to its "original" state: wasteland. If the wasteland wins, it mocks men's attempts at reviving it, attempts sullied by bloodshed. Daniel's desire to burn the orchard is echoed in Shenhar's "The Tamarisk" and Yehoshua's "Facing the Forests," as we saw.

The book concludes with a sweeping vision of the narrator:

> The orchard lands were bought by speculators for good money, and soon surveyors will arrive there to subdivide them. Then the tractors will

come to pull out the trees. After that they will dig foundations for houses, and some time later apartment houses will rise there, with electric posts jutting from their roofs and filthy garments waving in the wind from their balconies like the festival pennants of the city rabble whose clothes, even when they sleep, are loud in their garish colors.

New people will come gleefully to live in the new houses. And after a generation or two these people, too, will be dust and ashes. And the houses, too, will crumble. And in my mind's eye I see resurrection and destruction, destruction and resurrection, and it all has no end. Until the solver of riddles comes and solves this riddle, too, at the end of days. (pp. 87–88)

The Orchard touches on the mythic. If so, how do we resolve its irresolvable premise? Is its end a "solution"? Or, in the darkly ironic words of the narrator, are we to expect a solution only when life itself has come to an end? The sense of "ending" presents neither a solution nor a resolution. Instead, what the narrator does offer is an inconclusive piece of Nietzschean apocalyptic:

Whoever pursues justice in the empty expanse of an orchard that is not his is bound to be exterminated. It is not the triumph of justice that will emerge as white as snow, but the bones of the pursuer that will be as wool, evaporating before the empty wind. But he who masters life with joy, he will not sense or feel anything, even if the orchard is burned down around him. He will rejoice in the light of day just as he will sing in the darkness, because joy is his essence. And if I called the doctor, I did so in order to have no cause—then or ever—to accuse myself of daring to know what no man has the right to understand. (p. 85)

The concluding phrase "end of days" in the previous passage is a mocking reference to a messianic eschatology. The succession of destructions and resurrections, far from suggesting a positive note of rebirth, rather suggests the nihilistic emptiness of Nietzsche's "Eternal Return."

Tammuz's *Minotaur*[5] (1980) is a novel of the mingling of three Mediterranean peoples—Arabs, Jews, and Greeks—and the death of the Levant. It is also a novel of romantic aspirations and myth, that of the Minotaur. In their separate ways, the Jew and the Greek converge on Thea, a beautiful Englishwoman. The Greek (Nikos) and the Israeli Jew (Alex) believe Thea to be given to each of them, individually, as a mysterious act of grace. The novel involves the chronicle of a family, as well as suspense, love, and espionage. It can be read as a succession of unlikely occurrences. But it is also about the more commonplace desire on the part of Nikos and Alex to return to the soil of the East—although each is drawn to the West.

We might expect Tammuz to be drawn into the realm of biblical myth; instead, it is Greek mythology he now enters, perhaps as a way of uniting the different cultures, since at one time in the past all the peoples of the Mediterranean fed off the lore of Greece and Asia Minor. In the world of the mythic, all events are predetermined—as the meeting of Alex and Nikos would seem to be. There is an affinity between them, and they complement one another. Not only are they drawn to Thea, but both have romantic dreams of uniting the peoples of the East into an old/new unity. This dream of reviving the Levant is contrary to the prevailing nationalisms, each seeking its separate way. The unattainable dream creates a certain bond between the two men. But there is also an adversarial bond between the three men: Alex physically fights the Arab over the land (and kills him); and he competes with the Greek over Thea. At the end, Alex is killed by a secret agent, and Thea kills herself in remorse.

On the cover of the Hebrew edition of *Minotaur* is one of Picasso's etchings of the *Vollard Suite*. In the book's closing scene, Alex is shot. As he dies, he sees himself as a gladiator mortally wounded in the arena. Slowly he is turned into a large animal with the huge head of a bull, but he is a man from the shoulders down. He remembers the Picasso etching, a copy of which had hung in his room in childhood. The animal is crouching, a hand to his mortal wound, his horned head turned upward and bellowing. In the etching, a woman leans from the gallery, trying to touch his dying head. Alex sees her as Thea (p. 143).

Why did Tammuz choose this monstrous creature, half-man, half-bull, as his basic symbol? Was he fascinated by the theme of metamorphosis as man's escape from the self? There is the suggestion that had Thea touched the dying bull she might have saved him. (In Picasso's etching, the woman's outstretched hand does reach the bull; he is neither saved nor restored to humanness.) Much of Greek myth is concerned with metamorphosis: Tiresias being transformed into a woman; gods transforming themselves into animals; men becoming flora and fauna. It was all rather fluid, an extension of the vital Greek imagination that could dream up the imponderable, the Oedipus myth. In Judaism there is no transformation; in Christianity there is only God becoming the one man. Everyone else is fixed in what he is: mortal and sinning. The theme of the minotaur, then, is Tammuz's way of escaping from Judeo-Christianity: in the half-bull to escape humanity and its burdens, but at the same time to see that humanity all the more clearly.

Another central encounter is that between Alex and the Arab. Alex had been born in Palestine, to a middle-aged father and a young mother of eighteen who was a beautiful violinist. The home was cultured and musical. Alex meets reality with the Arab riots of 1929. The father of a girl schoolmate is killed by Arab marauders, and Alex takes an oath to avenge his blood (p. 90). At the age of fourteen, he kills a Bedouin:

> One evening, as he stood on the edge of the plantation and surveyed the slope that went down toward the Bedouin encampment at the other end of

the wadi, a figure rose up out of the furrows of earth close to the scorched bushes, and a young Bedouin—about twenty years old—stood facing him at a distance of about four meters. For a moment they looked at each other in silence and then the Bedouin opened his mouth and with the foulest words, words used to speak to those despised and hated, he told Alexander that he was a son of a bitch and doomed to die, and that now his last moment had arrived, and before he killed him he was going to rape him and then he would bury him in the ground. The Bedouin grinned and called Alexander to come closer to him.

"I've been waiting here for you for three days, Jew," said the Bedouin. "I swore to God that I would rape you and kill you like a dog. Come here you son of a whore, you won't get away from me." (pp. 104–105)

With his head, Alex rams the man in the stomach, immobilizing him. He straddles the fallen Arab and begins to strangle him. As he does so, he experiences an odor that takes him back to his childhood haunts:

It was a smell from the man's clothes, his body and hair. The smell of the smoke of an Arab stove that burned dung, the smell that used to fill the courtyard of their house at sunset in the days of his childhood, when the Arab workers left their work to go and bake bread and sit down to their meal. Unbeknown to his mother, he would be given pieces of warm pita by the workers, and as he ate it hungrily, he felt grains of sand being ground between his teeth.

Alexander saw before him bulging eyes, a swarthy face, and a final redness draining away from beneath the graying skin. Now the body twitched under him, as if wanting to be embraced and surrender. (pp. 105–106)

His killing of the Arab is Alex's initiation into an awareness of danger and death. He grows up, and serves in the defense forces of the pre-State days, then the regular army. He marries the girl whose father had been killed, and they have a child. In a chance encounter, however, he sees Thea, and he realizes that she is the materialization of everything he yearned for. For a long time after, he searches for her, unsuccessfully. His yearning for her is somehow linked with his restless fantasies about the West:

I must also be closer to the cities my father told me about, because in one of these cities I shall meet her. Lately she has almost been shouting, "Unless you reach out your arms I shall also keep away from you." (p. 124)

At the same time, he is deeply rooted in the East, and his love for Arabs is palpable:

I'm not apologizing. They regard us with deadly hatred and I'm just doing what is possible and necessary to do. But this does not alter the fact that in return for the friendship of one Arab I would give ten American, English, or French friends. With a European I can drink whiskey, do business, and come to an understanding that the state of Israel is in fact an extension of Europe in the east; but with an Arab I can once again roll about in the clods of earth in the plantation, inhale the smell of an oven burning goat dung, pick and eat thyme, run toward the horizon and find my childhood there, and perhaps also find a point to life—now almost aimless—within the place where the hill of my childhood stands. (p. 126)

At the same time, he realizes that this is not enough to resolve the conflict, or to materialize the dream of a revived Mediterranean people, however close he might feel to the Arabs:

In 1967 the Israelis conquered the whole of the West Bank of the Jordan, including the Old City of Jerusalem. Although he was very busy with his journeys, Alexander tried to stay in Israel as much as he could that year. He would journey to the conquered territories and go right out to the Arab villages where time stood still. He would enter into conversations with men sitting in the coffeehouses of the villages, listening to and telling Arabic legends and parables, which were partly ancient wisdom and partly obscenities. He had no qualms about speaking freely in the hearing of the Arabs and was grateful to them for giving back to him what he had lost and had long since despaired of retrieving. (p. 128)

The irony of all ironies is that the hostilities have locked the two contenders together in an indissolvable bond:

Who am I? It's easier for me to answer that now. What was once my private experience has now become collective experience. Formerly I was the only one out of all the children of Israel to wrestle with the Arab at his own private ford Jabok and emerge a sort of Pyrrhic victor. Now all the children of Israel are partners in this folly. Perhaps only a few know it, but they all feel it; they won and lost. They struggled and killed and slayed, and now both the victim and the victor long for each other, and there is no going back, since one of them was murdered. In fact, they were both murdered. (p. 129)

Tammuz carries a double message in his fiction: the fascination with the West and its Greek origins; the pagan Cana'anitic lore of man as *Ba'al* (owner) and the land as the woman he must have dominion over. And although he does not accept the entire ideological package of Yonatan Ratosh, he does embrace certain elements of it, especially the non-Judaic stance. And despite Tammuz's rejection of nationalism, the work of Ratosh (in his poetry) and Tammuz (in his fiction) contains elements of sanctified violence.

14. SAMMY MICHAEL

Born in Iraq, Sammy Michael came to Israel after the establishment of the State. Although he writes in Hebrew, his native tongue is Arabic. In the Iraq of his childhood, Jews suffered constant fear and oppression. He speaks of the government of that time as "corrupt and decaying, with an ideology made up of the darkest dictatorial Ottoman tradition, a romantic dream of a lost Arab empire, direct Nazi influence, and British colonial values."[1] In 1941, after a short-lived Nazi regime in Iraq, there was a pogrom marked by rape, slaughter, and pillage. All protest was stifled. Not a single voice was raised, in the Jewish community or outside it, against the persecution of Jews. There were, however, some close ties formed between Arab and Jewish Communist intellectuals (Michael being among the latter) who yearned for a better society. Many of them were jailed, tortured, and killed.

In Israel, Michael joined the Communist party, but he eventually left it, disgusted with what he felt was its anti-Jewish and anti-Israeli stance.[2] He earned a degree at Haifa University, where he majored in psychology and in Arabic literature. He has done some translating from the Arabic, notably the trilogy *A House in Cairo* by the Egyptian nobelist Nagib Mahfouz—and this after Michael declared his "divorce from Arabic," which he likened to the amputation of a limb. Despite the "divorce," Michael admits to the influence of Arabic on his Hebrew fiction, a blending of what he calls the pictoriality of Arabic with the modern functionality of Hebrew.

Michael is among a number of Hebrew writers raised in Arabic-speaking countries: there are Shimon Balas, Amnon Shamosh, Eli Amir, Yitzhak Goren-Gormenzano, and all have contributed to the broadening of Israeli vision by introducing the experience of the Jew in Arab society. Their treatment of the Arab, in their lands of origin and in the Israeli setting, is all the more realistic for their own experience, and contains insights from which the Israel-born writer is barred.

Michael's fiction is well within the tradition of the realistic novel, where plot, characters, and conflicts are presented in a fashion aiming at verisimilitude. The plight of people caught in a complex and obdurate reality, and shaped by powers beyond their control, is seen from the all-embracing point of view of the ever-present author. Jews and Arabs are caught up in personal and political entanglements. There are elements of innocence and violence, along with a subtle sense of the absurd.

We shall be discussing two of Michael's novels. The first, and more

179

important for this study, is *Refuge*.[3] The story is simple: Fathi, an Arabic poet and Communist, finds refuge in the Haifa home of Jewish friends, Marduk and Shula, at the time of the Yom Kippur War in October 1973. Fathi is divided by any number of concerns, such as his anxiety for the safety of his Jewish friends and his sorrow at the fact that Jews are going to kill Arabs.

Such ambivalence found its way into the attitude of Arabs outside Israel toward Israeli Arabs. In the view of Sammy Michael, Arabs in the greater Middle East were critical of Israeli Arabs after 1948: they felt resentment because they had fought on behalf of the Arabs in Israel, who did little and then continued to enjoy life in the "Israeli paradise." Consequently an Arab such as Fathi felt the need to apologize to the Arab world, to show that he is still an Arab who can stand on his own, and that he is actually suffering hardship and persecution in the "Israeli paradise."

The rift between Arabs in Israel and those in the West Bank widened with the Six-Day War. And with the rise of the Palestine Liberation Organization, the problem of self-definition for people such as Fathi worsened. However much they might wish to identify with the PLO, they nevertheless have come to realize that they are in some sense Israelis and thus different from all the other Arabs in the Middle East. But in order to convince the Arab world that they are still fighting Israel, some feel that they must "address" every article, poem, or story to Beirut, Cairo, or Damascus—rather than to Arabs in Israel.

Refuge is a political novel, in the better sense of that term. That is, it is not a mouthpiece for the author's political pronouncements. The characters are Jews and Arabs, intellectuals as well as plainfolk on both sides, those who live in Israel and those in the West Bank. They have ideas and they express them, but the ideas are not pasted onto their backs like labels.

We are taken to an impoverished refugee camp in the West Bank, and to the house of a wealthy dentist in the town of Jenin, who prospers amid anxiety and fear. The poet Fathi is a young Arab-Israeli intellectual who is emotionally impotent, suffering an estrangement from the people of his own village and from the Arabs in the West Bank, with whom he feels he no longer has a common language. On the other hand, he feels some sort of closeness to Jews: there is his Jewish girlfriend, Daphne; the city of Haifa, which has a rich mixture of Jews, Muslim Arabs, and Christian Arabs; and the Communist Party, which has served as one of the main political forums for Arabs in Israel.

Michael has remarked that in Israel, if an Arab is a Communist, it is because he is an Arab; in Iraq, a Jew is a Communist because he is a Jew. Thus Marduk was a party member in Iraq for that reason (as Michael was). Marduk believes that giving refuge is a transcendent value. He himself had found refuge in Baghdad, in the home of his poor Jewish relatives whose sons were Zionists, when his father was ready to denounce him to the Secret Police.

In Arab countries, Jews are often regarded as cowards, scum, a miserable lot—and this perception, as Marduk sees it, has infected the Jewish self-image there. For young Jews in Baghdad, the only way out of this negative self-image was through Communism (for the educated intellectuals) or Zionism (for the others). Communists took pride in being the same as other members of revolutionary movements; Zionists took pride in being different from the Arab majority, as Michael points out.

Michael's complex message in *Refuge* is that the Arab-Israeli problem is not to be resolved, whether by love or by enmity. The enmity between Jews and Arabs is not to be bridged, least of all by family connection. The three sons of a mixed couple create a war within the family: the first identifies with Israel, the two younger ones with the PLO. Only the two grandmothers, one Jewish and the other Arab, can find a mutual affinity, despite language barriers. Further, Michael suggests that humanism and understanding are weak forces indeed in this mythic war of collective memories. Neither side is capable of stepping over the line that divides them and embracing the other. Nor can political ideology be looked to as a possible source of brotherhood. And still further, there is an implicit message in the story's own lack of resolution. For example, we are not told if Marduk returns from the fierce battles in the Negev; we do not know what happens to Fathi. (Will he go to Beirut, like his friend Fachri, there to seal the cracks in his identity?) As we said earlier, the absense of a resolution to the story may suggest (to some readers) the irresolvability of the Arab-Israeli problem.

It is perhaps ironic that writers are less optimistic than politicians are when it comes to the solubility of the Arab-Israeli conflict. From Yizhar's "Hirbet Hizah," to the concluding chapter of Tammuz's *The Orchard*, to David Grossman's *The Smile of the Lamb*, the message is bleak indeed. *Refuge* tells us, however, that in the very world that denies the cogency of values, the search for operative values is necessary nonetheless—against all odds, and despite the fact that the message of the book is so unpromising.

In Israeli fiction dealing with the Arab-Israeli conflict and its implications, there is little if any satisfaction with military victory, nor indeed is there much satisfaction of any kind. (Whether this is to be praised or decried must remain an open question for the purposes of this study.) Some of the ambivalence has centered around the definition of the term *enemy*, which has practically disappeared in Israeli fiction since the 1970s. Apparently the term cannot be used when we enter into the "enemy's" many-sided complexity. An attempt to reach out to that complexity is to be seen in Sammy Michael's *A Trumpet in the Wadi*.[4]

The narrator is Hudah, a young Arab woman who lives in Haifa, in the *wadi*, the valley in the downtown section inhabited for generations by Arabs. She is thirty and single, and works in a Jewish travel agency, where she is loved and appreciated by her bosses and coworkers. She is fluent in Hebrew; her favorite poet is Yehuda Amichai. The young, sensitive woman lives at home with her mother, her Coptic Christian grandfather, and her young sister Mary. The 1948 War separated the mother from her two brothers, who became prominent public figures in Jordan. The mother was reduced to a meager subsistence. Both the girls grew up without a father; he died when they were very young, and the grandfather became the father figure for the two.

At the travel agency, the head clerk is Adina, a Jewish war widow. Her son has forced her to permit him to join a commando unit. (An only child, or a child of a bereaved family, is otherwise barred from commando units, which take only volunteers.) The boss, too, has a son in a commando unit, and Hudah thinks these same young men may be the ones to kill her Jordanian cousins, whom she has never met. As the novel proceeds, one of Hudah's cousins in Lebanon is killed.

Hudah's life changes when a new neighbor moves into the roof apartment. The young man, Alex, is a Jewish newcomer from Russia, a trumpet player; the two fall in love and begin to face the problems of a mixed couple, accepted by neither the Jewish nor the Arab neighborhood. The war in Lebanon is the main juncture of the novel: Alex is killed in the war; Hudah is carrying his child. She hovers in the zone of indeterminacy between the two communities. If she raises her child in the Arab street, it will be the child of a Jewish father, and born out of wedlock. If she raises her child in the Jewish street, it will inevitably have to face another war: if it is a son, he will want to prove himself by joining a select unit, just because he was born to an Arab mother. In any event, the child will feel a stranger.

Hudah's decision is not disclosed to us. Any clear-cut resolution—to give birth to the child or to abort it; where and how to raise it—would have been altogether too facile and too "fictitious." The book, in its indeterminate "ending," is an outcry against "solutions," and thus an outcry against heroism, slogans, and the power of words. The individuals on either side of the line are in a state of psychological siege; crossing the line would amount to a tragic flaw.

Although individual decisions are indefinite, Michael does believe in the determining power of instincts and societal restrictions. His characters are caught up in political entanglements. And the problems of self-identification faced by Jewish characters in Israeli fiction are now seen in the Arab in Israel and in the West Bank. The achievement, therefore, of Israeli fiction of the 1970s and '80s is in showing Arabs and Jews to be faced by similar and parallel predicaments.

In Israeli literature since Yizhar, the Arab has often evoked the image of the exile, the refugee. Being so close to Jewish historical experience is what gives this phenomenon its tragic dimension. Whether invited or not, whether friend or foe, the Arab has invaded the Israeli consciousness and has also become a part of its nightmare. Speaking from the vantage point of knowledge, Michael avoids giving solutions but only depicts people in the complexity of their situation.

Michael's choice of narrative technique is entailed by his general message, which is the vulnerability of human beings and human nature, their fragility and fallibility, as universal elements—and we have seen how these contribute to the inevitable indeterminacy of the narrative itself. But apart from technique there are certain elements of content that are inescapable for Michael, and for Shimon Balas as well. Both feel a great sympathy for the Arab intellectual in Israel, as a man on a tightrope. That sympathy, recognizing and respecting the bottomless wealth of Arab civilization, corresponds in its own way to their own situation as Jewish intellectuals in Iraq. We must realize that the Jews of Iraq are the descendants of the Jews of Babylon. Living there for more than two millennia, they produced the most extensive corpus of Jewish law and interpretation, in the Babylonian Talmud. Until the tenth century, Babylonia was the cultural and religious study center of the entire Jewish world. The departure of over 90 percent of its Jewish population (after 1948) is one of the epoch-making events of modern Jewish history. The ambivalent feelings toward their double homeland were resolved—but for Michael, at least, Baghdad will continue to be a city he dreams about.

15. SHIMON BALAS

Most of the Iraqi Jews (125,000 people) emigrated to Israel between 1948 and 1953. This wave of immigrants brought its middle class, its intelligentsia, its professionals, writers, and journalists. Born in Baghdad in 1930, Shimon Balas came to Israel in 1951. He had been in the Communist underground in Iraq, and joined the Israeli Communist Party. He became the correspondent for Arab affairs for the Hebrew Communist daily *Kol Ha'Am*. He went on to a doctorate at the Sorbonne, and today is a professor of Arabic literature at Haifa University.

This picture presents certain similarities to the literary and intellectual portrait of Sammy Michael: their Iraqi childhood and youth, membership in the Communist Party, and their mastery of Arabic literature. Both are translators of Arabic works into Hebrew.[1] Both have written novels giving a central position to the Arab, and portraying the experience of non-Ashkenazi Jews. Both aim to portray Arabs as intellectuals, whereas Hebrew fiction has all too often presented the Arab as a type. Both write of thoughtful Arabs, whose complex world they penetrate. In a conversation I had with Balas in Tel Aviv in January 1987, he discussed these points and also noted the contrasting picture of the Jew in Palestinian literature written in Israel, where the portrait is either negative or marginal: often, there might be a friendship between a Jewish and an Arab boy, the Jewish boy goes to the army, he is wounded, and a tension ensues; or, in a relation between a Jewish employer and an Arab employee, the Jew is cruel, and the image is that of a stereotyped "enemy."

An Arab intellectual is at the center of Balas's *A Locked Room*.[2] This is a first-person narrative by one Sa'id, who was born in a small Arab village in 1938; he is now thirty-six years old. In 1948, the village became a part of Israel. As a high school student, Sa'id joins the Israeli Communist Party. He moves to Tel Aviv and begins doing menial work for the Communist newspaper. He meets a Jewish girl who works as a proofreader there. They become lovers. He applies for admission to the Haifa Technion and is finally accepted in the 1960s, and his love affair with the Jewish girl, Semadar, continues. He joins an Arab nationalist organization and is expelled from the Communist Party. In 1967 he is arrested as a security risk, and he spends fourteen months in jail. In 1969 he leaves Israel, taking up residence in Germany and then in France, where he settles down with a French woman who is an anarchist. All this is presented in flashback, in

1974, when Sa'id comes to visit his dying mother. He is also gathering material for a book, which is to be either an autobiography or a study of the Arab predicament in Israel. The unfolding story comprises his two-week stay in Israel.

Sa'id is invited by Israeli friends to talk about the political Left in France. The question is raised whether nationality ought to be noted on Israeli identity cards (the basic document carried by everyone). When asked how he defines himself, Sa'id is uneasy. He poses a question: Is he to regard himself as an Israeli only because Israeli citizenship was forced upon him? Arabs, he says, did not take part in establishing the State, yet they were given the makeshift identity of Israeli Arabs—and as he sees it, "Israel" refers to a Hebrew tribe having no connection to Arabs. What is primary, to him, is the conflict between the two peoples, and their "labels" are of no importance.

Rather like Fathi in Sammy Michael's *Refuge,* Sa'id is wrestling with words as a part of his self-definition. It is interesting that Sa'id says he will never write a novel, and this contributes to the narrative ambiguity in the present novel. The narrating voice is unclear, as the flashbacks and the present monologue intermingle, telling the story of Sa'id's two-week visit and at the same time reconstructing past events. The story progresses and digresses simultaneously, so that it is up to the reader to recreate its continuity.

In our conversation, I asked Balas why he chose the title *A Locked Room.* He said that in essence his protagonist is a closed entity. Balas wished to depict an outsider—even more than an Arab—that is, a man who does not see himself as belonging to anything. Even in the relation to Semadar, Sa'id is locked within himself. In an analogous way, he has shut himself out of Arab society as much as out of Israeli-Jewish society. He cannot return to his village, and he is a foreigner in the new society; he can mix only with an international group of uprooted people. And although Sa'id has been a member of radical groups, he has been disappointed with them.

As we have seen throughout this study, the writer's choice of narrative technique can reveal his attitude to his protagonist's psychological or political stance, perhaps better than any mere pronouncement can. But can a Jewish writer—however close he might be to the Arab and Arab culture—portray the Arab intellectual in a fictionally satisfying manner? It cannot have been easy at all for a Jew to assume the voice of a young Arab intellectual, but fortunately, the resulting awkwardness of the narration, its abrupt regressions, can be seen to reflect something of the complex psychology of the Arab protagonist. Balas admitted to having had some hesitation concerning Sa'id, and doubts as to how close it was possible to approach him as a character. For this reason, he chose the city rather than the village as the main locus of the novel. Yet precisely such closeness to the intimate self of Sa'id is what Balas was aiming for, in order that Sa'id might not be seen merely in ideological (and thus non-literary) terms. That would have made Sa'id a stereotype, Balas said.

Yet it was impossible for Balas to avoid the ideological emphasis. For example, there is a conversation Sa'id has with an old-line Communist, Hassan, who reiterates the standard credo, that only the Communist Party offers protection to workers, fights for peace and brotherhood. Hassan is baffled by Sa'id, who seems to him so deeply rooted in Israeli society, living among Jews and speaking perfect Hebrew. Sa'id counters by saying that the Arab has no role to play in Zionist democracy; co-existence is a myth and an illusion, fostered by man's need to belong, to join.

Sa'id is beset by something like existential nausea and uprootedness. His belated return home is doomed to fail, despite the warm acceptance by family, friends, and fellow Communists. He is asked by Palestinians in Paris to explore the possibility of creating a link with the Israeli Left. But he fails to establish the connection. He is afflicted with a deep sense of estrangement—even from the Arab nationalist movement he had once belonged to. The once-active ideologue is now truly an exile. He cannot ignore the existence of Israel, he cannot live within the boundaries of Israel, and he senses the futility of his political life abroad. The short visit gives him perspective about himself as he re-evaluates his past and is distressed by his own blindness to his father's world. He has caused pain for all who loved him: his parents, Semadar, friends, and Party comrades, and he is barred from the self he wishes he could be, as a son, a lover, and a Palestinian.

Upon his return to Paris, he jots down his impressions of the visit, and these make up the content of *A Locked Room*. When he tells his French girlfriend that he is not writing a political treatise, but only to disclose himself to himself, she tells him that a man carries himself wherever he goes. He answers: "You don't understand me. Your world is open, and you are in the middle of it. My world is locked, and I'm outside it."

It is 1974, and in the aftermath of the October War of 1973, the emergence of an Israeli protest movement gives him a glimmer of hope. Yet his confrontation with radical youth only underscores his own age (36), his past experience as a political activist, and consequently his distance from the current scene. The discussions only underline his disillusionment with words that never lead to actions.

For Sammy Michael's Fathi and Balas's Sa'id, the encounter with Israeli society proved detrimental to their sense of self as Palestinians. Both protagonists experience the move from the traditional and strongly patriarchal Arab society to an open society in modern Israel. The transition is sharpened by the political dimension, as well as by the sense of estrangement from the younger generation and the old frustrations of the Arab nationalist movement. Is the final picture, then, one of inactivity for the

Arab intellectual? Someone has said, with some irony, that in an Israeli novel, the only thing an Arab cannot do is fall in love with an Arab woman. But this *môt* ignores the range and depth that Michael and Balas have given to their Arab protagonists in all their subtly variegated complexity.

Clearly, this has much to do with the fact that these authors are faced with the very complex range of emotions of the Arab intellectual who has grown up in Israel. Thus it is the "Israelization" of the Arab which makes such a many-sided portrayal possible. If the Arab has entered into the psyche of the Israeli, as A. B. Yehoshua has claimed, it is equally true that Israel has entered into the psyche of the Arab who was raised there. Thus Michael and Balas have filled some of the empty spaces in the depiction of the Arab intellectual.

16. DAVID GROSSMAN

David Grossman's novel *The Smile of the Lamb*[1] has established him as one of Israel's outstanding writers. The book is constructed as a series of monologues of the main characters. The time is 1972, or rather a suspended moment in it. At the opening of the book, one character is holding another at gunpoint, and the resolution of this moment will take place at the novel's end. Thus the book does not give us a gradual unfolding of events. Rather, it is about self-estrangement in psychological time, and how people can victimize others by means of love and hate; it is about psychological and political violence, and the human capacity to live with words which go counter to human nature.

The main characters are Hilmi, an old Arab who lives in a cave in the West Bank; Uri, a young idealist who becomes Hilmi's spiritual son; Shosh, Uri's wife, who is a psychologist; and Katzman, a friend of the two. What unites the major characters are words and the power of storytelling. But the power to dictate words becomes the power to dictate in the political sense, so that the personal drama is reflected in political drama.

Above all, this is a story about stories and texts. The inclination to see life as literature gives outline and structure to existence. When we add to this the elements of myth and fairy tale, the characters can radically modify their "text." Thus Hilmi—the hunchback, the old strange Arab—has woven an imaginary, heroic existence for himself, and he is the archstoryteller. He creates for himself a father and mother of legendary stature. With his repeated "Kan-ya-ma-kan" ("Once upon a time"), he weaves intricate webs of color and imagination that captivate and ensnare Uri, whose innocence and purity allow him to cross over into make-believe. The son of a poor Sephardic family, Uri is in search of a "text."

Shosh and Katzman can be said to have their "texts." Katzman, thirty-nine years old and military governor of a West Bank area, survived the Holocaust by living in hiding for three years with his demented parents. His father had been a professor of Italian and Spanish literature. Before the war broke out, he had been involved in a study of the ethical parallels between Ariosto and Cervantes. The manuscript was lost in the escape. In hiding, the father systematically recalled his research and committed it to memory. Later, the child was enlisted in the task of memorization—of ideas and facts beyond his comprehension. Thus the father and son created their own text, speaking in their own language of the language of Ariosto and

Cervantes. To the father, who had lost his mind, the windmills did not represent the external evils of tyranny and injustice; man's most lethal enemy lay within. To the young Katzman, the objective message lay in its very absence.

Shosh, Uri's young wife, was raised by loving parents who were idealistic fighters in the Jewish defense force during the time of the British Mandate. She has become a psychological victimizer. As a psychologist in a mental institution, she causes the suicide of one of her patients with her fanciful notion that we can reach the "kernel" of the psyche by peeling away its layers: her controlled violence, her sexual encounter with the opaque delinquent boy were what led to his suicide. Her desire for vindication leads her to acts of treason against herself: in her office, she tells her story to the tape recorder; like the stories of the others, it is made up of the most diverse formative experiences of her life. Her father, a public figure and a model to the young, is a poet who writes absurdist verse in sonnet form. He too has his "text": he realizes that his very example, his war exploits, his unyielding nationalist stance have sent boys to their death.

Uri has been searching for a father, his own father having rejected the oversensitive child. For a time, his father-in-law was his model. Then it was Katzman, whom he met when both were rescue workers after an earthquake in southern Italy. But finally it was the old illiterate Arab who could be his father and give him a text he could live by, however unreal. Hilmi, the recluse, was richer than the others in his connection to the land and the language, and Uri was therefore attracted to the physically repulsive man.

What these characters do is cross borders, psychological as well as political: Shosh crosses the border into the psyche of the patient she destroys. Katzman crosses a political border in an act that will lead to his death. He appoints Uri to the post of civilian liaison to the West Bank inhabitants. For Uri, a simple and dedicated soul, "justice" is not merely an abstract term. He does not live by a pre-conceived text or terminology, his existence is neither intellectual nor ideological, and he crosses over from the world of overheated political ideas into a non-political, humanistic realm. When Hilmi's adopted son is killed by Israeli soldiers, Uri crosses another border by going to Hilmi to tell him. Hilmi, in desperation over his son's death, takes Uri captive, threatening that unless the Israelis leave the occupied territories he will kill Uri with his son's gun. Uri calls for help. Katzman, deciding to avoid military action, goes up to Hilmi's cave alone. Hilmi points his gun at Katzman, who dies on his thirty-ninth birthday.

As we noted, this is a novel about language and storymaking, about how to weave existence and then justify it. This is a modern "fairy tale" about attempts to escape reality and to face it. Deterministic political factors leave little scope for independent self-definition outside the societal structure. Yet there is a yearning for authentic existence. Uri is the embodiment of innocence. His is the smile of the lamb. Everyone in the novel, without exception, is attracted to him, captivated by his quest for right and his uninhibited humanity.

Katzman had taken an altogether nihilistic approach to issues of "justice" and "truth." Having seen the collapse of a world of solid values as he lived in hiding with his parents, he preferred alienation as an alternative. It will be Uri, the innocent, who will prove Katzman right: Uri tries to attract Katzman's full military force to the cave by pretending that he is being held by a number of Palestinians. Katzman knows the truth as he goes to his last meeting. That is, he knows that the idealistic Uri can be corrupted into lying in an attempt to escape his situation; Uri too is a victimizer—his victims being his "father" Hilmi and Katzman. Hilmi speaks of Uri as "God's idiot," the naive young man who had been critical of the Israeli army and its actions in the West Bank.

The upshot is that on the interpersonal and political levels, words fail. All the characters are victims of deceit as well as perpetrators of it. Words become nothing better than personal myths, creating realities that do not have to hold up. Above all else, deceit is self-deceit. Hilmi believes he can fight the windmills in a single gesture. He wants—with a single word or sentence, as though it were an incantation—to expel the Israelis and return to a time when his world was not beset by the enemy. In a Cervantean sense, his act is at the same time heroic and naive, belonging to a world where reality could be eradicated by a word, and the past restored. At the end, everyone is victimized: Katzman and Hilmi's son are dead; Hilmi and Uri face arrest; and Shosh (who had been Katzman's lover) is devastated by what has happened.

How political is this novel? It is not so much about the Arab-Israeli conflict as about questions of language and reality. Clearly, it is not the conflict that creates this novel, or even its setting; rather, the story stems from the complexity of the characters. And yet the setting is an intrinsic element here, since this is the first novel involving the West Bank, and the first time a Palestinian Arab of Judea and Samaria is presented as a character enmeshed in a story of dark consequences. As to the setting, Grossman's rich mixture of sights, sounds, and smells evokes the unique nature of the Arab village. Hilmi, living in a cave, is in nature untouched by human hands, entirely outside the village and outside its restrictions of language and reality. As he bathes in his barrel under the fig tree, he is floating outside time and place.

What is remarkable as well in *The Smile of the Lamb*, in addition to its literary richness, is that the implied author takes no political, ethical, or ideological stance—showing that even in a conflict "between right and right" the boundaries may be blurred. Why *Lamb*? One critic has suggested a connection to the *Akeda* theme. But along these lines, I would think that the Christian Agnus Dei is more appropriate here. In any case, the link to the father-son connection, whether in Judaic or Christian tradition, is retained here. Fathers and sons are linked (in the Judaic tradition) in relations of obedience and independence, continuity and self-differentiation. And as for the *Akeda* theme, the victimization of the young by the old does make its appearance here.

The Israeli dimension of *The Smile* and other Grossman novels is created in the link between the young Israeli protagonist and the particular reality or fantasy the novel explores. His self-definition is marked by a reality that preceded his birth. Thus the Holocaust and the Arab-Israeli conflict loom over the young Israeli, who tries to weave for himself a private and authentic existence, where the spiritual and the human are not compromised and personal integrity is maintained.

In 1987, at age thirty-three, David Grossman went to the West Bank for a few weeks. His critical impressions were published in the 1987 Independence Day issue of a weekly journal. The wide reaction to his reportage took him back to the West Bank. Afterwards he added five chapters to the original manuscript and published it, in Hebrew, as a book. In English translation it appeared as *The Yellow Wind*.[2] In Israel, sections of the original were dramatized and performed by the Tzavta Theater in Tel Aviv.

Not unlike Amos Oz's *In the Land of Israel*, Grossman's *The Yellow Wind* is a political/literary document, with the reportage of the West Bank and the refugee camps giving the book a 1980s quality. In the third chapter, "What the Arabs Dream," the English translation omits the literary allusions that open the chapter in the Hebrew original. The Hebrew text reads: " 'But what do the Arabs dream about?' asks Anton Shammas in *Arabesques*. What do the twins, Aziz and Halil, dream about once they have completed their performance in Hannah Gonen's nightmares in the book of Amoz Oz?" (The Amos Oz book is *My Michael.*) The Hebrew text continues where the English text of *The Yellow Wind*, chapter 3, begins. The book's title is explained in chapter 6:

> The old man, Abu Harb, sighs a long sigh, passes his hand over his face, and presses it against his eyes. The small children watch him. Returning home did not turn the heart of any one of them into one which loves us, the Israelis. Maybe it was foolish even to hope for that. Abu Harb rises to his feet with difficulty, and sees me to the door. We stand and look together over the beautiful and peaceful valley, and the smoke from the straw fire curls up into the air, and the thistles and wildflowers bloom as far as one can see. Now is the time of the yellow flowers. I tell Abu Harb that I called my book *The Yellow Time* in Hebrew, and he asks me if I have heard about the yellow wind. I say that I haven't, so he begins telling me about it, and about the yellow wind that will soon come, maybe even in his lifetime: the wind will come from the gate of Hell (from the gates of Paradise comes only a pleasant, cool wind)—*rih asfar*, it is called by the

local Arabs, a hot and terrible east wind which comes once in a few generations, sets the world afire, and people seek shelter from its heat in the caves and caverns, but even there it finds those it seeks, those who have performed cruel and unjust deeds, and there, in the cracks in the boulders, it exterminates them, one by one. After that day, Abu Harb says, the land will be covered with bodies. The rocks will be white from the heat, and the mountains will crumble into a powder which will cover the land like yellow cotton. (pp. 75–76)

Chapter 11 is "Swiss Mountain View," and the title has a subtitle. In English it is "A Story," but in Hebrew it is "Perhaps a Story," and that conveys a tone of ambiguity the English title lacks. The story is the closest Grossman comes to the narrative of *The Smile of the Lamb*. Its protagonist, Gidi, is the realistic counterpart to *The Smile*'s Uri. Gidi is young, ambitious, and closely connected to the Arab village to which he was assigned in 1967 as a liaison for civil affairs. The time of the story is 1972. After an absence of six weeks, he returns elated: he has become a father. He wants to share his happiness with the villagers, the people to whom he is closest. But the last meeting with Abu Khatem, who has not left his house since 1967, points to the deep and unbridgeable rift. Gidi, who leans against a tree trunk, wants to shout, " 'I have a son, I have a son!' He felt that he had to shout it, in Arabic" (p. 143).

Grossman's depiction of the plight of the Palestinian also exhibits the essence of the tragedy when ordinary people are divided by the stream of history. Grossman, who speaks Arabic and stayed in the area for seven weeks for the original assignment, connects *The Smile of the Lamb* and *The Yellow Wind*:

Seven years ago, I felt I had to write something about the occupation. I could not understand how an entire nation like mine, an enlightened nation by all accounts, is able to train itself to live as a conqueror without making its own life wretched. What happened to us? How were they able to pass their values on to me during these years? For two years I sat and worked out those thoughts and dilemmas of mine. I wrote a novel, *The Smile of the Lamb*, and the more I wrote, the more I understood that the occupation is a continuing and stubborn test for both sides trapped in it. It is the sphinx lying at the entrance to each of us, demanding that we give a clear answer. That we take a stand and make a decision. Or at least relate. The book was a sort of answer to the riddle of my sphinx.

Years passed, and I discovered that one does not have to battle that sphinx. That you can go mad if you allow it to torture you with questions day and night. And there were other matters, and other things to write about and do. Because there are other sphinxes as well. (p. 212)

17. ARAB WRITERS OF HEBREW
Anton Shammas and Others

In an extended interview in the Hebrew daily *Ma'ariv*, the interviewer asked a number of writers what makes them Israeli writers.[1] The poet Yehuda Amichai responded with the unarguable answer that the fact that he writes in Hebrew and resides in Israel makes him an Israeli writer. A more interesting and problematic response came from an Arab writer, translator, and editor, Muhammad Rhanaim, who lives in the Arab village of Bakka El Garbiye. He translated A. B. Yehoshua's *The Lover* into Arabic, and is an editor of the Arabic-Hebrew publication *Miphgash*. His response ran:

> The question itself assumes that I indeed see myself as an Israeli and that I have to explain my Israeliness. I am an Israeli because I belong here. And in that case I can be an Arab and an Israeli too—depending on how one wants to relate to it. The Arab writer who lives in Israel and writes about life in Israel, who is an organic part of the area, will continue to belong to a minority group that has a sensitive position in the midst of a larger minority. . . . In the final analysis, what makes me an Israeli writer is the uniqueness of life here and now, a uniqueness which stems from the complexity of the existing Israeli situation, of which I am an integral part. . . .

All this must raise the profound question in what sense an Arab can be an Israeli writer. In the case of Michael and Balas, we have two writers raised in the Arabic language and culture but who are Israeli writers now, not only by virtue of their present residence and language but also because they are *Jews* in Israel. What we will now consider is the fact of *Arabs* writing in Hebrew, in Israel.

On the other hand, there is a considerable and impressive literature in Arabic written in Israel, concerned mainly with the problematic Palestinian identity of the writers. For the greater number of young Arab writers writing in Israel, the fact of their having attended Israeli schools, absorbed the Hebrew language, and immersed themselves in Hebrew literature has led to a crisis of their cultural identity, torn as they are between their Israeli, Arabic, and Palestinian sources. Does the fact of Arabs' writing in Hebrew give evidence of the Cana'anite vision of the eventual Hebraization of the region, and a non-national co-existence? Or is it a simpler phenomenon of cultural assimilation, the minority imitating the majority, as when Jews wrote in Russian or in German?

193

The puzzle is not resolved by considering the size of the readership, since the Arab readership is greater by far, including millions of potential readers all over the vast Arab world, while the Hebrew readership is minuscule by comparison. The choice of a language to write in, when the writer has such a choice, involves some element of identification with the language chosen, or with the readership. Compared to the large number of Arabs in Israel who write in Arabic, the number of Arabs writing in Hebrew is quite small: Atallah Mansour, Na'im Araidi, Muhammad Rhanaim, and, the most prominent one, Anton Shammas.

Na'im Araidi, a literary scholar, has tried to come to terms with Arabic literature written in Israel: should it be referred to as "Arabic-Israeli literature" or as "Arab literature in the Land of Israel"? He hastens to point out that many Arab critics prefer to call it "Palestinian literature," thereby giving emphasis to the political struggle, obviating the "Israel" connection, and placing that literature within the purview of literature written in the West Bank, Jordan, and other Arab countries and areas.

Araidi argues[2] that the Arabic literature produced in Israel cannot be considered "Palestinian" because it was not created in a Palestinian state and was not influenced by the tradition of Palestinian literature of the pre-1948 era, when Palestine did exist. Only after 1967 was there a surge in the quantity of Arabic literature written in Israel. But Araidi takes note of the fact that many of the writers in question were educated in the State of Israel; their formative reading was in Hebrew literature and world literature translated into Hebrew—thereby giving to Arabic literature written in Israel its "Israeli" character.

He goes on to distinguish between Arab writers who are connected to the Communist Party and those who are uncommitted. He finds strong elements of modernism and the avant-garde among those writers who are not a part of what he considers the Israeli political machine, i.e., the Israeli Communist Party—writers such as Michael Hadad, Anton Shammas, and Siham Daud. On the other hand, a poet such as Samich el Kassem was deeply influenced by modernist elements in Hebrew literature. Another writer, Mahmud Derwish, left Israel in the 1970s, resides in Paris, and was influenced by Pablo Neruda and Nazim Hickmat.

Na'im Araidi is the first Hebrew poet from the Druse community. He was born in 1948 in a village in the Galilee, was raised there, and after some schooling in Haifa returned to the village in 1978. His village represents, for him, the juncture between the two cultures. In his third collection of poems, he writes: "I returned to the village / as one who runs away from culture / and I came to the village / like one who comes from exile to exile."[3]

In the same issue as that of the Araidi article (see note 2), the Jewish poet and literary scholar Sasson Somekh, who teaches Arabic literature at Tel Aviv University and at Princeton, was asked to comment on the ways in which the Israeli experience has affected Arabic literature written in Israel. He pointed to the fact that 1948 saw the emigration of Arab intellectuals to Gaza, the West Bank, and other Arab areas. Only after 1967, he said, did the Arab world discover the militant Arabic literature written in Israel. Again, mention was made of Mahmud Derwish and Samich el Kassem, as well as of Touphic Ziahd. One of the most interesting of living Arab writers is Emile Habibi, whose political/picaresque novel the *Opsimist* (i.e., *optimist* plus *pessimist*) was translated into Hebrew by Anton Shammas.

Arab-Israeli literature has had three distinct wellsprings for its growth since 1967: the West Bank and Gaza; Arab countries; and Israel (regardless of whether the latter literature be called "Arab-Israeli" or "Palestinian"). The literature coming from the West Bank and Gaza has one thematic focus, the occupation by Israel. Writers have felt that their literature must be political—and that an *a*political literature serves only those who wish to forget the occupation. Further, some Arab poets have felt that there is nothing wrong with polemical poetry, and nothing wrong with slogans if they lead the Palestinian people to freedom.

Of the literature from the three main centers mentioned, that emanating from Israel is most original, modernist, and free of direct pressures and expectations. Written in Israel—by Arabs and Jews—it is a creditable part of the comprehensive body of literature in Arabic.

Atallah Mansour's 1966 book *In a New Light* was the first Hebrew novel written by an Arab.[4] A Christian Arab, Mansour was born in the Galilee. He lived for a time in a kibbutz that had a strong Socialist orientation. Later he was on the staff of the Hebrew daily *Ha'Aretz*, and after the Six-Day War he moved to Arab Jerusalem to report on West Bank news for his paper.

The book's narrator is a young Arab whose parents were killed when he was five. A Jew who was his father's friend raises him as a Jew. Later he goes to live in a kibbutz, but without disclosing his Arab origin. Yusuf Mahmud is known as Yossi Mizrahi, and he identifies himself with that persona. The book concerns his love affair with a blond California woman who has come to live in the kibbutz with her husband. He keeps his true identity from her as well, and when they go for a walk and an Arab passes, Yossi lowers his gaze. The woman is an ardent Socialist, and she tells Yossi that had she been an Arab, she would hate and fight the Jews. (Yossi tries to avoid the issue.)

The truth of his origin comes to light when he applies for full membership in the kibbutz. He is admitted, but in such a way that the issue of his true identity is ignored, since the politically vulnerable kibbutz wants to avoid giving political ammunition to its enemies. He is therefore admitted as Yossi-Mahmud, neither Jew nor Arab, and the deliberations will remain secret. The acceptance is half-hearted, and he is barred from a "security" meeting. Once again, the Arab is treated as something like a "stranger in our midst"—a condemnation of Israeli society as well as of the Socialist ideology that preaches universal brotherhood.

Anton Shammas, born a Christian Arab in 1950, is the most talented and versatile of the Arab writers writing in Hebrew. In an interview,[5] Shammas said that his problem is no different from that of any Jewish writer whose mother tongue is not Hebrew; moreover, there is a greater proximity between Arabic and Hebrew than between Hebrew and any other modern language. So much, then, for the formal problem of language difference. The problem of content, on the other hand, is much more complex. By means of irony, he feels, he can put a distance between himself and allusions having a canonic Jewish content. But this is only the tip of his iceberg. Shammas is a master of the familiar essay. His intimate style is studded with personal recollections, literary allusions, and cultural observations. In what seems a light manner he deals with issues of grave significance, allowing for humor and perspective—as well as what seems, often, a noncommittal stance.

Writing, for example, about the relation between majority and minority culture in Israel, Shammas employs the metonym of the wall:

> The Arab house in Israel, between whose walls I wish to examine the impact of the majority culture upon that of the minority, is one of many monuments to the "overwhelming" of the culture of the third world by the European kitsch—which, of course, does not acknowledge the "culture" of the third world. (This last sentence is unquestionably a typical product of the third world.) Before collapsing under the onslaught of the terrible kitsch, the Arab wall in our parts underwent several phases, which I shall divide schematically into three: the wall of the father, the wall of the son, and the wall of the grandson. We have said that there are very few Arab walls preserved from the beginning of the century, from the days before the Zionist fathers sought to push Europe's moral and cultural border eastward. The classical Arab wall is a creation in which the functional and the aesthetic coexist in a delicate balance. The wall divides and separates, defines and supports, while at the same time its white limewash, tinted with laundress's blue, inspires the space called "home" with an atmosphere of tranquility which characterizes not only the walls but all the components of classical Arab construction: the arch is functional (it supports the ceiling) as well as aesthetic; the keystone, which is the topmost stone that binds the other arch stones together, symbolizes better than anything else the balance which binds and consolidates all the elements of structure into one entity, from which the removal of a single component part may jeopardize the whole. (p. 23)[6]

The intercultural encounter was also the theme of an earlier essay.[7] Facing the Taunus Mountains in Germany as he wrote the article, Shammas mused about the no-man's-land in which he found himself; he imagined himself the Arab with his tongue cut out in Yehoshua's "Facing the Forests," sitting and thinking about the great fire, giving voice to his thoughts. When writers approach the Arab-Israeli conflict, certain metaphors reappear: Yehoshua talks about the infiltration of the Arab into the cracks of the Israeli psyche; Shammas speaks of himself in a no-man's-land.

Working in the no-man's-land between the two languages is his main activity. His "entanglement" with the Hebrew language began when a high-school teacher suggested that he do a matriculation thesis on the image of the Arab fellahin in Hebrew literature prior to 1948. "And so I arrived at the romantic plowshares of Hawaja Mussa (Smilansky), Burla, Stavi and Shami—who, in "The Vengeance of the Fathers," let Arab protagonists from Nablus and Hebron weave the plot, fifty years before the smile of David Grossman's lamb. . . . I come from a culture of words . . . the Arab within me still senses the power of words . . . the Christian within me believed in the sanctity of the Logos, the sanctity of words."

As Shammas sees the writers mentioned, those of the pre-State period were of a "Palestinian" mode, while those since 1948 are more in what he calls the "Jewish" mode. Thus he sees a transition from "Palestinian" (Hebrew) to "Jewish" literature, but no all-embracing "Israeli" literature as such—even though he admits that the writers of the "Jewish" mode are more important. Thus, S. Yizhar is more important than his uncle Moshe Smilansky, and Brenner is more important than Shami, in the view of Shammas—although the meeting point between Hebrew and Arab literature was closer when the "Palestinian" mode of Hebrew literature prevailed. On similar grounds Shammas argues that his novel *Arabesques* is more "Israeli" than Yehoshua's *A Late Divorce*.

A controversy has arisen between Shammas and A. B. Yehoshua, and it has aroused much public interest. In the view of Yehoshua (and the standard Zionist position), Israel must be a Jewish state; there alone can the Jew achieve full self-realization. Toward that end, the Law of Return (giving any Jew, anywhere in the world, the right to immigrate to Israel) is basic. Shammas rejects this law, as well as the tenet that Israel must be Jewish, and he has argued that he could achieve his fullest self-realization only in a non-denominational, secular democratic state. To this, Yehoshua retorted that if that is what Shammas wants, he need merely pick up his things and move one hundred meters to the east (i.e., east of Jerusalem), where the future Palestinian state will be set up.

Yehoshua's retort created an uproar, especially among the Israeli Left. In support of his views he has argued that bi-nationalism has failed wherever it has been tried in the world; and that it cannot succeed in Israel because of the deep differences between the two peoples. Earlier in the debate, Shammas wrote that Israel's Declaration of Independence is the "AIDS" of the State of Israel (the source of the "infection" being the declaration that Israel is a Jewish state and that the Law of Return is to be the law of the land).

Sammy Michael became the third participant in the debate.[8] To tell Shammas to pick up his things and leave would be no solution to the problem, Michael said, since Shammas would feel himself to be an exile in any future Palestinian state. (Shammas had said: "I feel an exile in Arabic, the language of my blood. I feel an exile in Hebrew, the language of my adoptive mother.") The problem stems from the fact that in addition to the "First Israel" (the Ashkenazi one) and the "Second Israel" (the Sephardic one), there exists a third Israel, the Arabic one. This division of Israel goes deeper, into the divided self of the Israeli Palestinian.

Michael finds a vulnerable element in Shammas's existence as a Christian, and as a secular and democratic person. The Christian Arab would not fare well in a Muslim Palestine: Shammas's father and forefathers had a taste of it under Ottoman rule, and Christian Arabs do not look forward to a unilateral Islamic solution. The Christian Arab is therefore left with a dream that verges on delusion. Moreover, there is an ambivalence in his actual situation: from the cultural standpoint, and because he feels superior to his Muslim environment, he resembles a Jew; but as a member of a humiliated minority, he resembles a Muslim.

Shammas's demand that Israel become a non-Jewish state—democratic, secular, and "belonging to all its citizens"—is not, in Michael's view, a viable solution in the Middle East, not if present-day Lebanon is taken as example, at one time the most thriving and democratic country in the region. In deference to Shammas, Michael suggests that Jews from all camps would be willing to go far to alleviate his suffering, but not to the extent of being willing to become a minority in Israel. Shammas's rebuttal returned to the issue of his identity as an Israeli. The only way that Israel could exist as a democratic country is if, *after* the establishing of a Palestinian state beyond the Green Line, the Jewish state *then* declares the establishing of a State of Israel, and on everyone's identity card there would be but one entry under "nationality"—"Israeli." Nothing less than this total removal of acknowledgment of national differences would constitute a democratic state, Shammas says.

For Yehoshua and Michael, the high-minded call for a secular democratic state, and the noble phrase regarding a state that "belongs to all its citizens," is an undisguised invitation to disaster—since it would, by "democratic" means, eliminate the Jewish homeland as such.

Shammas's first novel, *Arabesques*, written in Hebrew in 1986, touches upon the foregoing issues and upon the overall topic of this study.[9] In the novel itself, the narrator is a writer, telling about another writer—an Israeli,

Yehoshua Bar-On—who is writing a novel about the Arab. At first, the Arab narrator himself is the model; later, it is a true Palestinian, devoid of "Israeli bent," who is the model—suggesting that any Israeli Arab would be too "Jewish" to serve as a true model of the Arab.

Shammas admits to being influenced by David Shahar, whose series of novels *The Palace of Shattered Vessels* by now comprises six volumes.[10] Like Shahar, Shammas does not follow a temporal sequence: rather, the omnipresent narrator creates and recreates a realistic/fantastic map of time and place, as a mysterious thread interweaves the lives of the characters. Shammas displays a world which, although limited geographically, is filled with limitless possibilities. Often he uses the Proustian technique of focusing on one point in time, one incident, or one facet of an individual; and as the novel unfolds, the same moment or incident or facet is shown in a different mode, thereby adding another piece to the totality.

Often, it is time itself, the narrator's era, that is the protagonist in the novel. Time is selfhood in its passage, but since it is a function of freely flowing associations, it is not the irreversible and objective time. A stream of images triggers memory, and in a convoluted way these provide both matter and form, the what and the how. But the narrator can even go outside his own time frame, back to the Arab revolt in 1936, reconstructed in the past of the narrator's father and his family in the Galilean village where he was born. Thus the narrator serves in various functions, sometimes as part of the cast of characters, sometimes as observer, sometimes as investigator of past events. And at times he speaks to the reader, from within the book, as the author of the book.

The narrator's name is Anton Shammas, and he was born in 1950, as the author was. He senses that he has missed the "authentic" Palestinian experience of the 1930s and '40s. His fictional re-creation of the past is an homage to the time of his early childhood, to his village, to his family, and to the combined experiences that came to an end with the death of his Uncle Yusef, the creator and curator of family lore. This is the fantastic side of the novel, combining innocence and reverence, memory and substance. The novel's other side, interwoven in the same fabric, is the ironic. Here it is the Arab and his depiction in Hebrew literature that is the target. This introduces the novel's second location, Paris. (The third is Iowa City, where the narrator attends an international writing program at the University of Iowa.)

Shammas leaves the role of narrator when he turns to consider the depiction of the Arab in Hebrew literature. He pokes mild fun at the serious attempts of his Israeli writer, Yehoshua Bar-On, to present a rounded characterization of the Arab. Bar-On is going to incorporate the love story of the other Anton Shammas, the protagonist in his novel. But Shammas the author cleverly summarizes the Arab's history in Hebrew literature, enjoying the compounded interreferentiality. As he has Yehoshua Bar-On say:

> My Jew will be an educated Arab. But not an intellectual. He does not gallop on the back of a thoroughbred mare, as was the custom at the turn of the century, nor is he a prisoner of the IDF, as was the custom at the turn of the state. Nor is he A. B. Yehoshua's adolescent Lover. He speaks and writes excellent Hebrew, but within the bounds of the permissible. For there must be some areas that are out of bounds for him, so nobody will accuse me of producing the stereotype in reverse, the virtuous Arab. He might be permitted the *Kaddish*, as it were, but not the *Kol Nidre*. And so on and so forth. A real minefield.
>
> I can't remember where it was I read about the Arab as a literary solution. But it will come, ah yes, it will come. Some lurking critic like a mole planted in my path will accuse me, in a learned and rigidly reasoned article, that my Arab is nothing but a solution to my personal problems and not to the problems of fiction. So where does that leave us? In A.B. Yehoshua's phrase, "the continuous silence of the writer," as someone is bound to write, "was broken, which is a pity." (pp. 91–92)
>
> There has to be an Arab this time, as some sort of solution to some sort of silence. An Arab who speaks the language of Grace, as Dante once called it. Hebrew as the language of Grace, as opposed to the language of Confusion that swept over the world when the Tower of Babel collapsed. My Arab will build his tower of confusion on my plot. In the language of Grace. That's his only possible redemption. Within the boundaries of what's permissible, of course. (p. 92)
>
> Now it's coming to me—a possible opening line for the first chapter: "Having come to Jerusalem, from his village in the Galilee, he learned that, like the coffin, the loneliness of the Arab has room enough in it for only one person." (p. 93)

Underlying any psychological portrait, any complete identity, there must be the *search* for that identity. In the direction of the future, that search will have political implications; but in the direction of the past, the search has its roots in history. That history points to the village, above all else, and to the connection to the land, not only as the source of livelihood but as the source of myth and legend. In the words of Shammas (author and character):

> Our village is built on the ruins of the Crusader castle of Fassove, which was built on the ruins of Mifshata, the Jewish village that had been settled after the destruction of the Second Temple by the Harim, a group of deviant priests. It is said that they annulled the commandments pertaining to tithing and the sabbatical year, in which the land must lie fallow, and for this they were punished by four judgments: Plague, the Sword, Famine

and Captivity. In the words of the seventh-century Hebrew poet Eleazar Ben Kallir:

> From her land is banished the bejewelled bride
> Because of fallow laws and tithes:
> Quadruply punished for her crimes,
> All her finery stripped aside,
> The Harim of Mifshata.

The son did not rest until he had reached the place with the beautiful view that the Crusaders called Bellevue—as it is written: *Bellum videre quod Sarracenie vocatur Fassove*—and the villagers called Fassu-ta, as a sort of Jewish-Crusader compromise. (p. 11)

More than geological strata are exposed in any excavations; rather, they are historical and speculative. Anton Shammas is named after his dead cousin Anton Shammas, the son of his Uncle Jiryes, who sailed for Argentina, and his wife, Almaza, who went insane from grief. Anton is cared for by Almaza. While he is still very young, a woman appears, claiming to be his real mother, and demanding his return. The child has a nervous break-down, and the doctors advise sending him to America. There he becomes Michael:

> "Many years later, in 1978, I go back to Beirut and join the Palestinian Center for Research. At this point you might begin to get worried again, but let me reassure you that you have no reason for concern. There, I tell my story to Sami, who introduces me to Ameen, Uncle Yusef's son.
>
> "At that time I was thinking about trying to find my mother, the woman in black, but Beirut wasn't exactly the best place to do that then. I wasn't even sure she was still alive. The story of little Anton came up again. He was such an important figure in my childhood that sometimes I used to imagine that I was he. In Beirut this desire took hold of me again, to the point that I put myself entirely into his hands. Why shouldn't I be the son of Almaza, who raised me and loved me as much as if I really were her only little boy?
>
> "Ameen told me about you, and that you were named Anton after the child who had died. I decided to write my autobiography in your name and to be present in it as the little boy who died. A piece of the Palestinian fate that would confuse even King Solomon. I didn't tell Ameen what I had in mind, but during the days of forced leisure during the civil war, in Beirut, he patiently told me in great detail everything I wanted to know about you and about the family. You were still a child when he left the village, so I filled the gaps from my own imagination. Sami also provided me with information about the history and about the village.
>
> "I came back to America and I began to write my fictitious autobiography. I didn't tell anyone about it. I locked it all up in the closet again after I'd come out of it myself, you might say. And then a few days ago Larry

told me that the members of the International Writing Program were going to be visiting him. I glanced absently at the list of members, and I saw my fictitious name there. Which is also your name. Take this file and see what you can do with it. Translate it, adapt it, add or subtract. But leave me in. I didn't take time to arrange the material. I haven't even found a title for it. . . ."

If Michael were the teller, he would have ended it like this: "He opened a drawer and took out a pencil and wrote on the file: My Tale. He frowned at this a moment, then he used an eraser, leaving only the single word Tale. That seemed to satisfy him."

But maybe, out of polite arrogance, he might have finished with a paraphrase of Borges: "Which of the two of us has written this book I do not know." (pp. 258–59).

Interviewed for the *New York Times Book Review*,[11] Shammas was asked why he wrote *Arabesques* in Hebrew, not Arabic. He answered: "You cannot write about the people whom you love in a language that they understand; you can't write freely. In order not to feel my heroes breathing down my neck all the time, I used Hebrew."

Sammy Michael wrote a short review of the book two years earlier.[12] Had Shammas written the book in Arabic, in an Arab country, Michael said, it would have put him in first place in Arabic literature being written today. Michael related that when he told this to Shammas, Shammas retorted: "You too relate to me as an Arabic writer." Michael responded by asking, "You are an Arab, aren't you?" Shammas answered, half in jest, half bitterly, "Well, then one has to convert."

Michael underlined the deep sense of solitude that emanates from Shammas's novel. He added: "It is clear that many people would love to tear off Shammas' Israeli identity. . . . On the other hand, many Arabs in Arab countries will want his blood, for his pride in his contribution to Hebrew literature. Between the two camps, no wonder *Arabesques* conceals within it such pain. The only thing missing is the Jewish humor acquired during two millennia of solitude."

CONCLUSION

This study has examined the image of the Arab in Hebrew literature, in the hope of shedding light on the evolving presence and the many-sided significance of that image. A major aspect of that significance was mentioned: namely, the connection between the Israeli view of the Arab and the Israeli's self-definition and relation to the land. Directly or indirectly, the study has posed a number of questions. Among others: How has the Arab's literary image changed from the beginning of the century through the 1980s? What elements of that image have disappeared from view, and what elements have remained? There were questions relating to problems of form: In what ways is the writer's attitude toward the Arab reflected in the choice of genre and type of narrative?

As we saw in regard to the latter question, the use of the traditional folk-tale mode might be taken to reflect an escapist aim, while the more complex tale might in itself express a more ambivalent, ambiguous, or even divided attitude. All this has pointed to the function of the reader. In relation to the folk tale or another highly stylized mode, the reader's role is usually more passive, involving as it does the willing suspension of disbelief. In relation to more complex tales—involving irony, metaphor, metonymy, etc.—the reader's role is more active since numerous interpretations are possible (or even called for).

Frequently, a story might work on more than one level—realistic and metaphoric—thus encompassing some of the intricacy of image, action, or situation. What may have been a single image in the fiction prior to 1948 may become a metaphor after 1948, thereby reflecting a growing complexity in Arab-Israeli co-existence which defies a writer's attempt at reducing that co-existence to simple terms. Quite often, therefore, the texts are open-ended, the confrontation or conflict remaining unresolved—and this textual inconclusiveness might well be taken by the reader to signify the irresolvability of the Arab-Israeli conflict itself.

This study could have been subtitled *From Utopia to Dystopia* or *From Legend to Apocalypse*, thereby suggesting the difference between the rather naive representation of the Arab in pre-1948 Hebrew literature and the more complex treatment since 1948. Correspondingly, the Arab has moved from a place at the periphery to the center of Hebrew literature. But in addition to the linear change, there has also been an unfolding awareness of the complexity of what might be called the Arab-Israeli "situation." Something of that eventual complexity had already been adumbrated in the fiction of Brenner in the second decade of our century—and indeed, his fiction and polemic essays have been a blueprint of the various modes that evolved in literature up to the 1980s: the naive mode, the realistic/ethical mode, and the psychological mode.

Is it possible, with all this in view, to see a unifying factor in the perception of the Arab in Hebrew literature? There is, for example, the view advanced by Gershon Shaked suggesting that the stereotyping of the Arab in Israeli fiction is a transplant of the stereotyping of the Gentile in Hebrew literature in Europe.[1] Many of the writers of the second wave of immigration (1904–1914) had fled pogroms and revolution in Russia and the Ukraine; for them, the Arab skirmishes, the 1920–21 riots in Tel Aviv/ Jaffa and Jerusalem, as well as the 1929 massacre of Jews in Hebron, had evoked the echoes and collective memory of persecution of Jews in Europe over the centuries.

This metaphoric approach (i.e., seeing Jewish-Arab relations as the extension of Jewish-Gentile relations) would seem to have had implications as well for the romantic relation between Jew and Arab. Many stories in European Hebrew literature, from the late nineteenth century into the early years of the twentieth century, depict the attraction of the Jewish boy to the Gentile peasant girl. And although love affairs were rare involving Jewish men and Arab women, Hebrew literature from the beginning of this century into the 1980s has depicted love and erotic relationships between Jewish women and Arab men.

There is a further difference between European Hebrew and Israeli literature: Jews in nineteenth-century Europe faced the constant threat posed by the Enlightenment, the breakdown of the collective mentality, resulting in conversion, assimilation, and the piecemeal desertion of an integrated Jewish way of life. In Palestine conditions were different, because Jews there had no fear of losing their national identity through absorption into the host society. The Jew was Western-educated, multilingual, and motivated by Zionist ideology and conviction. The threat posed by Arab society was not cultural but physical—and the only romantic analogue was in the Jewish unrealistic fantasies about, and imitation of, the Bedouin.

An inverted extension of the persecution motif is the Israeli desire to become a "native son," with all the paradoxical implications this entails. Thus Yehoshua's "Facing the Forests" can be read as a display of Jewish guilt and self-hate; but there is also the possibility, as I suggested, of reading it as the spiritual odyssey of the alienated young intellectual on his way to becoming a native son. This desire is expressed as early as the 1890s in the fiction of Ze'ev Ya'abetz (1847–1924) and Hemdah Ben-Yehuda (1873–1951), and as late as the 1970s in the fiction of Benjamin Tammuz, for whom such themes as encounter with the land and wrestling with the angel carry a contemporary significance.

Myth and history seem to be clashing in the long struggle between Arab and Jew, between Arab and Israeli, and also between the Israeli Arab and the Israeli Jew. The mythic element can draw its patterns from biblical motifs—e.g., the struggle of two brothers vying for the privileges of the first-born; or the struggle between the one who is first-born and the one who is chosen. Classic myth, which does not accept compromise in its literary expression, is synoptic, timeless, whereas history is shaped and changed in the course of events. The modern myth of man's perfectibility does hold some promise; and historical considerations point to the possibility (however remote) of co-existence. For each of the "brothers," then, the mythic "reading" is countered by the advocacy of compromise.

Despite the substantive changes since the times of the Jews' vulnerability in Europe, the ancient motif of a recurring Jewish fate persists even in modern Israel. Although Jews constitute a majority in the State of Israel, they are a minority in the wider frame of the Arab Middle East, so that the mythic fear of vulnerability cannot be erased entirely. Against this, the Israeli's desire to become a son of the soil is at the same time a desire to disconnect all ties with these ancient images. In the 1980s, that desire can be seen from two different perspectives: there is the "Cana'anite" view that rejects both Zionism and pan-Arabism, as well as the view of a "Greater Israel" as an irredentist basis for reclaiming the land of the biblical forefathers.

These are political forces, and although they are quite vocal, the right-wing voice is rarely heard in Israeli literature. Most of the writers discussed in this study are (politically) positioned somewhere in the spectrum from left to center. The causes of this complex phenomenon are beyond our scope of discourse. Yet it is important to emphasize the fact that there are humanitarian as well as ideological elements at work in the Israeli's perception of the Arab, just as there are similar elements in the Israeli's desire to perceive himself as native son. Yet Israeli literature is not "ideological" if this means that a writer's political orientation dictates the content of his fiction. Israeli literature is not strictly a *littérature engagée*.

Political changes in Israel have to a great extent eliminated the Arab as a model for Israelis of the native son. (There are exceptions: in stories of Yizhar as late as the 1960s there is still some veneration of the Arab as native son.) At issue here is the more general topic of the treatment of the protagonist in Hebrew literature. In the literature of the pre-State era, we can detect two contrary movements: the mythicization and the de-mythicization of the protagonist. In a literature so infused with Zionism, the mythicization is in extolling the heroism of the pioneers, young men and women who sacrificed their lives in the struggle for the new land. The prototype is Joseph Trumpeldor, who died (1921) with his comrades, defending a Galilee farmstead.

The de-mythicized images appear as early as the fiction of Brenner, whose ironic outlook introduces doubt, self-questioning, and pessimism into the tone of the narrative. Yet Brenner was convinced, as early as the second decade of this century, that the Jew has no future in the Diaspora. Thus, despite Brenner's deep distrust of political solutions, political parties, and their manifestoes, he saw the only answer for the Jew in a territorial base in Palestine, where young Jews would be free of the Diaspora mentality and free to develop strong ties to the land.

A process of both mythicization and de-mythicization applies as well to the portrayal of the Arab. But here we must try to distinguish myth from mythology: the former, we may say, comprises the motifs of the eternal human condition, the repetitive timeless schemata that illuminate our confrontation with the cosmos and with one another; the latter comprises the innocuous folk tale, the idyllic interplay of human beings in their simplicity. In the early Hebrew stories, especially those inspired by Bedouin lore, the Arab is depicted within a literary "mythology," a highly stylized and a-realistic representation of a society that is closed, insular, and homogeneous.

There is also the mythicization of history itself, as in the visionary poetry of Uri Zvi Greenberg (1894–1981). One of the outstanding twentieth-century Hebrew poets, Greenberg expressed his reaction to the Arab riots against Jewish settlers in *The Book of Denunciation and Faith* (1937), unabashedly calling for revenge, and denouncing the complacency of the Jewish establishment: to Greenberg, "the cross and the crescent" are the eternal enemies of the Jew.

We pointed out that Israeli literature is not ideological (i.e., the writer's political orientation does not dictate the content of his fiction). But that is not to say that the pre- and post-1948 literature is non-political. The cultural context within which that literature was written has always been affected by its close ties to the political establishment: the founders of the political establishment came to Palestine in the early years of this century, at the same time that the eventual founders of the literary establishment were arriving, and all parties had been moved by a similar Zionist vision. The ethos of the pre-State settlement (the *Yishuv*) was simultaneously shaped by politics and poetics. The writers did not participate in the political machinery, but were its independent parallel.

Poets such as Uri Zvi Greenberg, Nathan Alterman (1910–1970), and Yonatan Ratosh (1908–1981) represent diverse political credos. Yet none of them ever contested the presence of the Jew in Israel. What impelled these writers was not a political manifesto, but the brute fact of the Jewish presence in an Arab milieu—a presence united by wars, bloodshed, and political unrest, and committed to its survival as a Jewish/Hebraic entity.

Since the 1970s, the overt political involvement of Israeli writers has grown considerably. They now participate in political protests; and since many of them are regular contributors to daily and weekly publications, their views are effectively voiced and heard. The War in Lebanon produced poetry directly linked to war for the first time in decades. There are novels revealing a hidden fear of annihilation, a fear first expressed in the 1970s, in the wake of the October War of 1973.

The writer's commitment to the Hebrew language carries with it an inescapable connection to a national/cultural/religious context. Thus the writer of Hebrew in the twentieth century conducts a dialogue, whether it be direct or indirect, affirmation or challenge, with the entirety of the past and present. Yet there were writers such as Brenner who presented their dissent, their break with much of the religious context. Thus the traditional role of the writer as guardian of the national ethos is both challenged and reinforced. Hebrew literature has reaffirmed the cultural context of Israeli/ Jewish society. At the same time, it addresses the political context and expresses its own dissatisfaction as well as the growing-pains of a society in continual flux and the consequent agony of self-assessment.

We have witnessed the emergence of the Arab writer of Hebrew within the existing literary establishment in Israel. This emergence has been matched by a new Israeli openness to Arabic literature—produced in Israel and elsewhere, and translated into Hebrew. The periodical *Miphgash* ("Meeting," "Encounter") began in 1960, with Yehuda Burla and Mordechai Tabib as editors, publishing Hebrew works in Arabic translation, and Hebrew translations of works written in Arabic, fiction and non-fiction. By 1985, this Arabic/Hebrew quarterly was printed in 1,500 copies, and its circulation now reaches beyond the borders of Israel. The attempt to trans-late into Hebrew some of the vast quantity of Arabic literature, written in Israel and the Arab world, has become a prominent factor in Israeli literary life in the 1980s. Also noteworthy has been the publication in Hebrew of an anthology of contemporary Arabic stories, *A Place on the Face of the Earth.*[2]

So far, then, we can regard these events as the *effect* of changing public attitudes. But what of the corresponding capability of literature to effect a change in public attitudes? Poetry has traditionally been utilized for its polemic power. Thus the novelist Haim Be'er wrote a strong poem titled "War Damage," in which he urges the State to return to the Orchard, to innocence.[3] The protest poetry of the 1980s has been in response to the Israeli incursion into Lebanon, condemning the war, its faulty *raison d'être* and its senselessness. Many of the poems were written by young poets who took part in the war and by fathers (such as Amnon Shamush) who had sons in combat. Poems by mothers whose sons fell in Lebanon have shaken the country, as have letters written to dailies by young men who died by the time their letters appeared.

In general, young writers differ from more established writers in being free of literary restraints such as the need to protect emotional national beliefs. But this generalization does not hold true for established writers such as Yehuda Amichai, Natan Zach, and Dalia Ravikovitch. Amichai is the father of anti-war poetry in Israel, beginning with his reaction to his own participation in World War II and the 1948 War. In his early poetry, he was still attached to the biblical/liturgical framework, which he ironized through multiple allusions.[4] Natan Zach, through analysis of the language associated with the war, challenges its very premises.

Yizhar, in a 1983 article, both challenged and affirmed the power of poetry to affect the war and the course of history.[5] Yet its effect need not necessarily be looked for in its polemical side: "The poem does not go to a demonstration, and does not change things in the world. . . . The poem is a poem. That's all. A poem with which man is man, and without which he is not."

This study began with the assertion that the Jewish/Israeli image of the Arab is connected with the self-definition of the Israeli. The implicit question to be asked is what the self-image of the Israeli will be toward the end of the century and after. We noted the emergence of the Arab writer who writes in Hebrew. Yet this is but one facet of the Arab as Israeli citizen, confronting his own problems of self-definition in relation to the Jew and to the Hebrew language.

It is a truism that language is shaped by reality and shapes it in turn. This is true of the language of politics, but even more so of the language of literature. Thus the romantic bent of the early days of Jewish settlement found expression in the romantic perception of the Arab in the literature of that time. The almost continuous state of war since 1948, combined with the ubiquitous presence of the Arab within and beyond the Green Line, has led to the view that the Arab-Israeli conflict amounts to a clash between the rights of two peoples. This new reality, in turn, has led to new ways of portraying the Arab. The Arab who was depicted in a realistic mode soon became a part of the Israeli conscience, and turned to be part of an extended nightmare in the Israeli narratives of the 1960s.

We also saw the growth of an allegorical/dystopian tone in fiction. With this, we might have had writers foregoing the creation of believable and three-dimensional characters, and reducing the conflict to a parable. In that case, the choice of genre would reflect the attitude of the writer, entailing a reductive approach to the subject, on one hand, and the fear of touching upon it, on the other. Here, historical reality and fictional myth-making are juxtaposed. Thus the writers who reject realism in fiction, and lean toward symbolism and allegory, are the ones most likely to take an *a*political stance in regard to the problem.

Clearly, it is the political/military situation that has led writers to a greater involvement and concern—i.e., the situation in the West Bank and Gaza, the plight of Arab refugees and Jewish settlement beyond the Green Line. All this has polarized national sentiment and provoked strong political statements from writers and others. The writers who are heard most often are those whose political leaning is left of center.

This brings us back to a more puzzling issue: As the awareness of the problem acknowledges its increasing complexity, does the portrayal of the Arab become more difficult? One way out of the impasse is already evident: In the 1980s, there has been a tendency toward the apocalyptic or sur-realistic in fiction, projecting catastrophe either in the subtext or in the text itself. Thus Yoram Kaniuk's title *The Last Jew* carries just such an apocalyptic overtone. There is also Yitzhak Ben-Ner's *The Angels Are Coming*, which portrays a futuristic dystopia in the twenty-first century. Two outstanding satirists, both ex-Cana'anites, have written of apocalyptic/surrealist dys-topias: Benjamin Tammuz's *Jeremiah's Inn*[6] envisages a grim future state of Israel run strictly along the lines of ancient Rabbinic law *(Halakhah)*.

Amos Kenan's *The Road to Ein Harod*[7] envisages the Israel of the future as a regime run by a military junta. Alongside Kenan's acid satire, there is a sentimental, almost obsessively nostalgic yearning for the beautiful Eretz Israel of his youth, for bygone days of innocence and wholesomeness. This is not the writing of an escapist: for years, Kenan has been a strong critic of the political and literary establishment of Israel. In his novel, the narrator tries to reach Ein Harod, where, according to rumor, freedom fighters have established a territory outside the reach of the regime. He finds an Arab who will guide him, and who is himself fleeing. Against the apocalyptic background, both Jew and Arab find themselves to be refugees in their own land, reaching Ein Harod to find that it no longer exists.

David Melamed's *The Fourth Dream*[8] is another novel in this genre. It envisions the conquest of Israel by the Arabs, followed by a new exile. The exiles are in Germany and Poland, and Israel is under Arab occupation. The Third Dream (i.e., the State of Israel as the Third Temple) is destroyed. At the novel's end, the protagonist and a few other exiles infiltrate illegally, suggesting the beginning of the Fourth Dream. Like those of Tammuz and Kenan, Melamed's book is suffused with a sense of fear and loss, although its tone is less scathing and less sanctimonious. Melamed does not refer to the catastrophe as Holocaust II, but rather adopts the term "The Fall." There is a characteristic reversal of roles: the Israeli Jew is the refugee/exile, the Arab is the occupier and rules the land.

For Tammuz and Kenan, Judaism is not what is at issue. In a symposium held in Jerusalem in May 1987 considering the topic "Cultural and Religious Pluralism," Kenan spoke of belonging to the human race, rather than acknowledging his identity as Jew, Albanian, or whatever. Melamed is a religious man, and by this he differs from the "Hebrews" (read: "Cana'anites") for whom Zionism and Judaism do not meet their cultural/political perceptions.

How can we account for the vast number of books depicting a new Fall, a new Holocaust as other than a vision of destruction in Hebrew literature in the late 1970s and 1980s? Some commentators have attributed it to the emergence of self-hate in the Israeli Left. In a newspaper interview, A. B. Yehoshua remarked:

> I'm afraid of this self-hatred, because I know that it can be exploited. When Englishmen or Frenchmen hate themselves—and some do—it doesn't put their countries at risk. They're in their countries unconditionally. Whereas here, self-hatred is always connected to something else, to another possibility, to packing my bags and leaving, or to a Jew in exile not coming. Of late, I've come to understand Jewish history better. We have this fear of being at home because home won't live up to our ideals. I didn't want to take part in that fear anymore. So I became much more forgiving towards Israelis.[9]

What can we foresee for the Arab in Israeli literature? Ever since the Arab Question became the Jewish Problem (to adopt, here, the Hebrew title of Gorny's book), the problem has become one of the major concerns confronting the Jewish population in Israel—sufficient to polarize and divide Israeli public opinion on the matter. If A. B. Yehoshua is correct (in remarks of his we cited earlier, in the chapter devoted to him), it would appear that it has become difficult, perhaps even impossible, to include an Arab character in an Israeli novel if that character is to be represented as a fully rounded, three-dimensional individual. This is because the situation, rather than the character, has become the main focus of Israeli fiction. This priority of situation over character lends itself to a more politicized treatment of the Arab in fiction—or to an apocalyptic literature in general.

Yet the cogency of such forecasts must always remain in doubt. With the situation as volatile as it is, the one reliable *donnée* is the truism that here predictions remain unreliable.

Notes

(E): sources in English
(H): sources in Hebrew

Introduction

1. Y. Sobol, *The Palestinienne* (Israel: Or-Am, 1985) (H).

PART ONE: *EARLY WRITERS—TO 1948*

Cultural Background

1. This division follows the plan of A. Hertzberg (ed.), *The Zionist Idea* (New York: Atheneum, 1979) (E).
2. I. Epstein, "The Hidden Question," *Mosaic* (periodical), vol. 1, no. 1 (Cambridge, Mass., 1986) (E).
3. Quoted in P. R. Mendes-Flohr (ed.), *A Land of Two Peoples: Martin Buber on Jews and Arabs* (Oxford University Press, 1983), p. 4 (E).
4. See Y. Gorny, *Zionism and the Arabs, 1882–1948* (Oxford: Clarendon Press, 1987), pp. 41–49 (E).
5. T. Herzl, *Altneuland*, trans. from the German by P. Arnold (Haifa: Haifa Publishing Co., 1961) (E).
6. See Y. Porath, "The Land Problem in Mandatory Palestine," *Jerusalem Quarterly* (periodical), vol. 1 (Jerusalem, 1976) (E).

1. Moshe Smilansky

1. See S. L. Hattis, *The Bi-National Idea in Palestine during Mandatory Times* (Haifa: Shikmona, 1979), pp. 144–54 (E).
2. Ibid., pp. 306–307.
3. Hawajah Mussa (M. Smilansky), *Bnei Arav* [Children of Arabia] (Tel Aviv: Dvir, 1964) (H).
4. M. Smilansky, *Zichronoth* [Memoirs] (Rehovoth, 1928), pp. 209–218 (H).
5. R. Domb, "The Arab in Fact and Fiction—as Reflected in the Works of Moshe Smilansky," *Jewish Quarterly* (periodical) (London: Winter 1981/82) (E).
6. M. Smilansky, "Hawaja Nazar," in *Palestine Caravan*, a collection of stories (London: Methuen, 1936), pp. 145–81 (E).
7. M. Smilansky, "Latifa," in *Palestine Caravan*, pp. 265–69.
8. See R. Domb (note 5, above).

2. Yehuda Burla

1. G. Yardeni, *Sixteen Conversations with Writers* (Tel Aviv: HaKibbutz HaMeuchad, 1961) (H).
2. Y. Burla, *In Darkness Striving* (Jerusalem: Israel Universities Press, 1968) (E).
3. Y. Burla, *Bli Kohav* [Starless] (Jerusalem, 1922) (H).
4. Y. Burla, *Bli Kohav and War Stories* (Masada Publishers, no date), p. 218 (H).

3. Yitzhak Shami

1. A. Barash (ed.), *Stories of Yitzhak Shami* (Tel Aviv: Newman, 1951) (H).
2. G. Shaked, *Hebrew Narrative Fiction, 1880–1980* (Tel Aviv: HaKibbutz HaMeuchad & Keter, 1983), vol. 2, p. 76 (H).

3. "Jum'ah the Fool" was translated into English twice: first as "The Simpleton" in I. Halevy-Levin (ed.), *Israel Argosy* (Jerusalem: Zionist Organization, 1953), pp. 33–69; then as "Juma the Simpleton" in S. Y. Penueli and A. Ukhmani (eds.), *Hebrew Short Stories* (Tel Aviv: Institute for the Translation of Hebrew Literature, 1965), vol. 2, pp. 274–302. Page numbers cited are those of the first translation.

4. Y. Shami, "The Vengeance of the Fathers," in A. Lelchuk and G. Shaked (eds.), *Eight Great Hebrew Short Novels* (New York: New American Library, 1983), pp. 59–163 (E).

5. H. Pesach, "Y. Shami: A Further Reading" (a review of the 1975 edition of "Vengeance of the Fathers"), in *HaAretz,* daily (Tel Aviv, January 6, 1976) (H).

4. Yosef Haim Brenner

1. Y. H. Brenner, "Nerves," in Lelchuk and Shaked (see note 4, chapter 3).

2. *Kol Kitvei Y. H. Brenner* [Collected Writings of Y. H. Brenner] (Tel Aviv: HaKibbutz HaMeuchad & Dvir, 1960), vol. 2, pp. 277–328 (H).

3. Ibid., vol. 1 (1964), pp. 293–320 (H).

4. Ibid., pp. 321–74.

5. Y. H. Brenner, *Breakdown and Bereavement* (Philadelphia: Jewish Publication Society, 1971) (E).

6. A. Eisenberg (ed.), *Modern Jewish Life in Literature* (New York: United Synagogue, 1968), Book 1, pp. 180–83 (E).

5. Yitzhak Shenhar

1. H. Hazaz, "The Sermon," in R. Alter (ed.), *Modern Hebrew Literature* (New York: Behrman House, 1975) (E). See also G. Ramras-Rauch, "The Re-emergence of the Jew in Israeli Fiction of the 1970s," in *Hebrew Annual Review* (periodical), vol. 2 (Columbus: Ohio State University, 1978) (E).

2. Y. Shenhar, "The Tamarisk" (published under Shenhar's birth name; Shenberg), in the *Jewish Spectator* (periodical) (Santa Monica, Calif.; March 1950) (E).

3. S. Hareven, *The City of Many Days* (New York: Doubleday, 1977), pp. 111–13 (E).

PART TWO: *WRITERS OF THE 1948 GENERATION*

6. S. Yizhar

1. S. Yizhar, "Ephraim Returns to the Alfalfa," in G. Shaked and Y. Golan (eds.), *Life on the Razor's Edge* (Tel Aviv: HaKibbutz HaMeuchad, 1982) (H). Translations given herein are mine unless noted otherwise.

2. S. Yizhar, "Paths in the Fields," *Gilionoth* (periodical) (Jerusalem, 1938) (H).

3. S. Yizhar, *On the Edges of the Negev* (Tel Aviv: Am Oved, 1945) (H).

4. S. Yizhar's novella "The Grove on the Hill" appears in a volume with that title (Merhaviah: Sifriat Poalim, 1947) (H).

5. S. Yizhar, *Four Stories* (Tel Aviv: HaKibbutz HaMeuchad, 1968) (H). "Midnight Convoy" and "The Prisoner" have been translated in their entirety (see notes 6 and 7 below). "Hirbet Hizah" has been translated in part (see note 14 below). "Before Zero Hour" has not been translated. Passages from the latter are my translation.

6. S. Yizhar, *Midnight Convoy and Other Stories* (Jerusalem: Israel Universities Press, 1969) (E). All quotations from "Midnight Convoy" are taken from this volume.

7. S. Yizhar, "The Prisoner," in R. Alter (ed.), *Modern Hebrew Literature* (New York: Behrman House, 1975) (E). Page references are to this edition.

8. See the report in *International Herald Tribune,* daily (Paris, February 8, 1978).

9. M. Segal, "The 'Hirbet Hiza' Row," *Jerusalem Post,* daily (Jerusalem, February 17, 1978) (E).

10. A. Shapira (ed.), *The Seventh Day: Soldiers Talk about the Six-Day War* (New York: Scribner's, 1970) (E).

11. R. Furstenberg, "The Man behind It All," *Jerusalem Post,* daily (Jerusalem, February 17, 1978) (E).

12. C. Nagid, "Interview with Yizhar," *MaAriv,* daily (Tel Aviv, February 10, 1978) (H).

13. H. Gouri, "Arav, Arav," *MaAriv,* daily (March 3, 1978) (H). See also M. Shalev, "Confusion and Sadism: Hirbet Hizah," in C. Nagid (ed.), *S. Yizhar: A Collection of Critical Essays on His Writings* (Tel Aviv: Am Oved, 1972) (H).

14. S. Yizhar, "Hirbet Hizah." Partial translations in *Jewish Quarterly* (periodical), vol. 4 (London, Spring 1957), and in *Caravan: A Jewish Quarterly Omnibus* (New York: Yoseloff, 1962) (E). All quotations given are from the latter.

15. S. Yizhar, *Days of Ziklag* (Tel Aviv: Am Oved, 1958), 2 vols. (H). Quoted passages are my translation, except for one passage by R. Alter, as noted.

16. R. Alter, "The Days of Ziklag: In Search of a Cultural Past," in his *After the Tradition* (New York: Dutton, 1962), pp. 221–22 (E).

17. S. Yizhar, *Stories of the Plain* (Tel Aviv: HaKibbutz HaMeuchad, 1963) (H). The translations given are mine.

18. Y. Smilansky (S. Yizhar), "What about Literature and the 'Israeli Situation'?" *HaAretz,* daily (Tel Aviv, April 5, 1985) (H).

19. Y. Smilansky, "The Poets of Annexation," *HaAretz,* daily (Tel Aviv, December 8, 1967) (H).

20. Y. Smilansky, "And Again Literature and Politics," *Politica,* weekly (Tel Aviv, February 1986) (H).

21. Y. Smilansky, "The Poem as Instrument," *Yedioth Aharonoth,* daily (Tel Aviv, February 4, 1986) (H).

7. Moshe Shamir

1. Interview with E. Mohar in *Yedioth Aharonoth,* daily (Tel Aviv, February 1973) (H).

2. G. Shaked, *A New Wave in Hebrew Fiction* (Tel Aviv: Sifriat Poalim, 1971), pp. 14–15 (H).

3. Interview with Y. Reuveni in *Yedioth Aharonoth,* daily (Tel Aviv, June 1987) (H). Translation mine.

4. M. Shamir, *With His Own Hands* (Jerusalem: Israel Universities Press, 1970), p. 1 (E).

5. G. Shaked, "Born of the Sea: The Hero in Modern Hebrew Fiction," *Ariel* (periodical), no. 65 (Jerusalem, 1986) (E).

6. M. Shamir's play *He Walked through the Fields* is to be found in H. S. Joseph (ed.), *Modern Israeli Drama* (London and Toronto: Fairleigh Dickinson University Press, 1983) (E).

7. M. Kohansky, *Israeli Theater, Its First Fifty Years* (New York: Ktav Publishing, 1969), p. 157 (E).

8. M. Shamir, *My Life with Ishmael* (London: Vallentine, Mitchell, 1970), p. 10 (E).

9. M. Shamir, *Under the Sun* (Merhavia: Sifriat Poalim, 1950) (H). Translations mine.

10. M. Shamir, *Not Far from the Tree* (Tel Aviv: Dvir, 1963) (H).

11. Y. Gorny, *Zionism and the Arabs, 1882–1948* (Oxford: Clarendon Press, 1987). See chap. 2 (d): "The Constructive Socialist Outlook," pp. 66–75 (E).

12. M. Shamir, *The Border* (Tel Aviv: Sifriat Poalim, 1966) (H). Translations mine.

13. See note 8 above.

14. A. Oz, "The Meaning of Homeland," *New Outlook* (periodical), vol. 10 (Tel Aviv, December 1967) (E).

15. See note 3 above.

16. N. Gertz, *Hirbet Hizah and the Morning After* (Tel Aviv: HaKibbutz HaMeuchad, 1984) (H).

17. D. Miron, *Four Facets of Contemporary Literature* (Tel Aviv: Schocken, 1962), p. 346 (H).

8. Aharon Megged

1. A. Megged, *The Turbulent Zone* (Tel Aviv: HaKibbutz HaMeuchad, 1984) (H).

2. A. Megged, *Fortunes of a Fool* (New York: Random House, 1962) (E).

3. S. Shifra, "Literature as an Act of Love: An Interview with Aharon Megged," *Ariel* (periodical), nos. 33–34 (Jerusalem, 1973) (E).

9. Nathan Shaham

1. N. Shaham, *Witness for the King* (Tel Aviv: Am Oved, 1976) (H). Translations mine.

2. N. Shaham, *The Gods Are Lazy* (Tel Aviv: Sifriat Poalim, 1949) (H). Translations mine.

3. N. Shaham, "The Seven," in S. J. Kahn (ed.), *A Whole Loaf: Stories from Israel* (New York: Grossett & Dunlap, 1963), pp. 86–102 (E).

4. See note 1 above.

5. N. Ben-Yehuda, *1948—Between Calendars* (Jerusalem: Keter, 1981) (H). Translations mine.

6. N. Ben-Yehuda, *Through the Binding Ropes* (Jerusalem: Domino Press, 1985) (H). Translations mine.

10. The Cana'anite Movement: Yonatan Ratosh and Others

1. See Y. Ratosh, "The New Hebrew Nation (the Cana'anite Outlook)," in E. Ben-Ezer (ed.), *Unease in Zion* (New York: Quadrangle Books; Jerusalem: Academic Press, 1974), pp. 201–234 (E). See also J. S. Diamond, *Homeland or Holy Land? The Canaanite Critique of Israel* (Bloomington: Indiana University Press, 1986) (E). See also Y. Shavit, *The New Hebrew Nation: A Study in Israeli Heresy and Fantasy* (London: Frank Case, 1987) (E).

2. H. Hazaz, "The Sermon," in R. Alter (ed.), *Modern Hebrew Literature* (New York: Behrman House, 1975) (E).

3. B. Kurzweil, "The New 'Canaanites' in Israel," *Judaism* (periodical), vol. 2 (New York, January 1953) (E).

4. See *Unease in Zion*, note 1 above.

5. N. Zach, "Ratosh, Last Interview," in *Monitin* (periodical) (Tel Aviv, March 25, 1981) (H).

6. B. Evron, "Uriel Shelah and Yonatan Ratosh," in *Modern Hebrew Literature* (periodical) (Tel Aviv, Winter 1981/82) (E). The two names are names he adopted, his birth name being Uriel Halperin. *Shelah* means "spear."

7. A. Shammas, in *Politica* (periodical) (Tel Aviv, October 1987) (H).

8. M. Dayan, *Story of My Life* (New York: Morrow, 1976), pp. 622–23 (E).

PART THREE: *WRITERS OF THE STATEHOOD GENERATION—1960s–1980s*

Cultural Background

1. A. Shapira (ed.), *The Seventh Day: Soldiers Talk about the Six-Day War* (New York: Scribner's, 1970) (E).

11. A. B. Yehoshua

1. See A. B. Yehoshua, "Brenner's Wife—as Metaphor," in *Modern Hebrew Literature* (periodical), vol. 8, nos. 3–4 (Tel Aviv, 1983) (E).

2. Interview, "To Write Prose," in *Siman Kri'a* (periodical), vol. 5 (Tel Aviv, 1976) (H). Translations mine.

3. A. B. Yehoshua, *Between Right and Right* (New York: Doubleday, 1981), pp. 75–106 (E).

4. Ibid., p. 163.

5. A. B. Yehoshua, "The Last Commander," in his collection of stories *Early in the Summer of 1970* (New York: Doubleday, 1977) (E).

6. A. B. Yehoshua, "Facing the Forests," in his collection *Three Days and A Child* (New York: Doubleday, 1970) (E).

7. For example, "The Crusades were Christian Zionism just as the political Zionism of today is a Jewish Crusade. In both cases we see a perversion of spirituality and faith." R. Garaudy, *The Case of Israel: A Study of Political Zionism* (London: Shorauk, 1983), p. 110 (E).

8. M. Shalev, "The Arabs as a Literary Solution," in *HaAretz*, daily (Tel Aviv, September 30, 1970) (H).

9. A. B. Yehoshua, *The Lover* (New York: Doubleday, 1978) (E).

10. G. Shaked, *Wave after Wave in Hebrew Narrative Fiction* (Jerusalem: Keter, 1985), pp. 41–52 (H).

12. Amos Oz

1. R. Alter, "New Israeli Fiction," *Commentary* (periodical) (New York, June 1969), p. 63 (E).

2. A. Oz, "The Meaning of Homeland," *New Outlook* (periodical), vol. 10 (Jerusalem, December 1967) (E).

3. A. Oz, in *World Authors*, a biographical reference work (New York: Wilson, 1975), p. 167 (E).

4. A. Oz, "Nomad and Viper," in his collection *Where the Jackals Howl and Other Stories* (New York and London: Harcourt Brace Jovanovich, 1981) (E).

5. A. Oz, *My Michael* (London: Chatto & Windus, 1972) (E).

6. G. Shaked, *A New Wave in Hebrew Fiction* (Tel Aviv: Sifriat Poalim, 1971), pp. 180–203 (H).

7. A. Shapira (ed.), *The Seventh Day* (New York: Scribner's, 1970) (E).

8. A. Oz, *Under the Blazing Light* (essays) (Tel Aviv: Sifriat Poalim, 1980) (H).

9. A. Oz, *In the Land of Israel* (New York: Harcourt Brace Jovanovich, 1983) (E).

13. Benjamin Tammuz

1. B. Tammuz, "The Swimming Race," in his collection *A Rare Cure* (Tel Aviv: HaKibbutz HaMeuchad, 1981) (E). The volume also includes the earlier collection *Sands of Gold*.

2. B. Tammuz, *Ya'akov* (Ramat Gan: Massada, 1971) (H). Translations mine.

3. B. Tammuz, "Second Encounter with the Angel," *Jewish Quarterly* (periodical), vol. 21 (London, 1973) (E).

4. B. Tammuz, *The Orchard* (Providence: Copper Beach Press, 1984) (E).

5. B. Tammuz, *Minotaur* (New York: New American Library, 1981) (E).

14. Sammy Michael

1. S. Michael, "On Being an Iraqi-Jewish Writer in Israel," *Prooftexts* (periodical), vol. 4, no. 1 (College Park, Md.: Johns Hopkins University Press, January 1984), p. 23 (E).

2. Interview with H. and B. Hakkak, *Turim* (periodical) (Tel Aviv, May 1981) (H).

3. S. Michael, *Refuge* (Tel Aviv: Am Oved, 1977) (H). *Refuge* (Philadelphia: Jewish Publication Society, 1989) (E).

4. S. Michael, *A Trumpet in the Wadi* (Tel Aviv: Am Oved, 1987) (H).

15. Shimon Balas

1. S. Balas (ed. and trans.), *Palestinian Stories* (Tel Aviv: Ekked, 1970) (H). See also his *Arabic Literature in the Shadow of War* (Tel Aviv: Am Oved, 1978) (H).

2. S. Balas, *A Locked Room* (Tel Aviv: Zmora, Bitan, Modan, 1980) (H).

16. David Grossman

1. D. Grossman, *The Smile of the Lamb* (Tel Aviv: Siman Kri'a & HaKibbutz HaMeuchad, 1983) (H).

2. D. Grossman, *The Yellow Wind* (New York: Farrar, Straus & Giroux, 1988) (E).

17. Arab Writers of Hebrew: Anton Shammas and Others

1. H. Nagid, in *Ma'ariv*, daily (Tel Aviv, May 2, 1986) (H).

2. N. Araidi, "The Contemporary Arab-Israeli Literature," in *Moznaim*, a literary monthly (Tel Aviv, October/November 1983) (H).

3. N. Araidi, *I Returned to the Village* (Tel Aviv: Am Oved, 1986) (H). Translation mine.

4. A. Mansour, *In a New Light* (London: Vallentine, Mitchell, 1969) (E).

5. Interview with S. Shifra in *Masa*, literary supplement of *LaMerhav*, daily (Tel Aviv, June 21, 1974) (H).

6. A. Shammas, "Kitsch 22: On the Problems of the Relations between Majority and Minority Cultures in Israel," *Tikkun* (periodical), vol. 2, no. 4 (Oakland, Calif., September/October 1987) (E).

7. A. Shammas, "The Encounter That Was, the Encounter That Will Not Be," *Moznaim* (periodical) (Tel Aviv, September 1985) (H).

8. A. B. Yehoshua, "An Answer to Anton," in *Ha'Ir*, weekly supplement (Tel Aviv, January 31, 1986) (H). And see S. Michael, "Arabesques of Zionism," remarks on the Yehoshua-Shammas debate, in *Moznaim* (periodical) (Tel Aviv, July/August 1986) (H). See Shammas's rebuttal in *Moznaim* (September 1986) (H).

9. A. Shammas, *Arabesques* (New York: Harper & Row, 1988) (E).

10. G. Ramras-Rauch, "Mixing Memory and Desire: The Visionary World of David Shahar," *World Literature Today* (periodical), vol. 57, no. 1 (University of Oklahoma, Winter 1983) (E).

11. A. Zusy, interview with Shammas, *New York Times Book Review* (Sunday, April 17, 1988).

12. S. Michael, review of Shammas's *Arabesques*, in *Kol Bo* (periodical) (Haifa, April 25, 1986) (H).

Conclusion

1. G. Shaked, "The Arab in Israeli Fiction," *Ariel* (periodical), no. 54 (Jerusalem, 1983) (E).

2. *A Place on the Face of the Earth* (Jerusalem: Van Leer Institute, 1986) (H).

3. H. Be'er, "War Damage," in *Moznaim* (periodical) (Tel Aviv, June/July 1982) (H).

4. *Selected Poetry of Yehuda Amichai* (New York: Harper & Row, 1986) (E). See especially "Jerusalem" (p. 32), "And as Far as Abu Ghosh" (p. 33), "Too Many" (p. 39), "Jerusalem, 1967" (pp. 47–55).

5. Yizhar Smilansky (S. Yizhar), "A Poet Goes to a Demonstration," *Moznaim* (periodical) (Tel Aviv, October/November 1983) (H).

6. B. Tammuz, *Jeremiah's Inn* (Jerusalem: Keter, 1984) (H).

7. A. Kenan, *The Road to Ein Harod* (London: Al-Sagi Books, 1986) (E).

8. D. Melamed, *The Fourth Dream* (Tel Aviv: Sifriat Poalim, 1986) (H).

9. *Jerusalem Post*, International Edition (April 11, 1987), p. 12 (E).

Selected Bibliography
of Works in English

R. Alter. *After the Tradition.* (New York: Dutton, 1962). See the chapter titled "The Israeli Novel".
———. "New Israeli Fiction." *Commentary* (June 1969).
W. Bargad. "The Image of the Arab in Israeli Literature." *Hebrew Annual Review,* vol. 1. Ohio State University, 1977.
E. Ben-Ezer. "War and Siege in Israeli Literature (1948–1967)." *Jerusalem Quarterly,* no. 2 (Winter 1977).
———. "War and Siege in Hebrew Literature after 1967." *Jerusalem Quarterly,* no. 9 (Fall 1978).
———. *Unease in Zion.* New York: Quadrangle Books; Jerusalem: Academic Press, 1974.
M. Buber. See Mendes-Flohr, below.
E. A. Coffin. "The Image of the Arab in Modern Hebrew Literature." *Michigan Quarterly Review* (Spring 1982).
R. Domb. *The Arab in Hebrew Prose, 1911–1948.* London: Vallentine, Mitchell, 1982.
A. Elon. *The Israelis.* New York: Holt, Rinehart & Winston, 1971.
S. D. Goitein. *Jews and Arabs: Their Contacts through the Ages.* New York: Schocken Books, 1974.
P. R. Mendes-Flohr (ed.). *A Land of Two Peoples: Martin Buber on Jews and Arabs.* New York: Oxford University Press, 1983.
D. Miron. "Modern Hebrew Literature: Zionist Perspectives and Israeli Realities." *Prooftexts,* vol. 4, no. 1 (January 1984).
G. Morahg. "New Images of Arabs in Israeli Fiction." *Prooftexts,* vol. 6, no. 2 (May 1986).
M. Perry. "The Israeli-Palestinian Conflict as a Metaphor in Recent Israeli Fiction." *Poetics Today,* vol. 7, no. 4 (1986).
G. Shaked. "First Person Plural: Literature of the 1948 Generation." *Jerusalem Quarterly,* no. 22 (Winter 1982).
———. "The Arab in Israeli Fiction." *Ariel,* no. 54 (1983).
———. "Challenges and Question Marks: On the Political Meaning of Hebrew Fiction in the Seventies and Eighties." *Modern Hebrew Literature,* vol. 10 (Spring/Summer 1985).
D. K. Shipler. *Arab and Jew: Wounded Spirits in a Promised Land.* New York: Times Books, Random House, 1986.
H. Wirth-Nesher. "Tragedy and the Arab-Israeli Conflict: Dangerous Misnomer." *Jerusalem Quarterly,* no. 9 (Fall 1978).
L. I. Yudkin. *Escape into Siege: A Survey of Israeli Literature Today.* London and Boston: Routledge & Kegan Paul, 1974.
———. *1948 and After: Aspects of Israeli Fiction.* University of Manchester, 1984.

Index

Page numbers such as 214*n*.6(10) should be read as page 214, note 6 of chapter 10.